ROOTS AND BRANCHES

Roots and Branches:
The Symbol of the Tree in the
Imagination of G. K. Chesterton

with

The Seven Moods of Gilbert:
Conversion Narrative in *The Flying Inn*

Deb Elkink

The Habitation of Chimham Publishing
Titusville, Florida
www.chimhampublish.com

www.chimhampublish.com
chimhampublish@aol.com

Paperback

Deb Elkink

Roots and Branches: The Symbol of the Tree in the
Imagination of G. K. Chesterton
with
The Seven Moods of Gilbert:
Conversion Narrative in *The Flying Inn*

ISBN-13: 978-0-9899-6962-8
Library of Congress Control Number: 2015935154
Library of Congress Catalog-in-Publication-Data

Book Cover:
    Illustration and Design by Lorenda Harder
        (lorenda.harder@gmail.com)

    Layout and Design by Averil Harder
        (averil.harder@gmail.com)

Author Photo:
    Nancy Yackel Photography
        (http://www.nancyyackelphotography.com)

To readers who seek *The Story* beneath the story.

FOREWORDS

I

The most famous poem about trees begins, "I think that I shall never see a poem as lovely as a tree." It was written by Joyce Kilmer and published in 1914. Most people today who might know the poem and might even know the poet's name assume that Joyce Kilmer was a woman. He was not. Not only was he a man, but a soldier who died heroically in World War I. He was also a great admirer of G.K. Chesterton, who was a direct influence on his poetry. Is it possible that Chesterton's many references to trees inspired Joyce Kilmer to write his famous poem?

The question, even though I am the one asking, is ridiculous. No poet needs another poet to inspire him to write a poem about trees. All he needs is a tree.

But the fact remains, as the present book shows, that the tree is a central symbol in Chesterton's writing. And while this book focuses on his fiction, the tree figures throughout his other prose and poetry as well. From the tree comes "the almighty stick," which, says Chesterton, is "the scepter of man," giving the mark of kingship to every man, but it is also "the wooden pillar of his house," which is as central and essential as any material object can be. The stick is "a universal thing, and has many functions. It is sometimes a crutch, sometimes a club, sometimes a balancing pole, sometimes a mere toy to twiddle in the fingers. Sometimes it is used for holding a man up, and sometimes for knocking him down" (*Daily News*, Oct. 23, 1910). Thus is wood "the most human of non-human things" (*New Witness*, Oct. 26, 1916), even as a tree is the most human of plants, rooted in the earth, yet reaching for heaven.

And yet, in a thundering contrast, Chesterton describes the tree as "a top-heavy monster with a hundred arms, a thousand tongues, and only one leg" ("Science and the Savages," *Heretics*). Nothing human about that. But this, of course, is Chesterton getting us to look at a familiar thing and see it as something strange, to see it for the first time. He also gives the tree a very unfavorable comparison with the human when he uses it to epitomize the vast difference between man and all other things. For man is the creature who makes dogmas. "Trees have no dogmas" ("Concluding Remarks," *Heretics*).

For the most part, however, we can rely on Chesterton using the tree for more positive roles than its lack of faith. He usually calls on it as a symbol of things human and divine. "A man's soul," he says, "is as full of voices as a forest; there are ten thousand tongues there like all the tongues of the trees: fancies, follies, memories, madnesses, mysterious fears, and more mysterious hopes" (*Illustrated London News*, July 2, 1910). The tree is mystical, obviously mystical, obviously pointing to things beyond itself, but even as we take hold of that, Chesterton trips us up with one of his paradoxes.

> The error of current mysticism is that mysticism, religion and poetry have to do with the abstract. There is a tendency to believe that the concrete is the symbol of the abstract. The truth, the truth at the root of all true mysticism, is quite the other way. The abstract is the symbol of the concrete. This may possibly seem at first sight a paradox; but it is a purely transcendental truth. We see a green tree which we worship. Then because there are so many green trees, so many men, so many elephants, so many butterflies, so many daisies, so many animalculae, we coin a general term "Life." And then the mystic comes and says that a green tree symbolises Life. It is not so. Life symbolises a green tree. Just in so far as we get

into the abstract, we get away from the reality, we get away from the mystery, we get away from the tree. And this is the reason that so many transcendental discourses are merely blank and tedious to us, because they have to do with Truth and Beauty, and the Destiny of the Soul, and all the great, faint, faded symbols of the reality. And this is why all poetry is so interesting to us, because it has to do with skies, with woods, with battles, with temples, with women and with wine, with the ultimate miracles which no philosopher could create. The difference between the concrete and the abstract is the difference between the country and the town. God made the concrete, but man made the abstract. A truthful man is a miracle, but the truth is a commonplace. (*The Speaker*, May 31, 1902)

The essence of paradox is that truth is unexpected. The reason that truth is unexpected is that we have the wrong expectations of truth. In an essay entitled "The Wind and the Trees," Chesterton gives a vivid description of the visual effect of a strong wind dramatically bending huge trees so that they look like giant dragons chained to the ground by their noses. A child who does not know any better or an adult who should know better might see these trees writhing and throwing their huge arms back and forth, and conclude that the trees, with all their gyrations, are stirring up the wind. This is a vital lesson in how we get things wrong, for the truth is precisely the other way around.

The great human dogma, then, is that the wind moves the trees. The great human heresy is that the trees move the wind. When people begin to say that the material circumstances have alone created the moral circumstances, then they have prevented all possibility of serious change. For if my circumstances have made me wholly stupid, how can I be certain even that I am right in altering those circumstances? (*Daily News*, Dec. 1, 1906)

The tree epitomizes the wonder of creation. The artist sees every tree telling a tale, or more poignantly, escaping with its tale untold. He knows that there is a truth behind all things, a truth independent of himself. "I enjoy stars and the sun or trees and the sea, because they exist in spite of me; and I believe the sentiment to be at the root of all that real kind of romance which makes life not a delusion of the night, but an adventure of the morning" (Illustrated London News, Nov. 22, 1913). The artist is almost overwhelmed by this. In his poem "Eternities," Chesterton talks of wanting to give a name to each leaf on every tree. It is a wonder that he naturally wants to share.

Thus, Deb Elkink rightly calls Chesterton "the didactic artist," and the almighty stick is not only a personal prop, it is the chief tool in his classroom. Indeed, the tree even figures in one Chesterton's principal essays on his economic philosophy of Distributism: "Reflections on a Rotten Apple." Here the tree represents ownership, self-sufficiency and independence. And in addition to serving as metaphor to address the modern world's commercial ideas, Chesterton also uses the tree to address our obsession with the notion of "progress." Whereas the metaphor for progress is usually the road, with the sense of going somewhere, Chesterton suggests that the tree is a better metaphor, "because the tree grows, so does society. Human society is more like a tree than a road. The trunk of this tree is country life" (*Christian Science Monitor*, Mar. 22, 1912).

And the tree serves as an object lesson in one of Chesterton's sublime precepts: "Do not try to bend, any more than the trees try to bend. Try to grow straight, and life will bend you" ("The Furrows," *Alarms and Discursions*).

Most notably, he uses trees to make his vivid points in the essential "Ethics of Elfland" chapter in *Orthodoxy*. Trees produce both the logical necessities, but also the very non-necessities, the magic of imagination. We cannot imagine two trees plus two trees not equaling four. It is a logical impossibility. We *can*, however, imagine candlesticks growing on trees, even if we might not expect it. Whatever we can imagine is a possibility. Logic says that if the apple hits Newton on the nose, Newton's nose also hits the apple. The one demands the other. But we can see a clear picture in our minds of the apple suspended in the air above Newton's nose. Gravity is not a necessity. It is merely the way to bet. Arithmetic and logic can only work one way, in this world and in fairy land. Imagination can work millions of ways, especially in Elfland, where the forests are full of magic.

Chesterton deals equally well with the hardness and complexity of reality on the one hand, and the hopes and dreams and fears of our imagination on the other. It is even debatable which is more complex. The exterior world created by God and the interior worlds created by us are fully fertile, and fully forested, and God dwells in both places.

Deb Elkink's choice of studying the tree in Chesterton's fiction [Part I] leads her to the same conclusion we would find if studying the tree in the rest of his writings. It is that the tree forms the great sign of contradiction, the cross, which is the symbol of the ultimate paradox: the God-Man. It is not surprising that Chesterton should be so consistent. And if we look at Chesterton's favorite time of year, we will see that there is a tree associated with Christ's birth that is also a paradox: the Christmas tree. It is not merely the symbol of the winter feast, the celebration in the bleak mid-winter. Bringing a tree inside is an act of defiance. It is defying death. Life contradicts death. Chesterton completes the paradox when he says that the cross is the tree of life.

*

There are few intellectual exercises more rewarding than the close reading of a Chesterton text. And too few critics have made the effort. Along with most exercise, it is avoided. Perhaps they are intimidated to offer a critical analysis of a writer who is himself a master literary critic. But Deb Elkink has risen to the challenge. She has not only gone very deep, she has gone deep on one theme in Chesterton, which illuminates the rest of his writing. The branches of the tree cover a wide area indeed.

But she has also has plunged into one particular text [Part II]: Chesterton's rollicking tale, *The Flying Inn*. With her essay, "The Seven Moods of Gilbert," she has presented a more penetrating analysis of this novel than has ever been written. But it is also the most creative, for she has chosen to interpret the story through the eyes of a minor character, so minor as to be forgotten by even the book's most ardent admirers, who are usually taken up with the heroes Dalroy and Pump, and their adversaries, Ammon and Ivywood.

But the character is not so minor after all. For Elkink's thesis, Dorian Wimpole represents none other than G.K. Chesterton. Dalroy, Pump, Ammon, and Ivywood, as amusing and entertaining and even exasperating as they are, are no different at the end of the tale as they are at the beginning. They all remain true to their characters. But one character undergoes a change, a conversion. It is Dorian Wimpole. That is what makes the story interesting. That is what makes any story interesting. Especially Chesterton's own story.

Dale Ahlquist, M.A.
President of the American Chesterton Society
www.chesterton.org

II

In Augustine's great treatise on teaching the Christian faith, *De Doctrina Christiana,* he begins strangely enough with semiotics: a discussion of "things" and "signs." In a world of things, we find that some things become signs of others things, such as the smoke that signifies fire, a natural sign, or the letters F-I-R-E (real sounds in the air, or ciphers on the page), a conventional sign. Signs become ever more complex as one considers figuration (signs of signs), such as when fire is itself symbolic: "Our God is a consuming fire." Augustine's intention in beginning with an erudite analysis of language was not academic. He sought to build up a hermeneutical theory for the reading of Holy Scripture governed by love, to show how all things (including things that signify) are meant to point us or convey us toward one final end, the love of God himself. In his autobiographical *Confessions*, Augustine reflected a similar outlook. He reported how he looked at all the things of this world and they seemed to reply in unison, "It is he that hath made us, and not we ourselves," pointing beyond themselves to God. And as he told the story of his own life, he seemed to incorporate his own life into the narrative and symbols of the Scriptures. Just as the fall from innocence in Genesis began with eating the forbidden fruit of a tree, so also he stole forbidden pears from a tree as an adolescent (even when he was not hungry) and somehow recapitulated the sin of Adam and Eve in his own person. When he surrenders himself to the grace of God in self-despairing faith, it is in another garden and it seems he was aware of the symbolism here again of returning to the original biblical garden to walk again with God.

It was for other later Christian writers such as Dante and Milton to take up the sacramental attitude in Augustine and to develop a Christian imagination that ranged more widely to develop the potential of the biblical narrative for imagining new stories and exploring the sign quality of the world given by God and narrated in Scripture. Indeed, the literary critic Northrop Frye argued that the overarching story and symbolic world of the Bible shaped the Western literary tradition from beginning to end. The Christian outlook that sees the "things" of the world as having a sign quality, pointing beyond themselves, is properly called sacramental.

The Enlightenment saw a flattening of the Augustinian world of signs and symbols into a flat world of surfaces, a modernizing world that seemed to be described comprehensively by materialist science and to which God was remote. If God was brought back, it was only at the end of a long argument. The result was what T. S. Eliot called a dissociated sensibility. G. K. Chesterton recognized this situation and wrote, "The huge modern heresy is to alter the human soul to fit modern social conditions, instead of altering modern social conditions to fit the human soul." In response, in the nineteenth century a number of Christian thinkers and writers, such as Samuel Coleridge and George MacDonald, sought not to demythologize the world but to remythologize it, recognizing the imagination itself as an organ of truth. Soon there were others. Among these remythologizers there was none more robust than Chesterton himself whose deeply sacramental imagination perceived God's presence everywhere in the world of things.

Deb Elkink has managed to find one particular magic thread to trace through the whole of Chesterton's life and writings to display the workings of this sacramental vision. Her focus might at first seem narrow or arbitrary. How much can we learn from the single image of the tree in Chesterton's oeuvre? The answer is, very much indeed. Just as in Scripture we begin the human story of the gift of life and the descent into evil with trees in a garden, and just as the climax of salvation history is enacted by the Son of God being nailed upon a tree, and just as the centre of the new creation is a tree whose leaves are for the healing of the nations—so also there is a profundity and fecundity to Chesterton's use of the imagery of the tree throughout his writing. Every tree is, so it seems, a burning bush. So, by tugging on this magic thread Deb is able to pull all the others along with it. The tree is domestic, an image of our true home, and it is anthropological, an image of our human nature. The tree is revelatory, a luminous sign of truth, and it is ecclesial, a place of veneration. The tree is anagogical, an image of ascent, and it is redemptive, an image of salvation. And so on. Deb traces this thread wherever it will go, and her exploration of the literature to do with Chesterton is comprehensive, her research thorough, and her writing crisp. We are given in the end a tremendous insight into the sacramental imagination of Chesterton as a whole. And what a remarkable imagination it is. There is much here to help the modern reader recover a vision of the Christian life that is joyful, hopeful, and redeemed. I know that Deb would be pleased if, as for Augustine, all these signs pointed, finally, to the God in whom our love can at last rest fulfilled.

Bruce Hindmarsh, D.Phil.
James M. Houston Professor of Spiritual Theology
Regent College, Vancouver

PREFACE

Gilbert Keith Chesterton (1874-1936) is a figure in the history of Christianity about whom many people in our day have only vaguely heard, often without recognizing his name until connecting it to popular media. ("Oh, so he's the one who wrote those televised Father Brown mysteries?") G. K. Chesterton's story, told mainly within the Roman Catholic Church since his reception in 1922, is being rediscovered by a wider audience. I myself found him at a Protestant seminary a dozen or so years ago when, resisting the empty nest, I threw myself into scholarship to kick-start my suspended writing career. *The Everlasting Man* hooked me and *Manalive* reeled me in. I quickly noticed a pattern to Chesterton's theologically informed fiction that I wished to investigate for mimicry in my own story writing.

This book, *Roots and Branches*, is adapted from my 2001 graduate studies, and in it I seek to contribute to the critical discussions on the symbolism of Chesterton. By examining the formation and expression of his aesthetic imagination so enriched by Scripture and Christian tradition, I demonstrate the wealth of sources upon which he drew. Part I provides an overview of Chesterton's life, then chronologically, thematically, and comprehensively examines the appearance of the tree motif throughout his short stories and novels. Part II looks more closely at a specific chapter of the novel *The Flying Inn* as a fictional conversion narrative or "testimony" consonant with Chesterton's own spiritual awakening.

By way of brief biography, Chesterton grew up in a late-Victorian London home, his highly creative father stimulating his early imagination partly through exposure to the Christian classics of English literature. A morbid childhood curiosity in the occult as well as the philosophies of pessimism, rationalism, and subjectivism contemporary to his time further propelled Chesterton towards metaphysical inquiry. He attended St. Paul's Preparatory School until age eighteen and his subsequent enrollment in the Slade School of Art trained him as a painter, but he soon found his way into the publishing industry and gained attention in 1900 with two poetry books. His popularity on Fleet Street grew out of prolific writing in all genres but, in reaction against the Impressionism encountered at Slade, he developed an allegorical model to satisfy his need for a clear form of expression that meaningfully represented underlying morals or ideas. His religious philosophy sharpened especially within his intimate marriage to Frances Blogg—a High Church Anglican whose practical faith encouraged him towards a personal understanding of orthodox Christianity.

The fiction growing out of his experiences is heavily analogical, employing among its referential imagery the picture of the tree that can be seen to integrate Chesterton's life and thought—an encompassing archetype that gives unity to his artistic imagination. The tree emblem, arising even in Chesterton's earliest juvenilia, illustrates themes that gained strength as his writing and spiritual life matured. Chesterton introduced and developed mythic concepts that began in his fragmentary childhood tales heavy with literary and biblical allusion (written in the 1880s), concepts that continued in his first novel (*The Napoleon of Notting Hill*, 1904) and on through his last story collection (*The Paradoxes of Mr. Pond*, published posthumously in 1937).

The tree's signification evolved with and paralleled Chesterton's basic convictions of Christianity: God's image in the created human, free will leading to the fall into sin, the yearning of the banished exile for a return to paradise, the promise of deliverance through the light of the gospel, the institution of the church, and the hope of the cross as passage between heaven and earth. Layer by layer, Chesterton's fiction added meaning to his iconic tree, which finally became an allegory itself for salvation by picturing Christ's incarnational, redeeming work and the continuing, sacramental presence of God in the world.

I am pleased to acknowledge and thank several people who have helped bring about this publication. Bruce Hindmarsh—expert in early British evangelicalism and conversion narrative, now teaching at Regent College, Canada—supervised my graduate research in historical theology at Briercrest Seminary, Canada (2001). Grant C. Richison—pastor, lecturer, and scholar committed to the expository study of Scripture—has grounded me biblically along the way for many years. Wayne Stahre—writer, publisher, and charter member of the Central Florida Chesterton Society—sniffed out my writing online and convinced me to throw my lot in with him at The Habitation of Chimham Publishing. My sister and niece, Lorenda and Averil Harder, employed their considerable artistic and technical skills to creating the cover. Above all, I am grateful for the patient care of my husband, Gerrit Elkink, and for the encouragement and prayerful support of our three children—all of whom continue to put up with my fictional and theological ramblings while their eyes glaze over.

Deb Elkink, M.A.
Author, *The Third Grace*
www.debelkink.com

CHRONOLOGY OF G. K. CHESTERTON: 1874-1936

1874

- May 29, Gilbert Keith Chesterton born, Campden Hill, Kensington, London

1881

- Chesterton family moves to new home at Number 11, Warwick Gardens, Kensington

1887

- Enrolls as a day student at St. Paul's Preparatory School
- Begins his notebooks, a collection of journals penned throughout youth and young adulthood incorporating miscellaneous writings and sketches

1891-3

- Contributes to *The Debater*, the informal organ of the Junior Debating Club (JDC) formed by Chesterton, E. C. Bentley, Lucian Oldershaw, and other school chums

1892

- Appears publicly for the first time in print (in *The Speaker*), with a short piece called "The Song of Labour"

1892-5

- Attends Slade School of Art and University College

1895

- Works in a publishing office, first briefly for Redway, and then for a larger firm, Fisher Unwin (for six years)
- Publishes a few book and art reviews, and three poems

1896

- Publishes his first two stories in the Slade School of Art's short-lived magazine, *The Quarto*
- Meets Frances Blogg in her bohemian community of Bedford Park

1899

- Leaves Fisher Unwin, settling on a career in writing
- Begins to publish in London's *Daily News* (until 1913)

1900

- Publishes his first two books, both poetry: *Greybeards at Play* and *The Wild Knight and Other Poems*
- Meets Hilaire Belloc, a lifelong friend

1901

- Marries Frances Blogg, and moves for a short while to a Georgian house at Edwardes Square, Kensington, then to Overstrand Mansions, Battersea Park
- Continues contributing essays, articles, and literature reviews to various journals, and begins regular Saturday column in *Daily News*

1903

- Commissioned to write a volume for "English Men of Letters" series, on Robert Browning, his first of eight biographies

1903-4

- Enters religious debate with atheist Blatchford, published in *The Clarion*

1904

- Publishes his first novel, *The Napoleon of Notting Hill*
- Meets John O'Connor—lifelong friend and spiritual mentor, as well as the model for Chesterton's detective, Father Brown

1905

- Publishes *The Club of Queer Trades*, a short story collection
- Publishes *Heretics*, a collection of controversial studies on prominent figures
- Begins weekly articles for *The Illustrated London News* (until 1936)
- Engages George Bernard Shaw in a public debate spanning thirty years

1907-8

- Publishes *The Man Who Was Thursday: A Nightmare*, a novel
- Publishes *Orthodoxy*, his first formal and personal defense of Christianity

1909-10

- *The Ball and the Cross*, a novel (serialized in 1905-6)
- Moves with Frances to a quiet country house called Overroads, in Beaconsfield, 25 miles west of London

1911

- Publishes *The Innocence of Father Brown*, the first of five collections of mysteries written for the popular magazine market, and featuring the theological "snoop," Father Brown
- Begins contributing to Shaw's polemical *Eye-Witness*, which in 1912 becomes *The New Witness* under the editorship of Cecil Chesterton and then (until 1922) of Gilbert himself

1912

- Publishes *Manalive*, a novel
- Begins to build "Top Meadow," a studio which eventually (1922) becomes the Chesterton home

1914

- Publishes *The Wisdom of Father Brown*
- Publishes *The Flying Inn*, a novel incorporating earthy pub poetry later collected under the title, *Wine, Water and Song*
- Falls seriously ill and lapses into a semi-coma for several months

1920

- Travels with Frances on their first of many trips to the Continent; also undertakes the first of two speaking tours in North America

1922

- Enters the Roman Catholic Church
- Publishes *The Man Who Knew Too Much*, a collection of philosophic mysteries previously appearing in magazines

1925
- Publishes *Tales of the Long Bow*, a collection of stories based on well-known sayings
- Starts up *G. K.'s Weekly*, which becomes the official organ for the Distributist League, and which he edits until his death
- Publishes *The Everlasting Man*, his outline of religious history

1926
- Publishes *The Incredulity of Father Brown*

1927
- Publishes *The Secret of Father Brown*
- Publishes *The Return of Don Quixote*, a novel

1928
- Broadcasts the Shaw-Chesterton political debates on BBC

1929
- Publishes *The Poet and the Lunatics*, a collection of stories

1930
- Publishes *Four Faultless Felons*, a mystery collection

1932
- Begins regular BBC broadcasts on literary subjects

1935
- Publishes *The Scandal of Father Brown*

1936
- June 14, G. K. Chesterton dies
- Posthumous publication of *Autobiography* (1936) and of the short story collection *The Paradoxes of Mr. Pond* (1937) as well as of other pieces; collection ongoing

CONTENTS

PART I

ROOTS AND BRANCHES: THE SYMBOL OF THE TREE IN
THE IMAGINATION OF G. K. CHESTERTON

PART II

PART I

ROOTS AND BRANCHES:
THE SYMBOL OF THE TREE IN THE
IMAGINATION OF G. K. CHESTERTON

ONE

INTRODUCTION

> Mr. Walter Windrush, the eminent and ec-
> centric painter and poet, lived in London
> and had a curious tree in his back garden.
> . . [It was] so squat in the trunk that the
> boughs seemed to spring out of the roots.
> . . . Sometimes it looked as if some huge
> hand out of heaven, like the giant in Jack
> and the Beanstalk, had tried to haul the
> tree out of the earth by the hair of its
> head. . . . It had never been planted in
> anybody's garden. Everything else had
> been planted around it. The garden and
> the garden-wall and the house had been
> planted around it. . . . The black and bi-
> zarre outline of the tree had really the ap-
> pearance of something more mystical than
> a natural object. . . . "I never before in all
> my life saw anything that I wanted to pos-
> sess [Windrush said]. . . . I have never
> seen before, in all my wanderings, any
> place where I wanted to stop and make
> my home."[1]

This excerpt from "The Honest Quack," a short story
written in the 1920s by "the eminent and eccentric" G.
K. Chesterton, introduces important components found
in his body of allegorical fiction as a whole. It illustrates
Chesterton's artistic eye and humorously descriptive
style. It focuses attention on the image of the tree in the
garden as a pre-existent literary motif, with enigmatic
significance inviting interpretation. It suggests metaphysical meaning, linking heaven to earth. Chesterton's

---

[1] G. K. Chesterton, *Four Faultless Felons* (New
York: Dover Publications, 1989), 59-61; first published
in 1930.

3

fiction offers theological stories that are entertaining, and an excellent opportunity to consider the themes in his life and thought as informed by prior English literature.

G. K. Chesterton is perhaps known best today as the author of the Father Brown mysteries in which an innocent-looking priest of a philosophic turn of mind solves crimes with pragmatic intuition rather than by scientific rationalism. The Father Brown stories were widely read in Chesterton's own day, about fifty of them appearing between 1910 and 1935 in popular magazines such as *Storyteller* and *Strand*. Yet Chesterton's notoriety on Fleet Street hung on more than his fiction stories (or his famously flamboyant appearance). Although he wrote profusely in most genres (including essay and article, play, verse, novel and short story, art and literary criticism, and biography), he called himself above all "a roaring journalist."[2] He illustrated several books. He entered vigorous political, social, and religious debate in print and over the airwaves. He lectured on tours at home and abroad. And he delighted his audiences with a paradoxical humor, a controversial viewpoint, and a quotable wit.[3] Today, Chesterton societies flourish in North America, Asia, Australia, and Europe. The publication of the scholarly journal *The Chesterton Review* and the ongoing issuing of *The Collected Works of G. K. Chesterton* are revitalizing interest in a great twentieth-century literary figure.[4]

---

[2] Christopher Hollis, *The Mind of Chesterton* (Coral Gables, FL: University of Miami Press, 1970), 20. As an example of Chesterton's prolificacy, he wrote over sixteen hundred columns for *The Illustrated London News* alone, according to David W. Fagerberg, "Chesterton on Ritual," *Worship* 71, (May 1997): 194, n. 1.

[3] Chesterton is seen as "the outstanding master" of paradox, although the term is often overworked by critics, according to Douglas J. Cock, "Chesterton in Fiction," *Chesterton Review* 18, no. 3 (1992): 385-9.

[4] The scholarly journal *The Chesterton Review* is published by the G. K. Chesterton Institute for Faith and

Yet the sheer volume of the work produced by Chesterton becomes a liability in comprehending the man and his message, making him a difficult author to catalogue. Even his official bibliographer, John Sullivan, did not claim to have included everything Chesterton wrote.[5] Many stories were missed in Chesterton collections through the years, untraceable partly due to the author's failure to take his own work seriously.[6] Lost manuscripts, given to friends or misplaced, are still being unearthed—some very recently. For example, Chesterton began keeping a series of notebooks while a boy at St. Paul's School in the 1880s. An extensive collection of the notebooks, which consists mostly of rough or intermediate drafts of work in progress, was presented to the library of St. Paul's School in the 1950s by Chesterton's secretary and literary executrix, Miss Dorothy Collins. However, more than two hundred more notebooks

---

Culture at Seton Hall University, New Jersey; its popular counterpart *Gilbert Magazine* is published by The American Chesterton Society. *The Collected Works of G. K. Chesterton* are being produced by Ignatius Press, San Francisco.

[5] John Sullivan's bibliographic works of note are as follows: John Sullivan, *G. K. Chesterton: A Bibliography* (London: University of London Press, 1958); John Sullivan, ed. *Chesterton Continued: A Bibliographical Supplement* (London: University of London Press, 1968). The lack of a uniform or definitive edition of Chesterton's work has been noted by several biographers; see e.g., Lawrence J. Clipper, *G. K. Chesterton*, Twayne's English Authors Series, ed. Sylvia E. Bowman (New York: Twayne Publishers, 1974), 175; see also Dudley Barker, *G. K. Chesterton* (London: Constable Publishing, 1973), 289.

[6] According to Denis J. Conlon, introduction to G. K. Chesterton, *The Collected Works of G. K. Chesterton,* ed. George J. Marlin, Richard P. Rabatin, and John L. Swan, vol. 14, *Short Stories, Fairy Tales, Mystery Stories, Illustrations* (San Francisco: Ignatius Press, 1993), 13-16.

languished overlooked in a long-stored trunk thought to hold only clothing, and were discovered in 1990 when the Chesterton estate sold remaining memorabilia to the British Library. The importance of this find is not yet fully appreciated, as not all manuscripts and stories have been published.[7]

Chesterton's preliminary notebook pieces gave way to publication of several stories in his college paper, *The Quarto*. His developing moral imagination produced tales in the classical short story form, as opposed to the "slice-of-life" vignettes just then coming into fashion.[8] Most of his stories were written for the magazine-consuming populace, intended for the appetites of robust readers who wanted quick-moving events and scenes with a point—demands that he could meet particularly well because his training as a painter prepared him to think in scenes rather than sequences. He used the short story specifically as "a form of parable for popular consumption."[9] His first of these story collections was entitled *The Club of Queer Trades* (1905); five collections ensued in addition to the Father Brown collections, most of the stories having previously appeared separately in magazines. They included *The Man Who Knew Too Much* (1922), *Tales of the Long Bow* (1925),

---

[7] According to the editorial office at Ignatius Press, in a telephone conversation on November 13, 2000 (confirmed by a follow-up email October 23, 2014), the forty-five volumes of *The Collected Works of G. K. Chesterton* (twenty-three currently available) are not being published in numerical or chronological order, and some of the gaps unfortunately fall in the area of fiction. At this point, one standard issue of the Chesterton fiction is not recognized.

[8] Donald Barr, introduction to G. K. Chesterton, *The Collected Works of G. K. Chesterton*, ed. George J. Marlin and Richard P. Rabatin, vol. 8, *The Return of Don Quixote, Tales of the Long Bow, The Man Who Knew Too Much* (San Francisco: Ignatius Press, 1999), 21.

[9] Conlon, introduction to Chesterton, *Collected Works*, vol. 14, 14.

The Poet and the Lunatics (1929), and *Four Faultless Felons* (1930), with his last of the short story groupings, *The Paradoxes of Mr. Pond*, published posthumously (1937).

When *The Napoleon of Notting Hill* appeared in 1904, popular opinion held that Chesterton had "awakened the novel just when it was feeling the reaction after the Victorian era, and was not quite sure in what direction it might go."[10] Its publication was followed by *The Ball and the Cross* (serialized in 1905-6) and *The Man Who Was Thursday* (1908), the biblical themes of which established Chesterton as a solid writer of religious fiction by 1910. *Manalive* (1912) and *The Flying Inn* (1914) are full of the vigour of a writer in his prime, but, by the time he turned forty years of age, Chesterton's novel-writing days had almost ended. *The Return of Don Quixote* (serialized in *G. K.'s Weekly* in 1925-6 and published as a book in 1927) was to be his last—and not considered his best—novel.[11]

Even a casual reading through a portion of this fiction reveals the saturation of symbolic detail. These "random illustrations of a central theme" can be almost overwhelming—even "heavy-handed" and "intrusive."[12] Perhaps our sensitivity to the copiousness of Chesterton's metaphors is a result of our era's dearth of symbols of age and tradition that, it has been noted, are "not flourishing but on the contrary are under siege to the point of extinction."[13] Scholars have inquired into his wide-ranging emblems—a glass of milk, a piece of chalk,

---

[10] Patrick Braybrooke, *The Wisdom of G. K. Chesterton* (London: Cecil Palmer, 1929), 58.

[11] According to David Lodge, "Dual Vision: Chesterton as a Novelist," in *G. K. Chesterton: A Half Century of Views*, ed. Denis J. Conlon (Oxford: Oxford University Press, 1987), 326.

[12] Ian Boyd, *Novels of G. K. Chesterton: A Study in Art and Propaganda* (London: Paul Elek, 1975), 196.

[13] Hal G. P. Colebatch, "The Meanings of *The Napoleon of Notting Hill*," *Chesterton Review* 25, no. 4 (1999): 446.

a red necktie. The focus of this book is on Chesterton's literary use of the tree image, which figures in many of the stories.[14] A preliminary review of his life will help to organize the chronologically ordered stories; a comprehensive sampling of his fiction will demonstrate the recurrent appearance of the tree in his symbolic imagination.

Chesterton's "story" is the subject of this study—both his writing of story and his life as a story. How then have Chesterton's life and writings been interpreted? His own *Autobiography*, published just before his death in 1936, is a significant work revealing the biographical—as well as the psychological, theological, and literary—influences upon his choice of imagery.[15] The most consequential of the early biographies came out within a decade of his death, when, in 1944, family friend Maisie Ward wrote a life that is still considered indispensable, making full use of letters, notebooks, and the personal memoirs of Chesterton's friends and associates. Ward concentrated on showing his "developing but integrated" personality and mind, interpreting his work as Catholic "propaganda" meant to instruct rather than entertain.[16] Preceding Ward's biography, the 1938 memoirs of Father John O'Connor (the "original" Father Brown) sketched out a partial portrait of Chesterton through a series of quick studies illuminating the meeting and friendship of the two men, and Chesterton's conversion

---

[14] Recurrence of the tree in Chesterton's fiction has been noted by Martin Gardner in his introduction to *Four Faultless Felons*, xii.

[15] G. K. Chesterton, *The Autobiography of G. K. Chesterton* (New York: Sheed and Ward, 1936).

[16] Maisie Ward, *Gilbert Keith Chesterton* (London: Sheed and Ward, 1944). For a critique of Ward's Catholic reading of Chesterton, see Boyd, *Novels of G. K. Chesterton*, 138. Several of the critics have attended to the question of Chesterton's denominational predilection, so that the biases of both Catholic and Protestant writers are often notable.

to Catholicism.[17] Cyril Clemens's 1939 collection of the testimonies of several literary and personal colleagues is full of anecdotal memorials from letters and interviews.[18] Contemporary biographies include those by Dudley Barker (1973), Michael Ffinch (1986), and British-Canadian Michael Coren (1989), with a fairly recent (1996) interpretation by Joseph Pearce correcting some misconceptions about Chesterton's turn-of-the-century political and social views.[19] Alzina Stone Dale's significant and readable biography (1982) promotes Chesterton's timely renewal of visibility that she found to be due to his commonsensical, balanced judgements made against the grain of even his own era.[20] Other biographies are emerging.

The biographical works on the life of Chesterton were supplemented by critical studies; the first appeared anonymously in 1909 and was written by Cecil Chesterton, whose early discussion of his brother's central ideas as a British thinker and writer is somewhat disapproving.[21] In 1929, a selective collection of essays by Patrick Braybrooke preceded more serious considerations of Chesterton's life.[22] One of the important early criticisms

---

[17] John O'Connor, *Father Brown on Chesterton* (London: Frederick Muller, 1937).

[18] Cyril Clemens, *Chesterton As Seen by His Contemporaries* (New York: Haskell House Publishers, 1969).

[19] Barker, *G. K. Chesterton*; Michael Coren, *Gilbert: The Man Who Was G. K. Chesterton* (London: Jonathan Cape, 1989); Michael Ffinch, *G. K. Chesterton* (San Francisco: Harper and Row, 1986); Joseph Pearce, *Wisdom and Innocence: A Life of G. K. Chesterton* (London: Hodder and Stoughton, 1996).

[20] Alzina Stone Dale, *The Outline of Sanity: A Biography of G. K. Chesterton* (Grand Rapids: Eerdmans, 1982).

[21] [Cecil Chesterton], *G. K. Chesterton: A Criticism*, American ed. (New York: John Lane Company, 1909).

[22] Braybrooke, *The Wisdom of G. K. Chesterton*.

is Hilaire Belloc's 1940 definition of his friend's place within the literati of England, emphasizing Chesterton's lucidity and unity, and the parallel connections between all of his work and his life.[23] Garry Wills gave a 1961 psychological reading of Chesterton's writing.[24] This was followed thirty years later by Ian Crowther's treatment, which notes that "in works about Chesterton we generally learn a great deal more about the life of the man than the life of the mind"; Crowther strove to redress the balance by presenting an intelligible translation of Chesterton's thoughts.[25] Christopher Hollis gave a Catholic interpretation in his 1970 criticism.[26] The theme of the unity between Chesterton's thought and work was picked up and furthered by Lawrence Clipper, whose 1974 discussion highlights the orderly philosophy and uniform evidence throughout Chesterton's writing while it criticizes the "absolutism" of his pre-modern viewpoint.[27]

In recent years, literary analysis of Chesterton's fiction has been carried out by an increasing number of contemporary scholars. Lynette Hunter traced his development of allegory as an art form suitable for expressing his theological philosophy in light of his understanding of the interdependence of art, life, and religion.[28] Ian Boyd explored the correlation between the socio-political meanings and the literary value in Chesterton's fiction, attending to the interplay between his artistry and his intellect, his imagination and his mind.[29] Boyd's serious

---

[23] Hilaire Belloc, *On the Place of Gilbert Chesterton in English Letters* (New York: Sheed and Ward, 1940).

[24] Garry Wills, *Chesterton: Man and Mask* (New York: Sheed and Ward, 1961).

[25] Ian Crowther, *G. K. Chesterton*, Thinkers of our Time (London: The Claridge Press, 1991), preface.

[26] Hollis, *The Mind of Chesterton*.

[27] Clipper, *G. K. Chesterton*.

[28] Lynette Hunter, *G. K. Chesterton: Explorations in Allegory* (New York: St. Martin's Press, 1979).

[29] Boyd, *Novels of G. K. Chesterton*.

and detailed literary treatment of the fiction is valuable for its wholistic approach. As founder and editor of *The Chesterton Review*, he continues to provide a medium for the contributions of many writers on the life, thought, and works of G. K. Chesterton.

In light of the biographical and literary work already completed and the continuing interest indicated by reissues of his works and current studies underway, this research investigating G. K. Chesterton is timely. It seeks to contribute to the critical discussions of Chesterton's symbolism by Hunter, Boyd, and others by tracing in some detail one particular recurrent and polyvalent symbol through Chesterton's life and fiction. Such an exposition advances reader understanding of his powerful symbolic imagination and demonstrates his indebtedness to the canonical Scriptures and to centuries of Christian tradition. By shedding light on the formation and expression of Chesterton's own Christian imagination, this study also points to the richness of the sources upon which he drew. This is all the more significant today because many of his allusions are now lost on modern readers of a more secular age.[30]

---

[30] To create order in this study, I first pay attention to the inception of Chesterton's symbolic imagination and to his resulting literary use of the tree image in his fiction; then I note the correlation between Chesterton's writing and the wealth of English literature that precedes it. Part II of this book was written as an independent article but fits nicely with the discussion of the tree in Chesterton's fiction. Consideration of the many themes in his life is beyond the scope of this book, and is only mentioned where immediately relevant to the fiction piece in question; other scholars have considered his essays and journalism, his political and social theories, his denominational quandary, and details regarding his later life, the extensiveness of his travels, and the decline of his health. For my purposes, Chesterton's fiction sufficiently shows the philosophical unity evident throughout his life and writings.

The motif of the tree in the life and fiction of G. K. Chesterton emerges as more than simply incidental background setting, coming to bear thematic meanings already established in antecedent literature. Returning to that "honest quack," for example, Mr. Windrush's tree (whose squat trunk hides a corpse) is identified as a central, archetypal device previously imbued through myth and Scripture with the significance of the adventurer coming home and of marriage as a sacrament.[31] The story is a satire on science, a comment on the intrusion of the city into rural England, and an analysis of the tree as worthy for its beauty and regardless of its use.[32] However serviceably the image showcases several of the writer's political, social, and moral philosophies, by the end of the tale its foremost purpose is theological. It becomes a reminder of the fall of humanity by free choice beneath the forbidden tree in the Garden of Eden, of the wind of God's will which vanquishes despair, and of the hope of a new creation in "a blending of the orders of nature and grace."[33] It ends:

> On top of the once accursed tree a small bird burst into song; and at the same moment a great morning wind from the south rushed upon the garden, bending all its shrubs and bushes. . . . And it seemed . . . that something had been broken or loosened, a last bond with chaos and the night, a last strand of the net of some resisting Nothing that obstructs creation; and God had made a new garden and [the lovers] stood alive on the first foundations of the world.[34]

---

[31] These two pivotal themes are further exposited in G. K. Chesterton, *Manalive*, G. K. Chesterton Reprint Series (Beaconsfield: Darwen Finlayson, 1962).
[32] Boyd, *Novels of G. K. Chesterton*, 161-3.
[33] Ibid., 162-3.
[34] Chesterton, *Four Faultless Felons*, 103.

A review of Chesterton's life story followed by a survey of his use of the tree image establishes the formation of his symbolic imagination, demonstrates several influences upon his aesthetic and spiritual progress, and explores the fiction that came to embody his spiritual and literary vision.

TWO

ROOTING AND BRANCHING: G. K. CHESTERTON'S LIFE (1874-1936)

The Rooting: Youthful Formation (1874-1900)

The parks of London and his own backyard garden in Kensington must have been in full leaf on May 29, 1874, the day Gilbert Keith Chesterton was born. He was the first son of Edward and Marie Louise, but the arrival of brother Cecil soon provided an audience for Gilbert's stories and a playmate on the "well-rubbed lawn" of their walled garden blooming with jasmine, roses, and irises.[1] Some of Chesterton's first recollections centred on the playground of his garden, supplying images for his fiction stories.[2] The tall trees standing as sentinels at the far end of the yard provided shade for Chesterton's summer reading, albeit little protection against the rainstorms to which he would abandon his book on running indoors, later finding "all that remained of a prized volume was a soggy mess."[3] On special evenings, Edward

---

[1] Ward, *Gilbert Keith Chesterton*, 19-20. For the setting of a walled garden, see, e.g., the insane asylum described in G. K. Chesterton, *The Ball and the Cross* (New York: Dover Publications, 1995); discussed below.

[2] Note that Chesterton's first and second childhood homes, at Campden Hill and Warwick Gardens, were both near Kensington Gardens, which was a lovely, tree-filled park offering him "the variety of the wide world in miniature," according to Dale, *Outline of Sanity*.

[3] Coren, *Gilbert: The Man Who Was G. K. Chesterton*, 16. Weather changes become indicators of emotional or spiritual activity in several stories; see, e.g., "The Crime of Gabriel Gale" in G. K. Chesterton, *The Poet and the Lunatics: Episodes in the Life of Gabriel Gale* (London: Cassell and Company, 1929); discussed below.

would hang out "fairy lamps" to twinkle among the trees.[4] The garden and its trees, in fact, formed a theatre for much of Gilbert's childhood, acclaimed as "one of the happiest in English literature."[5] To simply list each exposure to a tree in Chesterton's life would prove a futile and facile exercise, yet to take account of the recurrence of this emblem throughout his life story is not arbitrary. Rather, it illustrates how his aesthetic formation brought forth his artistic expression. The tree of his childhood came to symbolize the sacramental intertwining of the celestial with the terrestrial. In an introductory poem to his first novel, for example, he wrote,

> For every tiny town or place
> God made the stars especially;
> Babies look up with owlish face
> And see them tangled in a tree:
> . . . .
> Yea; Heaven is everywhere at home.[6]

Chesterton's preschool years were leisurely, full of wonder and delight in a secure and loving home. His mother provided domestic care, but it was his father who ignited the boy's imagination and creativity.[7] Mr. Chesterton relished his time at home and, though he

---

[4] According to Ada Chesterton, Cecil's wife, as cited by Dale, *Outline of Sanity*, 10. The illuminated tree becomes a reappearing theme in Chesterton's fiction; for example, "lanterns swinging from the garden trees," can be seen in "The Secret of Father Brown" in G. K. Chesterton, *The Complete Father Brown* (London: Penguin Books, 1981), 466.

[5] Coren, *Gilbert: The Man Who Was G. K. Chesterton*, 14.

[6] In "To Hilaire Belloc," introductory poem to G. K. Chesterton, *The Napoleon of Notting Hill* (Ware, U.K.: Wordsworth Editions, 1996).

[7] According to Kevin L. Morris, "Chesterton Sees Red: The Metaphysics of a Colour," *Chesterton Review* 21, no. 4 (1995): 506.

sold houses for a living, he "filled his own house with his life."[8] His hobbies overran the home, a "hundred hobbies, piled on top of each other."[9] The impression was not lost upon his sons. Gilbert's earliest visual memory was of the toy theatre his father constructed, upon which Edward performed for his sons the plays he had written, doubtless inspired by the English classics that were a part of the family life. The toy theatre, lit with candles that Chesterton described as a "forest of fairy trees," was a well-known influence on the boy's incipient imagination.[10] The puppet shows entertained him and his brother on many evenings and, as an adult and husband, the childless G. K. Chesterton would render his own versions upon the stage of his own theatre for the visiting youngsters of his friends and neighbours. He cherished these earliest memories—the fleeting images of childhood that stir the emotions—regarding "that mysterious state of innocence" as "the first and best spring" for later philosophy.[11]

Chesterton's early imaginative life was stimulated also by books. Although he did not begin to read until he was nine years of age, his father's love of the language, literature, and history of England ensured the boy's literary education, starting with fairy tales told in the

---

[8] Chesterton, *Autobiography*, 2, 36. Perhaps Edward's profession provided a model for "The Singular Speculation of the House-Agent" in G. K. Chesterton, *The Club of Queer Trades* (Hertfordshire: Wordsworth Editions, 1995), 48-64.

[9] Chesterton, *Autobiography*, 37.

[10] As quoted by Morris, *Chesterton Sees Red*, 506. For discussion on the formative influence of the puppet theatre, see, e.g., Christiane d' Haussy, "The Symbolism of the Key in Chesterton's Work," *Seven* 4 (1983): 38-44.

[11] G. K. Chesterton, *Saint Thomas Aquinas: The Dumb Ox* (New York: Doubleday, 1956), 131. For the importance of childhood memories, see also "The Man with the Golden Key" in Chesterton, *Autobiography*, 24-50.

nursery. Chesterton said in *Orthodoxy* (1908), "I knew the magic beanstalk before I had tasted beans."[12] First readings, he wrote, "made a difference to my whole existence . . . [and] helped me to see things in a certain way right from the start" by awakening a curiosity and joy in the ordinary—"staircases and doors and windows into magical things."[13] The island adventures of Robert Louis Stevenson and Daniel Defoe gave him a taste for romance, and Dickens was so familiar to the boy that he would stumble down the street, unaware of his surroundings, as he muttered long passages from memory.[14] From his earliest days, he was "steeped in literature"; yet he did not limit himself to the classics.[15] His reading was eclectic, and his pockets bulged even as an adult with pulp magazines and "penny dreadfuls" (which were cheap and sensational detective stories bought at the railway stations). Dale testified, "He refused—on principle—to be a highbrow."[16] He carried with him into his career this championing the literature of the common person, never disparaging the "uneducated" or boasting about the more serious essays he would later produce. He saw fairy tales, legends, and ancient as well as popular myths to be a reservoir of perspectives on

[12] G. K. Chesterton, *Orthodoxy* in *The Collected Works of G. K. Chesterton*, ed. David Dooley, vol. 1, *Orthodoxy, Heretics, Blatchford Controversy* (San Francisco: Ignatius Press, 1986), 252.

[13] Chesterton in his "Introduction" to *George MacDonald and His Wife*, quoted by Ward, *Gilbert Keith Chesterton*, 15.

[14] Chesterton's readings were so broad that a comprehensive listing is out of the scope of this paper: poetry, fiction, and essay include Dante and Donne, Macaulay and Milton, Aquinas and Bunyan and Chaucer, Swinburne and Spenser and Pope, Kipling, and Wells.

[15] E. C. Bentley's memoir of Chesterton in Clemens, *Chesterton As Seen by His Contemporaries*, iii-iv.

[16] Dale, *Outline of Sanity*, 21.

truth and sound morality.[17] Furthermore, Chesterton did not ignore the Christian Scriptures despite the nonreligious tone of his childhood home, especially enjoying the Old Testament. Cecil recounted that it was because his brother was not forced to read the Bible that he read it, "much to the advantage of his literary style."[18] In fact, the major literary influence in his work is seen to have been scriptural, as "it was the Old Testament which fed his imagination in its deepest recesses, colouring his mind ever after with the rhetoric of Isaias and Job."[19] Chesterton's expansive reading is evident in even his earliest stories, which are peppered with allusions and quotations from a remarkably wide range of authors.[20]

Not only his home but also his school life influenced Chesterton's imagination. Unlike most boys in late nineteenth-century England, he attended a day school that did not demand dormitory residence, but he found it difficult to fit into a formal program of study.[21] His transition from home to the classroom was not smooth and, in a way, never completely made; like his father, Gilbert was a homebody. He described his classroom education at St. Paul's Preparatory School (1887-1892) as that period "during which I was being instructed by

---

[17] See his early essays, such as "The Philosophy of Penny Dreadfuls," "Defense of Slang," and "The Value of Detective Stories," as noted by Clipper, *G. K. Chesterton*, 87.

[18] Cecil Chesterton, *G. K. Chesterton: A Criticism*, 8.

[19] Wills, *Chesterton: Man and Mask*, 33.

[20] For example, in one story written while still a teenager, he swept widely across the literature by mentioning—all in the one story—Chaucer, the medieval legend of the Holy Grail, Tennyson, Thackery, Browning, Whitman, Rosetti, Stevenson, and Kipling, as well as talmudic and biblical literature. See "Basil Howe" in Chesterton, *Collected Works*, vol. 14, 444-533; written in the early 1890s.

[21] According to Pearce, *Wisdom and Innocence*, 26.

somebody I did not know, about something I did not want to know."[22] His disinterest and unhappiness at school were obvious. Held back in a form with pupils two years his junior, he was a messy, absent-minded boy who shambled through the halls awkwardly towering above his shorter mates. His high, squeaky voice never fully deepened, eventually mellowing only into a tenor even as a man. Chesterton entered adolescence late, a fact used by some as an explanation for the troubling depression he was later to suffer. He was still slim and quite good-looking at school, but his mature physical appearance would be startling.[23] As a boy, he often wore a scowl due to the squint of short-sightedness, and even this experience affected his later descriptions of the tree.[24] The student brought home poor grades despite his evident ability, and spent his desk-bound hours sketching caricatures of his teachers or scenes from Shakespeare, giving the overall impression of being "asleep and dreaming."[25] Chesterton's worried parents even took him to see a brain specialist, who concluded that he had an equal chance of growing up to be either a genius or an imbecile.[26] All this while, however, in a tension between resisting and absorbing knowledge, he ag-

---

[22] Chesterton, *Autobiography*, 52.

[23] When boldly asked his dimensions after one of his lectures years later, Chesterton replied, "I am six feet three inches. As to my weight, no method has yet been found to calculate it." Quoted in "Our Mr. Chesterton: Glimpses of Gilbert," *Gilbert Magazine*, October-November 2000, 8. In fact, he eventually weighed nearly three hundred pounds.

[24] His character Adam Wayne, for example, is so short sighted that "the red and white and yellow suns of the gaslights thronged and melted into each other like an orchard of fiery trees." Chesterton, *Napoleon of Notting Hill*, 54.

[25] Chesterton, *Autobiography*, 67.

[26] Dale, *Outline of Sanity*, 19. For a fictive genius/imbecile, see "The Noticeable Conduct of Professor Chadd" in Chesterton, *Club of Queer Trades*.

gressively continued his learning at home—literature from his father, arts and culture from museum and gallery visits, and rhetoric from political debates around the kitchen table with his brother.

Despite his resistance to institutionalized education and his discontent in the classroom, the youth forged several close, lifelong friendships that influenced his writing. One, for example, was with E. C. Bentley, whose athleticism stood in stark contrast to Chesterton's own clumsiness—the source of many jokes in the school gymnasium.[27] Chesterton wrote in *Autobiography* that he found it "a poetic pleasure" to see Bentley walk "a little pompously" down the street and suddenly "scale a lamppost like a monkey."[28] Perhaps it is little wonder, considering Chesterton's physical limitations, that his fictional characters are constantly climbing trees.[29] Although the boys were unmatched in physical ability, Bentley's friendship provided Chesterton many opportunities to exercise at least his wit and artistry by putting to play his childhood "doodling" habit as illustrator and co-writer of a volume of poetry later published as *Biography for Beginners*.

---

[27] On one occasion, an exercise on the rings required hands and feet to be inserted and the body turned. Gilbert, hands in rings, could not get his feet up. The instructor seized his feet and pushed them in, whereupon Gilbert let go with his hands, leaving the instructor staggering under the full weight of his limp body; Pearce, *Wisdom and Innocence*, 15-16. In a fictive replay of this scene in *Manalive* (1912), Innocent Smith "would hook the rake on to the branch of a tree, and hoist himself up with horrible gymnastic jerks, like those of a giant frog in its final agony." Chesterton, *Manalive*, 147.

[28] Chesterton, *Autobiography*, 55.

[29] Chesterton's health was an obstacle restricting him from later military service; his contributions came in the form of supportive (or, more often, critical) articles, stories, and pamphlets.

The "clerihew," an example of Bentley's famous verse form, hints at the familiarity the boys had with classics of literature, even at this young age: "The people of Spain think Cervantes / Equal to half-a-dozen Dantes, / An opinion resented most bitterly / By the people of Italy."[30]

"Boys wander in threes," Chesterton said, explaining his principal friendships; "Three is certainly the symbolic number for comradeship."[31] So, at about fifteen years of age, he, Bentley, and Lucian Oldershaw founded the Junior Debating Club (JDC) with the intent of reading Shakespeare aloud, although its purpose changed to discussing literary topics and later included politics. The club routine consisted of tea at the home of one member followed by the reading of a paper on a literary figure and intensive (if juvenile) criticism and analysis. The JDC offered Chesterton an arena in which to evidence his wide reading and exercise his bookish memory, and it was formative in his social and literary life.[32] Every issue of *The Debater*, the club's informal paper, included his contributions of essay and verse

---

[30] Quoted by Ward, *Gilbert Keith Chesterton*, 41. Current clerihew writing is encouraged by the editors of *Gilbert Magazine,* who reserve a column for present-day contributions.

[31] Chesterton, *Autobiography*, 55. See also Morris, *Chesterton Sees Red*. The proliferation of symbolic numbers, colours, and names in Chesterton's work is evident at a glance through his fiction. See, e.g., Olive Ashley's search for medieval colour in *Tales of the Long Bow* (1925). Cf. Chesterton's essay, *G. F. Watts* (London: Duckworth, 1904).

[32] It has been noted that a "debating club quality" is a common feature of Chesterton's work and can be seen, for example, in the woodland discourses between Dalroy and Pump in G. K. Chesterton, *The Flying Inn* in *A G. K. Chesterton Omnibus* (London, Methuen, 1947), 725. See further John Coates, "Symbol and Structure in *The Flying Inn*," *Chesterton Review* 4, no. 2 (1978): 256.

that, Dudley Barker noted, indicated "how the years of solitary reading had shaped his mind."[33] His publishing efforts won him St. Paul's coveted prize, the Milton Award—a rare honour for a boy who had not achieved standing in the eighth form at school.[34] Chesterton's literary expression was beginning to surface just as he left St. Paul's at the age of eighteen and the end of his boyhood.

As he neared puberty, Chesterton's early love of home, his sense of wonder and imagination even in the ordinary things of life, and his yearning for romantic adventure were invigorated by a growing interest in the supernatural realm. Although he had been baptized into the Church of England as a baby, his general upbringing was not religious, for his freethinking parents were Unitarian.[35] Chesterton's educated household was situated in Kensington, an area of London that was a "hub of late-Victorian arts and letters" as well as the "symbol of prosperous and respectable middle-class virtue" (and the neighborhood where Queen Victoria herself had grown up).[36] Thus, the boy was raised at the historical locus of the Christian literary culture, yet his home was like many in that day when Victorian ethics and theology were "wearing thin throughout."[37] That is, he had very little practical experience of church doctrine; myths and legends had been substituted for orthodox Christianity that, as Dale noted, was increasingly seen as just one

---

[33] Barker, *G. K. Chesterton*, 31-32. *The Debater* had a circulation of sixty to one hundred; the papers were printed on a home duplicating machine and sold around the school for sixpence a copy.

[34] St. Paul's had been the school of the Puritan writer John Milton.

[35] Unitarianism was an eighteenth-century religious sect that denied the Godhead of Christ and that, by Chesterton's day, had degenerated into a system of ethics.

[36] Dale, *Outline of Sanity*, 16.

[37] Chesterton, *Autobiography*, 20.

story among many.[38] Yet the culture still retained a
sense of romance or, as Chesterton was later to say, a
yearning for significance and a desire to recreate that
love between man and woman that had been lost in
Eden.[39] In spite of the absence of Christian training at
home, his interest in the numinous was awakened
through his personal biblical readings as well as immersion in a literature rich in scriptural tradition that made
him "heir to a long English heritage."[40] Further to his

---

[38] Dale, *Outline of Sanity*, 15. See further Alzina
Stone Dale, "G. K. Chesterton, the Disreputable Victori-
an," in *G. K. Chesterton and C. S. Lewis: The Riddle of
Joy*, ed. Michael H. Macdonald and Andrew A. Tadie
(Grand Rapids: Eerdmans, 1989), 141-59.

[39] Chesterton, *Autobiography*, 142. For romantic
love re-created, see "The End of Wisdom" in Chesterton,
Collected Works, vol. 14, 372.

[40] Peter R. Hunt, "Dickens's Influence on Chesterton's Imaginative Writing," *Chesterton Review* 7, no. 1
(1981): 36-49. Hunt found especially Dickens's influence
everywhere in Chesterton's writing—in the romantic
style of his fiction, in the theme of journey, in descriptions of landscapes, in imagery, and in allegory. Moreover, the influence of biblical teaching upon the culture
and literature of England has been thoroughly substantiated; see further Lawrence E. Nelson, *Our Roving Bible:
Tracking Its Influence Through English And American
Life* (New York: Abingdon-Cokesbury Press, 1945); David Lyle Jeffrey, *People of the Book: Christian Identity
and Literary Culture* (Grand Rapids: Eerdmans, with The
Institute for Advanced Christian Studies, 1996); Abraham Avni, "The Influence of the Bible on European Literatures: A Review of Research from 1955-1965,"
Yearbook of Comparative and General Literature 19
(1970): 39-57; Abraham Albert Avni, *The Bible and Romanticism: The Old Testament in German and French
Romantic Poetry* in *Studies in General and Comparative
Literature* (The Hague, Paris: Mouton, 1969). For Chesterton's view on European culture preceding Victorian

broad independent reading, he received religious in-
struction at school.[41] Even at the young age of twelve,
his school fellows recognized this metaphysical hunger in
Chesterton; Oldershaw said, "We felt . . . that he was
looking for God."[42] Chesterton himself declared that he
was "a pagan at twelve and a complete agnostic by the
age of sixteen," yet he was "a struggling, thinking agnostic."[43] He left his boyhood on a quest.

Chesterton's creativity had a sound initiation in
his childhood home, school, and social life, with his
readings piquing an interest in larger philosophical ques-

---

literature, see G. K. Chesterton, *The Victorian Age in Literature* (London: Oxford University Press, 1955).

[41] Lucian Oldershaw made mention of the religious training (albeit by agnostic teachers) at St. Paul's,
as noted by Chesterton, *Autobiography*, 143.

[42] Lucian Oldershaw, quoted in Ward, *Gilbert
Keith Chesterton*, 26.

[43] Chesterton as quoted in Dale, *Outline of Sanity*, 34. See also Leo A. Hetzler, "Chesterton's Writings in
His Teenage Years," in *G. K. Chesterton: A Half Century
of Views*, ed. Denis J. Conlon (Oxford: Oxford University
Press, 1987), 296. Hetzler stated that Chesterton opposed the idea of divine inspiration of Scripture at four-
teen years of age and believed that the church holding
to this doctrine was simply the "salt required to keep it,
until men could appreciate grand literature for its own
sake." At this early point, Chesterton found the Bible to
be only a part of humanity's mystical experience and the
Judaeo-Christian belief too limited. But his maturing
writing is better characterized by the increasing use of
and allusion to Scripture, which can often be recognized
only by those readers very familiar with the Bible, according to Ian Boyd. Boyd claimed that, as a theological
writer, Chesterton was totally biblical; Ian Boyd, "Chesterton and the Bible," *Chesterton Review* 11, no. 1
(1985): 21-31. For Chesterton's opinion of the teaching
of the Bible as literature, see G. K. Chesterton, "The
Protection of the Bible," *Chesterton Review* 22, no. 3
(1996): 289-91.

tions. The answers he sought were not quick in coming, for his journey was circuitous and his conversion gradual. Late-Victorian England had lost much of its Christian ethos, and an unhealthy interest in the occult was being promoted by theosophists just as Chesterton began his spiritual query in earnest. He and Cecil had begun dabbling in occult activity while still in public school, playing with "planchette"—that is, the Ouija board. As a young man, Chesterton "blundered into rather queer and uncomfortable corners of Spiritualism" that led to a period of depression he described as "congestion of imagination" and "moral anarchy within."[44] These experiences, taking place over several years and acting as a detour, did however convince him of the reality of the devil, and of evil as not simply the absence of good but as a positive force in itself.[45] This experimentation with what he called "diabolism" was perhaps an extension of his emotional, intellectual sensitivity, for he said that even

> at a very early age I had thought my way back to thought itself. It is a very dreadful thing to do; for it may lead to thinking that there is nothing but thought. At this time I did not very clearly distinguish between dreaming and waking; not only as a mood but as a metaphysical doubt, I felt as if everything might be a dream. It was as if I had myself projected the universe from within, with all its trees and stars; and that is so near to the notion of being

---

[44] Chesterton, *Autobiography*, 82, 89. Although he avoided occult motifs after his childhood, the theme of anarchy became central in G. K. Chesterton, *The Man Who Was Thursday: A Nightmare*, ed. Stephen Medcalf (Oxford: Oxford University Press, 1996).

[45] *The Ball and the Cross* provides an example of how Chesterton pitted good against evil, picturing face-to-face combat between Michael and Lucifer, and between the asylum inmates and the keepers; see below.

God that it is manifestly even nearer to going mad.[46]

Chesterton ever after harboured a fear of this solipsistic belief that only the self exists, a belief that had led him close to the chasm of nihilism.[47]

Chesterton's early imaginative life, his surroundings of home and garden as well as his religious curiosity that nurtured an inner tension, produced a creative youth who was, above other activities, always drawing. His ultimate conversion to orthodox Christianity incorporated an aesthetic element; it has been said that he had an "imaginative conversion" in which he first discovered his "innermost intentional symbols" that then drove him to search for the ultimate meaning they represented.[48] One could say that Chesterton's moral imagination was baptized while still in its infancy, awaiting a later confirmation. In understanding his coming to Christian faith, one must take into account this generating of his artistic literary model, which was founded upon early readings and experiences but defined in his post-adolescent years.

Chesterton's period of young manhood was initiated by entrance into the Slade School of Art (1892), where his talents as draughtsman and caricaturist were

---

[46] Chesterton, *Autobiography*, 88.

[47] The powerful influence of his brush with lunacy became the basis of the madness, for example, of his character Lord Ivywood, driven insane by his own declaration of transcendent Godhood: "I have gone where God has never dared to go. . . . I walk in the heavens, as no man has walked before me; and I am alone in the garden." Chesterton, *The Flying Inn*, 725.

[48] David Leigh, "The Psychology of Conversion in Chesterton's and Lewis's Autobiographies," in *G. K. Chesterton and C. S. Lewis: The Riddle of Joy*, ed. Michael H. Macdonald and Andrew A. Tadie (Grand Rapids: Eerdmans, 1989), 300.

refined and later applied in commercial endeavors.[49] Art training laid a foundation for his budding style in fiction as well, his writing employing colourful verbal scenes with the perception of a painter. Dale noted that it was Chesterton's lifelong fascination with light that led to the memorable verbal descriptions of sunrise and sunset, misty streets and shadowy lanes, "'setting the scene' by means of a very Impressionist imagination."[50] Even his childhood scribbling had shown him how to be "an artist in thought"; he drew pictures of his fiction ideas before he started writing the fiction, as if his mind "saw" the story ideas and "seized instinctively upon the essences of them."[51] His fiction is not simply descriptive but also reflects some underlying meaning or purpose. This propensity to look beneath the surface gives nuance to his scene setting and alerts the reader to watch for the meanings behind even his most casual mention of such images as the tree.

---

[49] Chesterton's cartoons were printed in various London papers and in his own *G. K.'s Weekly*. He illustrated both his own works (e.g., *Greybeards at Play*, one of his first books to be published, in 1900), and those of other authors (notably the novels of Hilaire Belloc). George Bernard Shaw, another of his famous friends, was later to coin the term "chesterbelloc" to describe the close intellectual relationship between the other two men, who produced a great quantity of written work together. Ffinch, *G. K. Chesterton*, 75; Pearce, *Wisdom and Innocence*, 51-63; Ward, *Gilbert Keith Chesterton*, 195, 466.

[50] Dale, *Outline of Sanity*, 31. Note that Chesterton himself would likely have resisted the comparison of his work to Impressionism, even if only in technique. For an example of Chesterton's own Impressionist technique, in a story that condemns Impressionist philosophy, see *The Man Who Was Thursday*.

[51] Ronald Knox, "G. K. Chesterton: The Man and His Work," in *G. K. Chesterton: A Half Century of Views*, ed. Denis J. Conlon (Oxford: Oxford University Press, 1987), 46.

At the Slade School of Art, Chesterton encountered Impressionist painting, which was just coming into
vogue. The "art for art's sake" movement, with its emphasis on form over content, was being advocated in the
studios and classrooms of London in a time when "the
avant-garde in the arts were nearly unanimous in seeking to purge the arts of morality or doctrine of any
kind."[52] He reacted negatively to Impressionism, which
he regarded as a philosophy or ideology rather than just
an art technique—"a denial of the value of the world
outside us," as Stephen Medcalf put it.[53] Chesterton explained in *Autobiography*:

> But I think there was a spiritual signifi-
> cance in Impressionism, in connection
> with this age as the age of scepticism. I
> mean that it illustrated scepticism in the
> sense of subjectivism. Its principle was
> that if all that could be seen of a cow was
> a white line and a purple shadow, we
> should only render the line and the shad-
> ow; in a sense we should only believe in
> the line and the shadow, rather than in
> the cow. He tended rather to say that he
> had only seen a purple cow; or rather that
> he had not seen the cow but only the pur-
> ple. Whatever may be the merits of this as
> a method of art, there is obviously some-
> thing highly subjective and sceptical about
> it as a method of thought. It naturally
> lends itself to the metaphysical suggestion

[52] Thomas Peters, *The Christian Imagination: G.
K. Chesterton on the Arts* (San Francisco: Ignatius
Press, 2000), 48.
[53] Stephan Medcalf, "Introduction" to G. K. Chesterton, *The Man Who Was Thursday: A Nightmare*, ed.
Stephen Medcalf (Oxford: Oxford University Press,
1996), xv.

that things only exist as we perceive them, or that things do not exist at all.[54]

The Impressionists, with their vagueness of meaning and lack of limitation, seemed to be saying that, because the artist cannot know what reality actually is, he should therefore avoid realistic representation, for "the most he can hope to draw is the image of his own mind—his impression."[55] In response to this prevalent school, Chesterton began exploring his own theory of art—literary as well as visual—that sought the meaning behind the image.[56] He rejected the notion that, in a sort of boundless creativity, the "imagination is supposed to work towards the infinite," becoming convinced instead that "the object of opening the mind, as of opening the mouth, is to shut it again on something solid."[57] There was a solid, objective reality underlying the universe, he felt. He recalled the theatre plays of his father, and the street-side Punch and Judy puppet performances in which cloth and wood concealed the animating force, for

> the magic figures could be moved by three human fingers . . . which [also] hold the pen and the sword and the bow of the violin; the very three fingers that the priest lifts in benediction as the emblem of the Blessed Trinity.[58]

The tangibility of the puppet shows of his nursery days had translated truths and principles concerning the underlying reality of good and evil. Now, in contrast, Chesterton saw the nebulousness of Impressionism as

---

[54] Chesterton, *Autobiography*, 87.

[55] Hollis, *The Mind of* Chesterton, 28.

[56] For an examination of Chesterton's theories of art and the imagination, see further Peters, *The Christian Imagination.*

[57] Chesterton, *Autobiography*, 103-5, 288-9.

[58] Ibid., 45.

expressing its own latent message of meaninglessness. He believed "that the form is not superficial but fundamental; that the form is the foundation."[59] In other words, the external structure of artistic expression is not important solely for its own sake, but reveals much about the artist's internal intentions, motives, and beliefs.

The fiction story, then, by its very form tells something important about the storyteller. Chesterton created a form for himself that he described as "the romantically inclined philosophic" or "allegorical comedy," in which rapid, symbolic scenes take the place of long arguments to communicate thoughts.[60] This form accurately expressed his expanding inner views, for the ideas were more significant than the art; he declared that he never took his fiction as seriously as he took the ideas behind his fiction.[61] The Impressionist separation of art from reality had not given him a satisfying model, for its solipsistic philosophy portrayed the artist as supreme creator, unencumbered with any external reality. Neither had he subscribed to the prevalent scientific rationalism, unwilling as it was to admit to the existence or authority of something beyond its own system of understanding. In rejecting the options of Impressionism and rationalism, Chesterton adopted the ritualistic and allegorical philosophies of the literary giants he had been reading— Chaucer and Aristotle, Aquinas and Dante.[62] He would come to say, "Every great literature has always been

---

[59] Chesterton, *Saint Thomas Aquinas*, 158.

[60] Chesterton, *Collected Works*, vol. 14, 769.

[61] Chesterton, *Autobiography*, 107, 332. In fact, Chesterton never regarded his fiction as highly as some others have, believing himself to be more of a journalist than a novelist; he liked to see "ideas wrestling naked," not "all dressed up in a masquerade as men and women." Chesterton, *Autobiography*, 298.

[62] For a discussion on Chesterton's development of allegory as an art form suitable for expressing the interdependence of art, life, and religion, see Hunter, *Explorations in Allegory*.

allegorical. . . . The Illiad is only great because all life is a battle, the Odyssey because all life is a journey, the Book of Job because all life is a riddle."[63]

Of course, as a youth and before his debut as a career writer in 1900, Chesterton's definition and application of a religious literary philosophy had not yet acquired the depth it would later reflect in his declaration that "art is the signature of man."[64] In *The Everlasting Man*, he would argue that it is the ability to create that differentiates the human from other creatures; the *imago Dei* mirrors God's creativity.[65] But at even the most tender age, he felt "the ache of the artist to find some sense and some story" in the beauty of life, a "hunger for secrets" and an "anger at any tower or tree escaping with its tale untold."[66] Every tree had its tale, and Chesterton, even in his earliest fiction, could not resist the urge to allow the underlying philosophical ideas to dictate the storyline, characters, and images. He was developing, through parable and allegory (between which he made no distinction, using the terms interchangeably), a story form that sought to teach and persuade.[67]

---

[63] Barker, *G. K. Chesterton*, 91; quoting an unnoted edition of *The Speaker*.

[64] G. K. Chesterton, *The Everlasting Man* (San Francisco: Ignatius Press, 1993), 34.

[65] See also Brian L. Horne, "'Art: A Trinitarian Imperative?'," in *Trinitarian Theology Today*, ed. Christoph Schwobel, 80-91 (Edinburgh: T&T Clark, 1995).

[66] Peters, *The Christian Imagination*, 104.

[67] Boyd, *Novels of G. K. Chesterton*, 8. Chesterton's art as propaganda, indicating the tension between his imagination and his mind, was thoroughly exposited also in Ian Boyd, "Philosophy in Fiction," in *G. K. Chesterton: A Centenary Appraisal*, ed. John Sullivan (London: Paul Elek, 1974). See further Ian Boyd, "In Search of the Essential Chesterton," *Seven* 1 (1980): 28-45. An examination by Chesterton on the way words assume value can be seen in the short story "A Crazy Tale" in Chesterton, *Collected Works*, vol. 14, 69-75.

As Chesterton left art school in 1895, and with "little help from philosophy and no real help from religion," he formulated a functional world view based on gratitude; he found that "even mere existence, reduced to its most primary limits, was extraordinary enough to be exciting."[68] He remembered the optimistic theism he had learned in the nursery under the esotericism of such fantasy writers as George MacDonald and now, as a young man, he began to look at things with "a mystical minimum of gratitude."[69] This new optimism, love for humanity, and thankfulness for his mere existence can be seen in his notebooks, which at this time displayed a deepening notion of the divinity of God, though the influence of his brush with spiritual darkness gives realism especially to his later murder mysteries.[70] He had "wandered to a position not very far from the place of [his] Puritan grandfather, when he had said that he would thank God for his creation if he were a lost soul."[71] But at this point thankfulness—and not Christian doctrine—described his beliefs. His previous dabbling in the occult had led to a pessimism common to the age; he now climbed out of that into a mysticism and optimistic realism as he "hung on to the remains of religion by one thin thread of thanks."[72]

The finding of Chesterton's orthodox faith related to the formation of his artistic vision; it has been said that it is impossible to exaggerate the importance of the idea of art within his spiritual thought and views.[73] His earliest, pre-Christian understanding of God, then, had to do with His performance as Creator of the world: God

---

[68] Chesterton, *Autobiography*, 89-90.

[69] Ibid., 90.

[70] For example, in "The Wrong Shape," Father Brown solves the "twisted, ugly, complex" mystery through his knowledge of "the crooked track of a man"; Chesterton, *The Complete Father Brown*, 100.

[71] Chesterton, *Autobiography*, 90.

[72] Ibid.

[73] John Peterson, "The Nutshell," *Gilbert Magazine*, December 2000, 7.

was defined not as Father, Judge, or Saviour, but rather as an artist. Chesterton believed that a personal God had made a world that was separate from Himself, for

> God was a Creator, as an artist is a creator. A poet is so separate from his poem that he himself speaks of it as a little thing he has 'thrown off.' Even in giving it forth [as in birth] he has flung it away. . . . All creation is separation.[74]

The creation of the universe (as a production of the Creator), and of the person as "a statue of God walking about the garden," became the aesthetic basis of Chesterton's Christian conversion and literary expression, explaining the unity that characterized his life and writing.[75] His conviction that God was to be found in the physical, material objects of the world merged with a mystical understanding of revelation to form in him a sacramental view of life in which "apparently profane realities are really sacramental signs from God."[76] His ongoing curiosity in the created order was met by Christian teaching as "instinct after instinct was answered by doctrine after doctrine," which he came to express through his fiction in corresponding story after story.[77]

---

[74] Chesterton, *Orthodoxy*, 281.

[75] Ibid., 298.

[76] Ian Boyd, "The Legendary Chesterton," in *G. K. Chesterton and C. S. Lewis: The Riddle of Joy*, ed. Michael H. Macdonald and Andrew A. Tadie (Grand Rapids: Eerdmans, 1989), 64. Sacramentalism was a central principle in Chesterton's fiction; see, e.g., the discussion regarding "Apotheosis" and "The Point of a Pin," below.

[77] Chesterton, *Orthodoxy*, 282-3. See also Boyd, *Novels of G. K. Chesterton*, 14. According to his brother, Cecil, the major doctrines of Chesterton's theology include man as the image of God, free will, the fall and original sin, incarnation, and sacramentalism; Cecil Chesterton, *G. K. Chesterton: A Criticism*, 138.

The Branching: Mature Expression (1900-1936)

Chesterton emerged into public sight in 1900 with the printing of his first two books of poetry, *Greybeards at Play* and *The Wild Knight*. He had previously produced a few book and art reviews and several short stories, but the completion in 1899 of his six-year job as a reader at the publishing house of Fisher Unwin allowed him to enter into a fulltime career in writing. By the turn of the century, his journalistic essays and articles began to appear regularly in London's *Daily News* and in *The Speaker*.[78] Commissioned in 1903 to write his first of eight biographies for the "English Men of Letters" series—a volume on Robert Browning—Chesterton received censure from the editor for his factually inaccurate, loose quotations made without reference to exact wording used by the subjects. He defended himself: "I quote from memory both by temper and on principle. That is what literature is for; it ought to be part of a man."[79] Despite his carefree approach to scholarship, Chesterton's literary criticisms were well received by a public that applauded his transparency.

By the time he was in his mid-twenties, the subject of religion became increasingly interesting to Chesterton, who was seeking integration between spirituality and his artistic vision.[80] He did not yet call himself a

---

[78] Chesterton had retained close ties to this small weekly paper since his school days, when he published his first nonfiction article in it. He and his friends used the paper largely to attack British Imperialism, specifically as it pertained to the Boer War.

[79] Quoted by Barker, *G. K. Chesterton*, 128. See also "Chapter One: Romance of a Man Reading" in Clipper, *G. K. Chesterton*.

[80] Chesterton, claimed by Catholics to be a Catholic writer and by Protestants as one of their own, did not join the Catholic Church until he was almost fifty years old. The bulk of his best fiction had already been written, and some say his Father Brown stories began to

Christian, for, although he was "tending towards the more Christian elements in his surroundings," his spiritual transformation was not complete before his relationship with Frances, whom he described as having "brought the Cross to me."[81] Frances Blogg lived in Bedford Park, London's first garden suburb and a bohemian community of artists and poets.[82] She was a religious woman who had been educated at a local High Church convent and who was diligent in prayer and Bible reading.[83] Chesterton said that Frances had "a sort of hungry appetite for all the fruitful things like fields and gardens and anything connected with production," and her practicality impressed him.[84] The specifics of Frances's influence upon her husband's conversion are not well known, as she treasured her privacy and asked him to leave her

---

deteriorate at this point. Others argue his "conversion" to Catholicism marked the beginning of his true orthodoxy. It has been a heated debate, but most agree that Chesterton presented a very unified, although maturing, spirituality from a young age. See e.g., Douglas Cock, "A Protestant View of Chesterton," *Chesterton Review* 17, no. 1 (1991): 25-31. See also Leigh, "Psychology of Conversion," 290-304.

[81] Ward, *Gilbert Keith Chesterton*, 76.

[82] In Bedford Park, Chesterton hobnobbed with Victorian writers including James Barrie (who wrote *Peter Pan*) and William Butler Yeats. The innovative planned community—the first of its kind in London—became the setting for several stories. See, e.g., "The Tremendous Adventures of Major Brown" (written in 1905), in which the main character meets, and later marries, a mysterious lady who bears remarkable resemblance to Frances—"a graceful, green-clad figure, with fiery red hair and a flavour of Bedford Park." Chesterton, *Club of Queer Trades*, 7.

[83] According to Dale, *Outline of Sanity*, 52

[84] Chesterton, *Autobiography*, 152.

out of *Autobiography*.[85] It has been suggested that what he learned from her was the practice of personal belief rather than the intellectual theorizing of it.[86]

Chesterton expressed his awakening sense of a personal God in the agrarian language of re-creation in a love letter to Frances during their long courtship (1896-1901), in which he wrote, "There is one kind of beauty which begins inside and works out: first it makes spring in the heart and then the whole blossoms like a tree, on every twig and spray." [87] The long process of this "blooming" of his conversion from the inside out had begun with the troubling doubts and anxieties he experienced while a schoolboy at St. Paul's in about 1892. This had been followed by an interval of horror over the possibility of his own madness, which he related to the Impressionist philosophies he encountered while at Slade School of Art. He had begun to emerge into an understanding of traditional Christianity by 1894 or 1895, and during the next ten years he moved towards a spiritual solidification between the intellectual and emotional comprehension of Christianity, finally piecing together "the fragments of the old religious scheme."[88] He had

---

[85] According to Russell Sparkes, ed., *Prophet Of Orthodoxy: The Wisdom of G. K. Chesterton* (London: HarperCollins Publishers, 1997), 18.

[86] Ibid., 37.

[87] Pearce, *Wisdom and Innocence*, 40; quoting from a letter reproduced by Maisie Ward.

[88] Chesterton, *Orthodoxy*, 177. Clipper believed that by 1900, the year of Chesterton's emergence into public sight, his "childhood, education, and milieu" had already secured his orthodox Christianity; Clipper, *G. K. Chesterton*, preface. His faith was certainly secure by 1908, the year of the publication of his spiritual biography, *Orthodoxy*, written to "celebrate his conversion to Christianity," according to Alzina Stone Dale, "Some Ideas on a Christian Core Curriculum from the Writings of G. K. Chesterton, T. S. Eliot, and Dorothy L. Sayers," in *Permanent Things: Towards the Recovery of a More Human Scale at the End of the Twentieth Century*, ed.

been "blundering about" since his childhood to find a connection between the world and Christian tradition, to somehow "find a way of loving the world without trusting it."[89]

He finally made his connection between a philosophy of art (that loved the creation) and traditional Christian doctrine (that distrusted it) after his marriage to Frances in June of 1901. This synthesis of art and doctrine is seen in both his fiction and journalism, and it achieved his mounting popularity. His first novel, *The Napoleon of Notting Hill*, appeared in 1904, and about the same time *The Clarion* published his famous debate with the atheist Blatchford (which gave rise to the 1905 novel, *The Ball and the Cross*). One interview expressing his mature religious stance follows (with Blatchford's questions in italics):

> *Are you a Christian?* Certainly.
> *What do you mean by the word Christianity?* The belief that a certain human being whom we call Christ stood to a certain superhuman Being whom we call God in a certain unique transcendental relationship which we call sonship.
> *What do you believe?* I believe . . . a large number of. . . mystical dogmas ranging from the mystical dogma that man is the image of God to the mystical dogma that all men are equal. . . .
> *Why do you believe in it?* Because I perceive life to be logical and workable with these beliefs, and illogical and unworkable without them.[90]   Now   publicly

Andrew A. Tadie and Michael H. Macdonald (Grand Rapids: Eerdmans, 1995), 257.

[89] Chesterton, *Orthodoxy*, 282.

[90] Cecil Chesterton, *G. K. Chesterton: A Criticism*, 111-2; first appeared in *The Clarion*, 1903-4. Dale maintained that these two basic tenets of Christianity—the fall and the incarnation—were present already in Ches-

defined by his orthodox Christian stance, his journalism attracted the surprised attention of his readership, to whom he gave his opinions on a wide range of subjects—from modern decadence to patriotism, from philanthropy to morality. His convictions were delivered with a generous twist of his characteristic, paradoxical humor, but "his real business was not entertainment but salvation."[91] By the time he began contributing weekly articles to *The Illustrated London News* (1905), he was in the heyday of "his golden years on Fleet Street," a time period that was framed on one end by his marriage to Frances and on the other by their move away from London.[92]

Meanwhile, Chesterton was proving to be as jumbled a husband as he had been a bachelor. He forgot his tie for the marriage ceremony and even lost his way back to the honeymoon suite during a solo walk on his wedding night. Frances took care of him regarding his hapless appearance—he was a mountain of a man whom she ceased trying to make tidy in favour of making picturesque. She encouraged him to don what would become his trademark outfit of a great cloak, a wide-brimmed slouch hat, and a swordstick. To this, he later added a walking stick of Birminghamshire ash that he regarded as a "pilgrim's staff."[93] More than dressing

---

terton's childhood belief system; Dale, *Outline of Sanity*, 103, 121.

[91] Michael Asquith, "G. K. Chesterton: Prophet and Jester," in *G. K. Chesterton: A Half Century of Views*, ed. Denis J. Conlon (Oxford: Oxford University Press, 1987), 122.

[92] Wills, *Chesterton: Man and Mask*, 80.

[93] Barker, *G. K. Chesterton*, 246. Both the sword and the walking stick appear in fiction; see e.g., "The Secret Garden" in Chesterton, *The Complete Father*

him, she organized his life for him, planned his engagements, and took care of every need. He was literally lost
without her, as confirmed in a celebrated correspondence between them. He sent a telegram to her: "Am in
Market Harborough. Where ought I to be?" She desper-
ately wired back: "Home."[94] And home, again, he would
come.

The newlyweds moved into a quaint house in
Edwardes Square, Kensington, for the first few months
of their marriage, yet friends found that even this temporary dwelling had the feel of home, "with its garden of
old trees and its general air of Georgian peace."[95] The
Chestertons soon transferred, for the rest of their eight-
year London tenancy, to Overstrand Mansions—a medi-
um-sized block of flats that overlooked Battersea Park
"with its Thames-side walk under the trees, its lake, its
lawns, flower borders and shrubberies."[96] Barker wrote,
"There was tranquility under the shade of the trees in
the garden," and domestic serenity with a view was becoming a theme in Chesterton's life and fiction.[97] The
home with a back garden, the city park, or the forest
grove would furnish the setting for many of his tales.[98]

His sojourn on Fleet Street exposed Chesterton to
many of the instrumental writers of his day, one of them
George Bernard Shaw—playwright, debater, Fabian, and

Brown; see also *The Ball and the Cross* and *Manalive*,
below.

[94] Ward, *Gilbert Keith Chesterton*, 222. Frances
found it easier to get him back home and then "start
him off again," according to "Our Mr. Chesterton:
Glimpses of Gilbert" in *Gilbert Magazine,* December
2000, 6.

[95] According to Bentley, quoted by Ward, *Gilbert
Keith Chesterton*, 134.

[96] Coren, *Gilbert: The Man Who Was G. K. Chesterton*, 126; Barker, *G. K. Chesterton*, 118.

[97] Barker, *G. K. Chesterton*, 115.

[98] See, e.g., "The Crime of Gabriel Gale" in *The
Poet and the Lunatics*, *The Man Who Was Thursday*, and
The Trees of Pride, below.

colourful public figure—with whom he engaged in a thirty-year public debate on theological, philosophical, and political issues (1905-36).[99] Perhaps it was one of Chesterton's occasional appearances at the Fabian Society that provided him another close friendship; Noel Conrad was a radical Anglican curate with outspoken Christian convictions.[100] Chesterton met the Catholic politician, Oxford scholar, and novelist Hilaire Belloc, who was to be one of the strongest influences upon his embracing of Catholicism later in life and whose politically liberal writings focused Chesterton's attention on the rights of the individual over the state.[101] The Chestertons attended parties at the home of Maurice Baring, a fun-loving writer from a wealthy upper class banking family whose courtyard sported a fig tree and a secret underground passage to Westminster Abbey.[102] But perhaps no meet-

---

[99] Clipper described their relationship: "Linking arms with Shaw, Chesterton the Catholic moralist joins Shaw the Puritanical Socialist, the Right joins the Left, to announce that art's purpose is not art but the serious presentation of ideas." Clipper, *G. K. Chesterton*, 27.

[100] There is no evidence that Chesterton ever officially joined the Fabian Society (which advocated economic and social reform, favouring the gradual spread of socialism by peaceful means), although his earthy drinking songs from *The Flying Inn* (in which the woods ring with the cheerfulness of Robin Hood's "Merry Men") found their way into some of the meetings and became extremely popular among the people in a Britain threatened with the Prohibition modelled by America. Hollis, *The Mind of Chesterton*, 154.

[101] Herbert Race, *Gilbert Keith Chesterton: Essays*, Notes on Chosen English Texts, ed. Norman T. Carrington (London: James Brodie, 1961), 6; Dale, *Outline of Sanity*, 50. For a wry attack on state interference, see, e.g., Chesterton, *Flying Inn*; written in 1914.

[102] Barker, *G. K. Chesterton*, 151. Note Chesterton's use of subterranean passages or forest tunnels as escape routes in several of his stories; see, e.g., "Father Brown and the Donnington Affair" in Chesterton, *Collect-

ing was as influential as that with Father John O'Connor (in 1904), who within six years became the intellectual model for Chesterton's detective, Father Brown. Elements of all his relationships made their way into Chesterton's fiction, which he was now publishing at a brisk pace. In the summer of 1909, he and Frances moved to the small village of Beaconsfield, twenty-five miles west of London, where the rhythm of his life took on a more leisurely cadence. The mature integration between his literary aesthetic and his religious convictions produced an expression of his symbolic imagination that was fully refined in his fiction.

"The return to the real England with real Englishmen would be a return to the beech-woods, which still makes this town like a home," Chesterton said of Beaconsfield, named after the forests surrounding it.[103] If choosing an entirely British emblem, he said, he would choose the beech tree even over the great oaks that had made the battleships of Britain.[104] The Chestertons rented a small house (named Overroads), and the view from their window—of forests, fields, and farmlands far from the hustle of the city—gave them the privacy that Frances, especially, craved. They were disappointed that

---

ed Works, vol. 14, 139. See also *The Trees of Pride* in Chesterton, *Collected Works*, vol. 8, 634. See further an important scene in *The Flying Inn* (722-3), in which the valiant Christian, British, rebel forces emerge from a tunnel of refuge to crush the attacking Turkish forces.

[103] Chesterton, quoted in Ward, *Gilbert Keith Chesterton*, 449.

[104] Ibid. The influence of the elm is seen in "Father Brown and the Donnington Affair" (1914), in which "Adam's thicket" is part of a great dark forest of "magnificent beeches," a "primeval woodland" with "undergrowth so thick that the foot of man might never have been set therein"; Chesterton, *Collected Works*, vol. 14, 130-1. This particular Father Brown mystery was commissioned by Max Pemberton's *The Premier Magazine* and did not appear in Chesterton's five collections of the Father Brown stories.

they could not have the children they both desired, yet they gave their house at Beaconsfield the "stamp of a real home."[105] Their schedule of London engagements had been demanding, and Frances had worried about her husband's declining health, due in part to a habit of heavy drinking.[106] The move refocused Chesterton's attention on the pastoral. He retained a gardener to help Frances keep the yard green and growing, and would wander about the grounds firing arrows at his trees or knocking the heads off the dahlias with his unsheathed swordstick. He wrote prolifically in the tranquillity of his new surroundings.

The couple continued to entertain friends in their country home, and testimonies survive through letter and interview of their hospitality and cheery household.[107] The pastoral lifestyle afforded a closer prospect of nature and increased opportunity for Chesterton to

---

[105] Ward, *Gilbert Keith Chesterton*, 211.

[106] While at Fisher Unwin, Chesterton had gained a reputation for being a drinker, although never a drunk. Coren mentioned the speculations about whether or not Chesterton was an alcoholic and concluded that his addiction was to overindulgent quantities in anything he could consume—food or drink—and that this is what damaged his health. Coren, *Gilbert: The Man Who Was G. K. Chesterton*, 71, 214.

[107] See, e.g., Clemens, *Chesterton As Seen by His Contemporaries*. It is a simple book, authored by the cousin of Mark Twain ("Dedicated with his kind permission to Benito Mussolini, a warm admirer"). In a famed meeting between Mussolini and Chesterton, when the Italian leader asked the writer about his views on politics and his interesting theory of Distributism, Chesterton found himself doing all the talking; but in *The Resurrection of Rome*, Chesterton made clear that he was not a fascist; Pearce, *Wisdom and Innocence*, 377-9. His outspoken nationalism is a theme that comes up often in stories such as *Napoleon of Notting Hill*, in which a small land holding is protected against the rest of the world system.

ponder and express a view of God as revealed in creation. As Marshall McLuhan noted, all of Chesterton's
work is informed by this "sacramental sense of the life of
earth and sea and sky, of tillage and growth, and of food
and wine."[108] His old theme of the stars in the trees is
seen again, for example, in a story he wrote about one
spring evening at Beaconsfield, when the telephone
rang. Chesterton listened in vain to understand the gar-
bled voice on the other end of the crackling line, for the
telephone connection was very poor. With the snatches
of this strangled voice in his ears, he went out into the
garden. The night was clear, a night of

> startling and blazing stars—stars so fierce
> and close that they seemed crowding
> round the roof and tree-tops. While hot
> and speechless they seemed striving to
> speak, like that voice that had been
> drowned amid the drumming wires.[109]

Chesterton's move to the country refreshed his perspective of nature as a riddle spoken by the Creator and
fuelled his own resolve to communicate to his readers
this secret of the presence of God.

For the most part, country life suited Chesterton,
who hoped that all ordinary Englishmen would someday
return to the time when each could possess his own private property.[110] His assuming the rural life dismayed
his brother, Cecil, and his Fleet Street friends, who ac-

---

[108] H. Marshall McLuhan, "G. K. Chesterton: A
Practical Mystic," in *G. K. Chesterton: A Half Century of
Views*, ed. Denis J. Conlon (Oxford: Oxford University
Press, 1987), 1.

[109] Ffinch, *G. K. Chesterton*, 185; originally printed in *The Illustrated London News*.

[110] Chesterton detailed his advocacy of the socio-
political system of Distributism (a medieval scheme re-
establishing ownership of land for all) in *Outline of Sanity* (London: Methuen, 1926), in which he argued for
"three acres and a cow" for every landholder.

cused Frances of jealously hoarding her husband's attention. But Ward denied their indictments; Chesterton, after all, "did not want a desert, he did not want a large landed estate, he wanted what he had got—a house and a garden."[111] Of course, he did not abandon his associations with the publishing industry but continued to write abundantly in all genres and made the trip into London regularly. One such excursion inspired a reflection on his love of the city but his preference for the countryside. The poem, entitled "When I Came Back to Fleet Street" (1915), says in part:

> I had been long in meadows,
> And the trees took hold of me,
> And the still towns in the beech-woods,
> Where men were meant to be.[112]

His attachment to the country was permanent, and one summer day, while sitting in the garden of their rented home in Beaconsfield and snacking on gooseberries from a bag, Chesterton pointed across the road towards a particular tree at the top of the meadow, declaring to

---

[111] Ward, *Gilbert Keith Chesterton*, 213-4. A short story character conjured up by Chesterton just a few years before his move to the country expresses some of this desire for home. Major Brown (who finds love with a woman who, again, sounds like Frances) equates a "little sunlit garden" with a "harbour in heaven," and is looking for "a little house and a little hobby; in the Bible, you know, 'There remaineth a rest' "; Chesterton, *Club of Queer Trades*, 5, 17. Chesterton's direct biblical quote refers to the promise of Sabbath rest for the people of God and reminds the reader of the creation story and its seventh day, of the temporary rest offered in the land of Canaan, and of the eternal rest found in Christ.

[112] G. K. Chesterton, "When I Came Back to Fleet Street," in *The Works of G. K. Chesterton*, The Wordsworth Poetry Library (Hertfordshire: Wordsworth Editions, 1995), 138.

Frances that he wanted to build a home around it.[113] In 1912, using wood from that very tree as supporting timber, the Chestertons began construction of a studio that eventually (1922) became their final residence, "Top Meadow."[114] Fittingly, 1912 was also the year he finished the novel *Manalive*, about which he later said,

> There are two ways of getting home; and one of them is to stay there. The other is to walk round the whole world till we come back to the same place; and I tried to trace such a journey in a story I once wrote.[115]

In summary, the context of Chesterton's early life stimulated his visual and literary imagination, with the home supplying both imagery and themes for his writing. The culture and education of Victorian/Edwardian London further roused his aesthetic and religious curiosity, largely due to his panoramic reading in literary and biblical classics. Art training influenced his evolving style of fiction, with Impressionism clarifying his cultural and moral philosophy. Relationships, too, played an important role in Chesterton's spiritual, social, and artistic formation. As he made his way through the prevalent pessimistic atmosphere created by subjectivism and rationalism to a place of orthodox Christian belief, his marriage to Frances and the home they made together further anchored him emotionally and spiritually. His life and writings are characterized by themes of wonder and

---

[113] He sounds just like his "Honest Quack," Mr. Windrush.

[114] Coren, *Gilbert: The Man Who Was G. K. Chesterton*, 214. See also Dale, *Outline of Sanity*, 136. After Frances's death, Top Meadow was given to the Roman Catholic Church to be used as a retreat/hostel for Roman Catholic priests converting from Anglicanism.

[115] Chesterton, *Everlasting Man*, 9; written in 1925. In fact, he was to trace this journey theme in many stories.

delight in the ordinary and commonplace, and of love for romance and adventure, and by a synthesizing desire to communicate his faith. He placed priority on the ideas over the artistry of his fiction—he was a purposeful writer. The foundational experiences of Chesterton's youth yielded a mature expression of Christian belief through his substantial body of work.

The theme of the tree consolidates Chesterton's life and thought, emerging throughout both stages of his formation and expression, and becoming an encompassing archetype that gives unity to his symbolic imagination. His application of the tree image increasingly illustrates the elements of plot, setting, and moral in his allegorical parables. The record of his story—from the first puerile fables through the mature religious fiction—gives evidence of his spiritual conversion (from agnosticism to orthodoxy), and of his social shift (from liberalism to conservatism), and of his literary integration (of art with religion).[116] A commentary follows on Chesterton's use of the tree in his fiction, and it will provide insight into his development of the symbol for literary and philosophical means throughout his life.

---

[116] Ward, *Gilbert Keith Chesterton*, 63; Hunter, *Explorations in Allegory*, 47.

THREE

SEEDLING: SHORT STORIES OF YOUTH
(1888-1896)

Chesterton's fragmentary notebook juvenilia indicates the importance of his childhood experiences by bringing to light the initial emerging themes regarding home, the creation, and man's place therein, which were informed by his literary and biblical readings and which can be illustrated by his introduction of the image of the tree. The notebook stories reveal the process of much of Chesterton's growth, for most of his fiction "had its roots firmly planted in what he had written in the 1890s."[1] A brief survey of this exuberant (if incohesive) segment is preliminary to a closer examination of later fiction. In his early stories, written while still a teen, the tree is implicated with subjects of death, self-discovery, and religious mysticism through his pictures of trees in forest and garden, beneath the night sky, or full of creatures.

"Thou hast waken [sic] from the nightmare, which is Superstition and the death and burial of the Soul," penned fourteen-year-old Chesterton in "Flickerflash" (1888), a scrap of a story in which the hero escapes from his own funeral and climbs a tree for its food and shelter, to find freedom beneath "the crests of the pine forest tossing like a dark ocean in the wind."[2] Chesterton's earliest picture of the tree, written in a tone of pessimism characteristic of the era, introduces religious themes that might have been evoked by his family's reaction to the death of his older sister when he was just a toddler. Eight-year-old Beatrice's passing traumatized the parents and led to a complete silence in the home on the subject of funerals. Ward mentioned Chesterton's

---

[1] Conlon, note in Chesterton, *Collected Works*, vol. 14, 437-8.

[2] "Flickerflash" in Chesterton, *Collected Works*, vol. 14, 573; written 1888.

own sense of loss and sorrow in connection with his nursery days.[3] "Flickerflash" is a curious reversal of the fairy tale "The Babes in the Woods," in which two children are lost in the forest, seeking their home that is eventually found only in their demise. Perhaps young Chesterton was thinking of this fable or even of his early Scripture readings, for biblically the tree, often a figure of providence and safety, was scaled by Zacchaeus who "sought to see Jesus."[4]

Death of a spiritual nature is next suggested in a striking sketch accompanying another of the first tales, entitled "Half-Hours in Hades" (1891), detailing Chesterton's fanciful notions of the evolution of demons.[5] The drawing depicts a devilish dance of snake, winged demon, and Mephistophelean gent in top hat and tails swirling about a fruit-laden tree. In addition to the biblical influence, it denotes Chesterton's precocious morbidity that was perhaps the result of his experimentation with the Ouija board.[6] The sketch and story evoke Milton's temptation of Eve in *Paradise Lost* as well as the biblical account of the fall as Chesterton must have read it.[7] His use of the image of the tree implies the death

---

[3] Ward, *Gilbert Keith Chesterton*, 13.

[4] Ezek. 34:26-28; Luke 19:3. These and all subsequent biblical quotes, unless otherwise noted, are to the King James Version.

[5] "Half-Hours in Hades: An Elementary Handbook of Demonology" in Chesterton, *Collected Works*, vol. 14, 23-36; written 1891. Previously printed in G. K. Chesterton, *The Coloured Lands* (New York: Sheed and Ward, 1938).

[6] Chesterton's father occasionally joined him and his brother in the "game," perhaps indicating lack of parental concern or awareness about the occult, as seen in Chesterton, *Autobiography*, 77-79.

[7] Gen. 3; cf. Milton *Paradise Lost* 9.568-838. All references to Milton are to the following edition: John Milton, *Paradise Lost and Paradise Regained*, ed. Christopher Ricks, Signet Classic Poetry Edition (New York: Penguin Books, 1968).

delivered through the Tree of Knowledge of Good and Evil.

The influence of his love for adventurous travel tales is seen again in the journey theme of "The Wild Goose Chase" (1892), in which a boy seeking courage embarks on an expedition, chasing a goose through forests that, even at this early stage of writing, are used as more than simple backdrop.[8] The pursuer pauses for breath beneath an elm and again under a "magnificent flowering fruit tree" to speak to the Bird of Paradise while, nearby, a hang-man's gibbet serves as a fear-inspiring "Tree of the Vultures."[9] A nightingale remembers the time "when I too was free in the free forests and sang my songs as the free gift of God. But now . . . the beauty of the woods has died out of me."[10] She warns the boy not to linger but to seek wisdom from the owl who lives in the Tree of Knowledge, a "great mystic

---

[8] "The Wild Goose Chase" in Chesterton, *Collected Works*, vol. 14, 37-44; written in 1892. Many of Chesterton's stories, such as the early "Prince Wild-Fire," use the tree image on an ad hoc basis, seemingly for literary purposes of setting and atmosphere. Not *all* trees can be assigned metaphysical meaning; moreover, the remarkable number of occurrences of tree imagery in almost every story would make an impossible listing.

[9] The connection between the gibbet, tree, and cross is made also by Jennifer O'Reilly, "The Trees of Eden in Mediaeval Iconography" in *A Walk in the Garden: Biblical, Iconographical and Literary Images of Eden*, ed. Paul Morris and Deborah Sawyer, Journal for the Study of the Old Testament: Supplement Series 136 (Sheffield, U.K.: JSOT Press, Sheffield Academic Press, 1992), 186. Chesterton's gibbet-tree full of vultures perhaps echoes his reading of the Arthurian tales, in which the evil Knight of the Red Lawn conquers forty of his enemies one by one, hanging each dead armour-clad knight in a tree.

[10] "The Wild Goose Chase" in Chesterton, *Collected Works*, vol. 14, 38.

oak."[11] Already in this childish piece Chesterton was alluding to themes he would expand in later fiction—of
home as a place from which to embark upon the adventure of self-discovery, of the Garden of Eden with its
tree of death and diabolical knowledge that destroys
freedom and beauty, and of the dark forest as the world
at large in which to inquire into the meaning of life. Wisdom, or at least knowledge, is to be sought.[12] The way-
farer entering the forest to find happiness or victory is a
familiar theme in tales such as *Goldilocks and the Three
Bears* and the Arthurian legends of the questing knights,
both accessible to Chesterton in whom spiritual interest
had been aroused by this age.

In the ancient tale of the search for the Holy
Grail, seen in the twelfth- and thirteenth-century ro-
mances, the main character also takes a forest excursion, forming a literary motif that links the image of the
tree with the image of the sacrament of communion.[13]
This might have been in young Chesterton's mind as he
penned "The Wine of Cana: A Sketch" (early 1890s).[14]
Madge is a sixteen-year-old whose pessimism and ego-
ism show on her face, and who has not claimed her
rightful place of honour in her family. Before her "trans-
figuration" at the conclusion, she is considered a little
lazy, and always looks sleepy in "a drifting twilight, be-
fore-breakfast state of mind" reminiscent of Chesterton's
pre-conversion description of himself as a teen who was
"asleep and dreaming" with an occupied mind and an
idle appearance.[15] She meets Mr. Hope, who shares
Chesterton's appreciation for the ordinary objects of life

---

[11] Ibid.

[12] Cf. Gen. 2:8-10; Pr. 4:5. Wisdom and the Tree
of Life are explicitly connected in Pr. 3:18, 11:30,
13:12, and 15:4.

[13] Eleanor Simmons Greenhill, "The Child in the
Tree: A Study of the Cosmological Tree in Christian Religion," *Traditio* 10 (1954): 323-71.

[14] The title implicates the gospel miracle; see
John 2:1-10.

[15] Chesterton, *Autobiography*, 67.

by finding even a garden to be a religious symbol of heaven.[16] He is a "masterful young moralist" with a "distinctively Puritan temper" who speaks in biblical-sounding language.[17] For example, Hope calls the loaf of bread itself a parable embodying all Christ's miracles— the sower, the seed, the harvest. He then mentions the crust broken by "the fisherman," when "in that dark garret, knowing that the gibbet hung above him, he gave those he loved a last symbol and memory" that stood for "the central miracle of man, the miracle compared with which the . . . cursing [of] the fig-tree [was] a

---

[16] Ibid., 562.

[17] "The Wine of Cana: A Sketch" in Chesterton, *Collected Works*, vol. 14, 563-4. As seen here, Chesterton's frequent, and surprising, comments about Puritans are not always negative, nor his Puritan fiction characters always the villains. In contrast, the Reverend David East is a Puritan minister and criminal in "The Man Who Shot the Fox," also in *Collected Works*, vol. 14, 418-34. Chesterton saw the main problem with what he labelled "Puritan" to be its doctrine of determinism bordering on fatalism. His later friendship with George Bernard Shaw, "who was everything that Chesterton was not: Irish, Socialist, rationalist, Puritanical and teetotalling," provided much theological banter on the subject; Clipper, *G. K. Chesterton*, 26. For a Chestertonian review (on a book contemporary to his time) regarding the subject of Puritanism, see G. K. Chesterton, "Puritan and Anglican," *Chesterton Review* 9, no. 4 (1983): 304-7, first published December 15, 1900. On the other hand, Dale warned against reading Chesterton's terms as though they mean exclusively and completely what common definitions or church dogma say. He had a private meaning for many words; for example a "Puritan" was a sober ascetic committed to a doctrine of determinism—a definition that threatened to put one of its ranks in closer relationship to fundamentalist Moslems than to practicing Catholics. Dale, *Outline of Sanity*, 19, 129.

scientific experiment."[18] Chesterton again drew attention to the tree as an instrument of death. Its relevance to the eucharist and the last supper proves his early intellectual comprehension of the facts of Christ's life (the miracles) as well as His death (the crucifixion).

A more whimsical piece written at age fifteen, "The Queen of the Evening Star" (1889-90) echoes Chesterton's childhood fascination with magic and mysticism and reflects his interest in a Miltonic lost paradise, which is here announced through a vision from heaven. Seven children enter a wood to see an unusually bright star "between the dark tree-stems" appearing very near to them.[19] Mysteriously, the star takes angelic shape to deliver a proclamation "about a garden on an island where all life was perfect."[20] When the children later argue over the details of her dress, she returns as an old gypsy, saying to one of the children who recognizes her, "My externals appear different to everybody; but there are some . . . who look at my face and remember it, and these [are] the prophets and poets of the world."[21] The

---

[18] "The Wine of Cana: A Sketch" in Chesterton, *Collected Works*, vol. 14, 560-1. Cf. John 2:1-11. The cursing of the fig tree speaks of judgement for hypocrisy; see Mark 11:12-14. Note the recurrence of the cross as a gibbet.

[19] "The Queen of the Evening Star" in Chesterton, *Collected Works*, vol. 14, 575; written in 1889-90. In his similarly entitled poem, "To the Evening Star," Blake pictured his own understanding of the divine influence of the "fair-hair'd angel of the evening"; William Blake, in Alexander W. Allison and others, eds., *The Norton Anthology of Poetry*, 3 ed. (New York: Norton, 1983), 497.*

[20] "The Queen of the Evening Star" in Chesterton, *Collected Works*, vol. 14, 576. Cf. Milton *Paradise Lost* 4.207-9.

[21] "The Queen of the Evening Star" in Chesterton, *Collected Works*, vol. 14, 578. Chesterton showed the influence of George MacDonald's *Princess* stories. He

theme of the disguised trickster is not new; consider the crone who visits Snow White at the dwarves' forest cottage, or the fraud who calls to Aladdin's princess, "New lamps for old!" Yet the image in this story is one of the natural hiding the supernatural—the tree delivering, as it were, the light to the children. Perhaps Chesterton intended to project a mystical picture of the Virgin Mary; the theme of a lady in the sacred wood as a figure translating salvation is found in Dante's Beatrice, whose eyes reflect the very light of God.[22] The tree is thus implicated in the communication of the heavenly to the earthly; the forest is the place of meeting.

Chesterton's growing awareness of historical and political issues, and the early exercise of his paradoxical style, surface in a short story published in *The Debater* school paper. "The White Cockade" (1891) is a soldier's tale in which a black-hatted Jacobite visits the home of a friend who is involved in an insurrectionist plot.[23] While the hero, Maxwell, contends against an immoral (but white-hatted) suitor for the love of the girl of the house, the themes of good and evil become loosely attached to the setting of wild, open moor. This early suggestion that the landscape and sky interact in a supernatural communication is seen in the hero's retirement to the "desolate moorland" where, in spiritual contemplation,

---

developed the theme of "prophets and poets" in Chesterton, *Everlasting Man*.

[22] Dante *Purgatory* 29-30; *Paradise* 28.1-42. All references to Dante's *Divine Comedy* are to the following edition: Dante, *The Comedy of Dante Alighieri the Florentine*, trans. and ed. Dorothy L. Sayers, 3 vols. (London: Penguin Books, 1949). A further example in an anonymous, thirteenth-century poem expresses a relationship between Mary, Christ, the tree and light: "Now goes the sun under the wood— / I pity, Mary, thy fair face. / Now goes the sun under the tree— / I pity, Mary, thy son and thee"; "Now Go'th Sun Under Wood" in Allison and others, *Norton*, 3.

[23] "The White Cockade" in Chesterton, *Collected Works*, vol. 14, 545-6; written in 1891.

he wanders "like a lonely ghost under the stars," and from which he returns to save the innocent girl (named Mary) from the pantheistic villain.[24] The wrongly labelled victim, sacrificially accepting blame to preserve the honour of a home, is likened to Christ in an allusion to the "thief in the night."[25] But the story also brings to mind such mystics as St. Francis of Assisi, who wandered the wilderness with his contemplative brother monks and suffered persecution for his refusal to join in with the ruling authorities.[26] The romance of the saint had been introduced to Chesterton in the nursery by his parents.[27] "The White Cockade" involves the tree only as a part of the general landscape, but it introduces the setting of the wilderness, as well as the private back garden (that, in many future stories, accommodates a tree to apply a moral lesson). Perhaps this story indicates Chesterton's reading in medieval literature, with its "garden of the soul" motif: John Scotus Eriugena divided the garden of human nature into two regions—the inner containing the Tree of Life and the outer the wiles of Satan.[28]

Despite his unpolished style, Chesterton's first stories reveal that his childhood provided ample artistic material for his conception of the tree image, which he incorporated with his youthful pursuit for the meaning of life. His wonder-filled home life, literary enrichment, and incipient social and spiritual condition were budding into a powerful imagination. His adolescent stories, while not clearly Christian at this point, exhibit the influence of his readings and show also the beginnings of a creative literary theory that would come to express his later religious beliefs. By the time Chesterton left public school in 1892 at eighteen years of age, he had already been

---

[24] Ibid.

[25] Chesterton, *Collected Works*, vol. 14, 547; cf. 1 Thess. 5:7.

[26] See also "Le Jongleur de Dieu" below.

[27] Pearce, *Wisdom and Innocence*, 292.

[28] David Lyle Jeffrey, ed. *A Dictionary of Biblical Tradition in English Literature* (Grand Rapids: Eerdmans, 1992), 224.

writing fiction using the picture of the tree to illustrate several themes—good and evil, blessing and curse, humanity and creation, self-awareness and religious mysticism. The landscape or the forest of humanity is a meeting place between the heavenly and the earthly, with the tree mediating communication and light, and providing food and shelter for the questing adventurer, far from home. The loss of perfection, beauty, and freedom, as well as the physical and spiritual death of the fall, are tentatively connected to the Tree of Knowledge in the Garden of Eden. Moreover, the tree roost of the vultures has become the very "gibbet" of crucifixion. Chesterton also implied that the tree, as an object of nature, is hiding another identity.

The preceding fragmentary notebook entries and short stories characterizing Chesterton's transition from dreamy wondering to urgent religious probing show the image of the tree illustrating his developing aesthetic and religious philosophies. Further short stories were written during or just after his training at the Slade School of Art (in the mid- to late-1890s). At this time, scientific rationalism, agnosticism, and the theosophy of Madame Blavatsky were infringing upon the romantic culture of waning Victorianism, and Chesterton was battling his own spiritual depression brought on in part by involvement with the occult.

"A Picture of Tuesday" (1896) explores Chesterton's views on the philosophy of art, discussing "the techniques of impressionism, realism, and symbolism," as Lynette Hunter demonstrated.[29] The tale features a club that meets regularly to challenge its members with an inventive subject to paint. This time, the choice of

---

[29] Hunter, *Explorations in Allegory*, 31. Cf. "A Picture of Tuesday" in Chesterton, *Collected Works*, vol. 14, 60-63. This and "A Crazy Tale" were Chesterton's first two short stories to be published, appearing in 1896 in *The Quarto*—the paper of the Slade School of Art. They both contain themes that were reworked in *The Man Who Was Thursday*, according to Conlon in introduction to Chesterton, *Collected Works*, vol. 14, 14.

topic is especially nebulous: Tuesday, the day of the week. The group includes several philosophic types. A realist, believing nothing exists but the material, interprets the assignment by painting a picture of his mother, who is always at home on Tuesday. The names of two members are especially noteworthy, because they describe emblematic function. The Impressionist, who paints gaslight on an early morning, is named Plumtree; this stands for the creative act of art in its own right ("art for art's sake"), just as his name conjures visions of a tree that produces fruit out of its own essence. Starwood is a dreamy visionary with a symbolistic approach to art, who balances the other two by spanning the distance between earth (realism) and sky (etherealism). His picture of Tuesday has form as well as content—he paints a human figure in the act of separating the firmament from the waters, quoting Genesis 1:7.[30] "A Picture of Tuesday" exhibits Chesterton's early awareness (as Hunter explained) of "the fusion of form and essence accomplished by symbol and the metaphors that make it up"; his symbolism by way of the tree names establishes "a relationship between the word and the object."[31] The tree here stands for the essence of a person, illustrating Chesterton's opinion of the hollowness behind the faulty philosophy that produces Impressionism and his preference for a mediating symbolic approach to art that communicates a real truth. His thought is consistent with Jesus' parable of the tree producing fruit in kind.[32]

In "The Human Club," Chesterton's characters form a fraternity suggesting his own involvement with the JDC, whose members discussed important issues. The goal of the fictive young men's club is to aim for perfection, which gives rise to religious debate. One

---

[30] "And God divided the waters that were under the firmament from the waters that were above the firmament: and the evening and the morning were the second day." Chesterton, *Collected Works*, vol. 14, 62.

[31] Hunter, *Explorations in Allegory*, 33.

[32] Matt. 7:16-18.

character makes a strange, circular sign in front of his face with his hand, and says,

> It is my new symbol. . . . In moments of thanksgiving, such as before meals . . . you make the sign of the circle. . . . The circle is the type of the infinity which includes without confusing. It is the mathematical formula for God.[33]

When a fellow member protests that he knows of another ritualistic sign that the hand would make with more satisfaction, the first counters (in the prevalent religious spirit of Chesterton's Unitarian home), "Those four points are all included upon my circumference, just as my Christianity is included in my universality."[34] The other club member rebuts this with a tale of epic adventure, describing the tree for its triple use—"the pole to which was lashed a blade of flint, the first weapon of war," the bark for a boat to carry humanity over the serpent-like river, and "the flaming brand of fire which was to light a world of cities."[35] Perhaps Chesterton was here alluding to the Lord's rebuke of Satan, in speaking of the light-bearing, Christ-prefiguring Joshua as "a brand plucked out of the fire."[36] The tree imagery gave Chesterton the chance to compose this short redemption history suggesting the "pole" of the cross that pierces,

---

[33] "The Human Club" in Chesterton, *Collected Works*, vol. 14, 671-2; written in mid-1890s. His attention to shapes and outlines is further explored in *The Ball and the Cross*, below.

[34] Ibid., 672.

[35] Ibid., 685.

[36] Zech. 3:2. Chesterton elsewhere recounted the story of the flaming brand, snatched from the fire, which Aquinas used to chase from his room a courtesan sent there by his brothers to test his celibacy, in Chesterton, *Saint Thomas Aquinas*, 65; written in 1933.

offends, transports, and gives light.[37] Although the tree's
multi-fold usage can be put to evil and idolatrous ends,
here it illustrates Chesterton's rejecting the "circle" of
Universalism in favour of accepting the overarching purpose that unites the narrative of the world.[38] His later
explication in both *Orthodoxy* and *The Everlasting Man*
pictures another "tree" at the centre of man's worship,
which is "the crux of the whole matter."[39] The tree in
"The Human Club" represents the historical, transcendent cross of traditional Christianity.

A madman with a God-complex narrates "Apotheosis: A Primeval Legend" (1896), which is set in a forest like the "dark wood" near the mouth of hell in Dante's *Divine Comedy*.[40] The centre portion of "Apotheosis"
is the only part of the tale in which the narrator is aware
of being delusional; in the opening and closing frames
he speaks as in the voice of God: "I am the Beginning
and the End."[41] A woodcutter, with "his colour . . . like
red clay," is the true Saviour calling the deluded narrator back home to the pine hut, out of the deep woods
that are being harvested: "The pine is fallen, but the hut
stands. Come home."[42] But the narrator falls back into
his solipsistic hopelessness, believing himself again to be
God. He says,

> Many times I had heard him in the high
> grey pinewood on the slopes. The thud of
> his axe, the snap of the twigs and the

[37] See also pole imagery in "The Garden of
Smoke," below.

[38] Cf. Isa. 44:13-20.

[39] Chesterton, *Everlasting Man*, 87-88, 134.

[40] Dante *Hell* 1.1-6.

[41] "Apotheosis: A Primeval Legend" in Chesterton,
Collected Works, vol. 14, 625; written in 1896. Christ is
the beginning and the end in Rev. 1:8, 17.

[42] "Apotheosis: A Primeval Legend" in Chesterton,
Collected Works, vol. 14, 624, 631. Cf. *Napoleon of Not-
ting Hill*, below, for imagery of the red clay of Adam
Wayne.

clear sound of the strange woodman's
song he sang, a song of trees, without
beginning or end like the forests it
seemed to catalogue. Shouldering bundles
of wood. . . .[43]

The narrator's tone of hopelessness is poignant as, in a
moment of sanity, he glimpses the truth of the woodcutter's eternal identity, his harvesting of the fallen creation, and his bearing of the burden of humanity. The
narrator's return to madness recalls Chesterton's early
fear of insanity, which becomes characteristic in several
writings.[44] Yet "Apotheosis" is a beautiful story of revelation, incarnation, and redemption in which the forest becomes a symbol for fallen humanity, creation, and eternity. Usually the biblical theme of the felling of timber
connotes judgement (as in Jesus' warning that "an axe
is laid unto the root of the trees" that produced no
fruit); one exception is of the acacia wood God pre-
scribed for the tabernacle furnishings, which was redeemed—made holy with its covering of Egyptian gold in
a typological picture of the incarnation.[45] Along with allusions to the incarnation, "Apotheosis" also continues a
hint from Chesterton's earlier work that a riddle—a message—is written in the creation.[46] The narrator of the
forest says,

A bird flies to and fro among the low
leaves. . . . So it is read in the language of
men. Only now and again they see a half-
recognition, feel that they all but know it,
a great and staring word in the language
of the mountains. Every rank in the

[43] "Apotheosis: A Primeval Legend" in Chesterton,
Collected Works, vol. 14, 631.
[44] For example, it is a main theme in *The Ball and
the Cross*, below.
[45] Matt. 3:10; Exod. 25:10.
[46] For a later tree used to deliver a message, see
"The Point of a Pin," below.

hierarchies of heaven and hell read it plainly, but each in a different tongue: it is a hieroglyphic in a thousand languages: a bird flying among the trees.[47]

Although the character of the woodcutter appears as a Saviour in the familiar folktale of *Little Red Riding Hood*, the themes in "Apotheosis" go beyond Chesterton's youngest bedtime stories. He might not yet have reached his full, personal experience of Christianity, but the influence of the scriptural tradition upon him was strong. In addition to affirming his deepening belief in the divine nature of God, the story is emotionally evocative. The cry of the woodcutter might be the cry of the writer.

In another brief tale of this period, Chesterton tied the forest of the universe to the church. Vivid scene painting learned at Slade illuminates "Le Jongleur de Dieu" (mid-1890s), which applies the metaphor of the tree to the physical description of a cathedral. Chesterton wrote,

With its domes like the domes of eclipsed worlds, with its marbles rich with all the colours of forgotten sunsets, with its columns of nameless hues clustered like autumn forests, it is like a graven allegory of the universe.[48]

Into this forest-like setting Francis of Assisi, the "brother of every living thing," has come "to found the Church of

[47] "Apotheosis: A Primeval Legend" in Chesterton, *Collected Works*, vol. 14, 630-1.

[48] "Le Jongleur de Dieu" in Chesterton, *Collected Works*, vol. 14, 659, written in mid-1890s. For an earlier picture of aged trees composing cathedral walks, see "Cowley, The Garden" in *Imitations of English Poets* in Alexander Pope, *The Works of Alexander Pope* (Hertfordshire, U.K.: Wordsworth Editions, 1995), 7. All further references are to this edition.

the whole world."[49] He is a jongleur ("troubadour" or "tumbler"), a "King's son" unjustly killed. Perhaps Chesterton was thinking of Manasseh's setting up of a "graven image of the grove" in the temple, or he might have read Luther's (or the Puritans') speculation that Adam's grove formed the first temple, altar, and pulpit.[50] Chesterton's symbolism might seem weak until one considers two subsequent stories that relate the tree to the church. At the risk of breaking up the fictional chronology, and in order to support Chesterton's probable intention in "Le Jongleur de Dieu," they should be mentioned.

The cosmological form of the column seen by Ezekiel as he stood before the new temple has been considered by scholars to be related to the tree.[51] The archetype of tree as column is repeated in "The Paradise of Human Fishes" (1925), a whimsical yarn in which Mr. Peter Paul Smith, a deep-sea diver, discovers an underwater city like "a garden" of "smooth and serpentine columns of titanic seaweed . . . quite as natural as trees."[52] The underwater garden-city is peopled with humans who are surrounded by water as Mr. Smith is surrounded by air, and who have air pumped to them as Mr. Smith's people have water pumped to them— through hoses so numerous as to look "like a forest of very thin trees of almost infinite height."[53] Both realms are dependent on "gods who sit above [them] in the heights and give [them] the very breath of life."[54] This

---

[49] "Le Jongleur de Dieu" in Chesterton, *Collected Works*, vol. 14, 661-2.

[50] 2 Kings 21:7 ("grove" in KJV becomes "asherah" in NIV); Luther *Lectures on Genesis* regarding Gen. 2:9, 17. See also Joseph E. Duncan, *Milton's Earthly Paradise: A Historical Study of Eden* (Minneapolis: University of Minnesota Press, 1972).

[51] Ezek. 40:48; see further Greenhill, "The Child in the Tree," 337.

[52] "The Paradise of Human Fishes" in Chesterton, *Collected Works*, vol. 14, 340; written in 1925.

[53] Ibid., 342.

[54] Ibid.

aquatic world mirrors Chesterton's dry-land world much as the Renaissance system of correspondence saw creation as an earthly paradise—"a little model of heaven and a sign of the great Heaven."[55] Chesterton's breathing tubes are tree-like columns delivering life from the upper to the lower realms. This sounds like a motif suggested by Eleanor Simmons Greenhill (in her excellent study of the cosmological tree). She cited a twelfth-century legend by St. Hildegard of Bingen that saw Ezekiel's columns as connecting the temple with "the mysterious realm directly above . . . the throne of God."[56] In a slightly different form, and invoking Jesus' parable of the mustard tree, is Chesterton's "A Nightmare" (1907).[57] Here, the shape of the tree is proposed as a prototype by an architect who is striving to improve the stability of St. Paul's Cathedral, which he says should have "in the first floor two domes, in the second floor three domes, in the third floor and so on, ever branching, ever increasing, each landing larger than the last one."[58] "The Paradise of Human Fishes" and "A Nightmare" continue Chesterton's earlier comparison of tree to cathedral.

Chesterton used his picture of the forest (related to fallen creation, the universe, and the church) as a frame upon which to hang an argument against one of his archenemies, scientific rationalism. In "My Uncle the Professor" (mid-1890s), Chesterton featured an eccentric evolutionist who tells "fairy tales from biology," and who promotes his "great Arboreal Theory"—that people were meant to live in the treetops.[59] The professor tests his hypothesis by packing up a Robinson Crusoe-style

---

[55] Duncan, *Milton's Earthly Paradise*, 247.

[56] Greenhill, "The Child in the Tree," 367.

[57] See Luke 13:18-21. For Milton's comment on the tree as the reign of Jesus on the Davidic throne, see *Paradise Regained* 4.346-8.

[58] "A Nightmare" in Chesterton, *Collected Works*, vol. 14, 89; written in 1907.

[59] "My Uncle the Professor" in Chesterton, *Collected Works*, vol. 14, 652; written in mid-1890s.

list of supplies (that includes copies of both a Bible and Grimm's fairy tales "for when it rains"), and moving into a tree at the back end of the garden identified as the "Tree of Life."[60] He and his nephew settle into a "hollow cup hung between heaven and earth" that "emerge in [the nephew's] memory clearly distinct as the three levels of the Universe in Dante's epic." [61] The tangled boughs represent in order hell, the never-ending forest purgatory, and the top-most branches heaven (affording a celestial vista). Chesterton's strong reference to Dante's literature has been argued on the basis of his love of medieval literature.[62] The tree of "My Uncle the Professor" acquires the significance of home, halfway to heaven, that the characters must climb to reach their goal. In this, Chesterton added to his earlier intimation (of the forest as the meeting place of heaven and earth) the identification of the forest with cathedral imagery. The tree resembles the church.

In these writings of Chesterton's teens and early twenties, the tree takes on the meaning of a fallen universe. It tells something about the essential nature of the person, or represents mankind—the flesh of humanity shouldered by the woodcutter. Furthermore, Chesterton's youthful stories hint at the use of the wooden pole as weapon, transportation, and illuminating light that guides the wanderer. The church is analogized as a tree that can take the climber to celestial heights; furthermore the tree, as an object of nature, carries a hidden message. Chesterton's ensuing novels all continue to advance the themes introduced by the short stories.

---

[60] Ibid., 648, 654.

[61] Ibid., 651.

[62] Dominic Manganiello, "'Where in Hell Are We?': Chesterton on Dante," *Chesterton Review* 20, no. 1 (1994): 65-81. Manganiello showed surprise that a review of Dante's influence upon Chesterton's writings was undertaken only recently, given Chesterton's reputation as a medievalist.

FOUR

SAPLING: EARLY NOVELS (1904-1909)

The Napoleon of Notting Hill (1904)

Chesterton's first and possibly best-loved novel, *The Napoleon of Notting Hill*, had its beginnings, in part, in two events: a childish daydream in which he had planned a strategy to defend his little neighbourhood of North Kensington, and the outbreak of the Boer War in 1899.[1] Consequently, it exposes his strengthening coherence in socio-political themes of nationalism, local patriotism, anti-imperialism, and anti-industrialism (all of which were being concurrently promoted in his journalism and essays).[2] He paraded his views on the rights of the citizen against the demands of the state, and the value of individualism over collectivism.[3] His character, Adam Wayne, tells us that Notting Hill is symbolic of the common earth, home of the common man.[4] In speaking of the novel, Chesterton clarified his point further:

> My idea in *The Napoleon of Notting Hill*
> was that men have a natural loyalty for
> their own home and their own land. I do
> not see why, instead of progress lying in
> the direction of bigger and bigger every-
> thing, it should not be found in the oppo-
> site direction, in local patriotism. I say let

[1] Chesterton, *Napoleon of Notting Hill*; Boyd, *Novels of G. K. Chesterton*.

[2] See e.g., Chesterton, *The Collected Works*, volumes 4, 5, 27-37.

[3] For a full explication of political and social allegory in Chesterton's novels, see Boyd, *Novels of G. K. Chesterton*.

[4] Chesterton, *Napoleon of Notting Hill*, 46.

a man go on loving his own home, he will all the better recognize the other fellow's right to do so.[5]

It has been claimed that *The Napoleon of Notting Hill* is alone in having no religious significance, but in spite of the strength of the first level of allegory seen in the story, and although there is less direct reference to religion in this novel than in subsequent ones, the use of the tree reveals a deeper meaning than simply the political and social.[6] The tree becomes more closely associated with Chesterton's conception of home—that is, his understanding of the nation as home, and of the city as physical picture of spiritual home. That Chesterton himself intended a metaphysical reading of *The Napoleon of Notting Hill* can be seen in the identification of Notting Hill as "an Earthly Paradise" and in the hero's sacramental comment, "Nature puts on a disguise when she speaks to every man; to this man she put on the disguise of Notting Hill."[7]

To understand Chesterton's use of the tree within the theme of the city, it is helpful to acknowledge that the larger theme of city was well established in the antecedent literature. Augustine's influential *City of God* explicated the biblical teaching of the city of the faithful "whose builder and maker is God" and compared it to the merely earthly city of man, built upon self-love and pride.[8] Dante's road takes his travellers through cities of torment (for example, through Desolation and the "city of the woe-begot" named Dis) to the heavenly city of the White Rose, symbol of divine love fulfilled.[9] Bunyan's pilgrim travels from the City of Destruction, through

---

[5] Chesterton quoted in Clemens, *Chesterton As Seen by His Contemporaries*, 80.

[6] See, e.g., Hollis, *The Mind of Chesterton*, 111.

[7] Chesterton, *Napoleon of Notting Hill*, 31, 53.

[8] Heb. 11:10.

[9] Dante *Hell* 3.1-42, 9.32; *Paradise* 30.130. The significance of the rose is mentioned in "The Garden of Smoke," below.

Vanity Fair, to Zion. Milton's lost and regained cities represent the earthly Babylon and the heavenly Jerusalem, first allegorized by Paul the Apostle.[10] In his turn, William Blake equated England with Jerusalem.[11] Within this larger theme of city, the tree appears as an identifying element, an obvious example being Milton's trees in Eden: "The middle Tree and highest there that grew, / . . . and next to Life / our Death the Tree of Knowledge grew fast by."[12] The centrality of the tree in the city is echoed by Chesterton in *The Napoleon of Notting Hill*.

In the novel, eccentric Auberon Quin, the new king of London, elaborates a bizarre and humorous plan to restore the heraldry and pageantry of medievalism. Adam Wayne, chosen as the provost of Notting Hill, takes the jest seriously and leads his community in revolt against the plans for industrialization, which would annex his Pump Street at the expense of its small shops. The armies of the entire city are beaten by the nationalistic Notting Hill forces, but Adam Wayne eventually falls in a final battle beneath a tree, only to be resurrected at the end. In a revealing discussion on the two-fold nature of man, this revivified Adam (Wayne) is equated with the biblical second Adam, and described by Chesterton as the "equal and eternal human being" who can justify the disparity between the fallen and the divine.[13]

---

[10] Milton *Paradise Lost* 12.51-62; *Paradise Regained* 2.306-14; Gal. 4:21-31.

[11] See, e.g., William Blake, "England! Awake! Awake! Awake!" in *Jerusalem*, in Allison and others, *Norton*, 510. Cf. "The Oak Tree Song" in *The Flying Inn*, 702-3 (reproduced below), for Chesterton's equation of England with Christianity through the picture of the tree.

[12] Milton *Paradise Lost* 4.195, 220-1.

[13] Chesterton, *Napoleon of Notting Hill*, 128-9. Chesterton's meaning behind the "two lobes of the brain of the ploughman" or the "two lobes of the same brain that has been cloven in two" has been argued through several approaches—psychologically, artistically, and relationally. See, e.g., Dale, *Outline of Sanity*; see further Lynette Hunter, "A Reading of *The Napoleon of*

Religious allusion is first introduced in the novel through Chesterton's choice of colour; this symbolism can then be extended to his picture of the tree. Boyd noted that Chesterton was aware of the significance of his hero's name meaning "red earth," which is a biblical prefiguring of Christ in the first Adam.[14] This adds nuance to Notting Hill's choice of yellow and red as its heraldic colours, previously established in the story as political symbol as well as religious (the church having her own "symbolic colours").[15] That Adam Wayne was intended by Chesterton as the Christ-figure can be seen in the novel's final battle, when Adam thrusts forward his victory banner and points to his own red blood before giving up his life beneath the great oak tree that stands atop the hill.[16] Against this oak tree, the rush of the enemy has carried Adam by force, with the cry "Kill him!" echoing as though from the biblical crucifixion crowd.[17] "He caught hold of the oak . . . getting his hand into a wide crevice and grasping, as it were, the bowels of the tree" in anticipation of his own death, as Christ grasped the tree of the cross in anticipation of the joy to come.[18] As Christ at the last supper comforted his disciples, Adam says, "There is good wine poured at the inn at the end of the world."[19] He continues,

---

Notting Hill," Chesterton Review 3, no. 1 (1976-77): 119-28. The pivotal importance to Chesterton of the fallenness of humanity and original sin is seen again. For the unifying effect of Christ upon the double-sided nature of the flesh and spirit, see Romans 7:15-8:11.

[14] Boyd, *Novels of G. K. Chesterton*, 201, note 23. Cf. Gen. 1; 1 Corinthians 15:45.

[15] Chesterton, *Napoleon of Notting Hill*, 14-15.

[16] The tree on the hill is seen in Milton's *Paradise Lost* 4.226; see also Dante *Purgatory* 22.

[17] Chesterton, *Napoleon of Notting Hill*, 123; cf. Luke 23:21.

[18] Chesterton, *Napoleon of Notting Hill*, 124; cf. Phil. 2:8; Heb. 12:2.

[19] Chesterton, *Napoleon of Notting Hill*, 124; Luke 22:18.

"I am doing what the truly wise do. When a child goes out into the garden and takes hold of a tree, saying, 'Let this tree be all I have,' that moment its roots take hold on hell and its branches on the stars. The joy I have is what the lover knows when a woman is everything. It is what I know when Notting Hill is everything. I have a city. Let it stand or fall."

As he spoke, the turf lifted itself like a living thing, and out of it rose slowly, like crested serpents, the roots of the oak. The great head of the tree . . . swept the sky . . . like a broom, and the whole tree heeled over like a ship, smashing everyone in its fall.[20]

Thus, Adam Wayne dies for "the truth that is also a riddle," written "in the darkest books of God."[21] What is this truth? Is it, as Colebatch suggested, the achievement of human happiness by the awakening of "all London to a sense of colour, splendour, and pageantry"?[22] Is it merely a political argument told through medieval story, which is the extent of the analysis some writers expend upon it? For his part, Ian Boyd found the novel an allegory concerning a balanced political view; yet he insisted that Chesterton's work should be considered religious allegory and all of his writing read "as an expression of his search for God."[23] Lynette Hunter noted that Adam Wayne's perception of the value of ordinary objects in the novel underscores Chesterton's conviction

---

[20] Chesterton, *Napoleon of Notting Hill*, 124. The uprooted tree is featured also in the opening scene of *The Flying Inn* (431) as a symbol that death is preferable to peace at the cost of truth.

[21] Chesterton, *Napoleon of Notting Hill*, 125.

[22] Colebatch, "The Meanings of *The Napoleon of Notting Hill*," 441.

[23] Boyd, "In Search of the Essential Chesterton," 39.

that art must communicate "an essential value or truth of God." [24] The tree in *The Napoleon of Notting Hill*, then, can be seen to stand for more than merely a political or moral belief. The tree of Adam Wayne, planted in the city, looks more and more like the cross of Jesus Christ, made of the stuff of the earth and essential in the journey to the heavenly city.

The symbolism of the oak tree in literature substantiates a religious interpretation. The oak, known for its sturdiness and strength, was considered sacred in the days of the Druids and represents the theme of death in *The Pardoner's Tale*.[25] In Chaucer's influential work, the oak tree is very significant, a "sign, in the Augustinian sense, guiding the reader's understanding of the action of the story" and a common medieval symbol of despair evocative of biblical connotations.[26] The tree's imperial and sacrificial associations implicate it with royal coronations and with worship that is both godly and idolatrous.[27] In Adam Wayne's action of uprooting the oak, one can hear the cries of a biblical poem lamenting the destruction of the nations caused by the rejection of God's messianic provision: "Howl, O ye oaks of Bashan; for the forest of the vintage is coming down."[28] Zechariah's lamentation in turn brings to mind Nebuchadnezzar's dream of an enormous tree, the felling of which represents the sovereignty of God over the nations of

---

[24] Hunter, "A Reading of *The Napoleon of Notting Hill*," 127.

[25] As noted by Jeffrey, *Dictionary of Biblical Tradition*, 780. *The Canterbury Tales*, according to Chesterton, was "already pregnant with the promise of the English novel"; Chesterton, "The Victorian Age in Literature," 61.

[26] Carolyn P. Collette, "'*Ubi Peccaverant, Ibi Punirentur*': The Oak Tree and the Pardoner's Tale," *Chaucer Review* 19 (1984): 39-45.

[27] See, e.g., Judg. 9:6; Gen. 12:6 and Josh. 24:25-27; Ezek. 6:13.

[28] Zech. 11:1-3.

the world.[29] That Adam Wayne uproots (instead of cuts down) the tree might have further significance; the book of Job pictures a felled tree as retaining the hope of sprouting again, and an uprooted one means judgement with the removal of all hope.[30]

Notting Hill stands for the centre of the cosmos; as Wills put it, "The stars were made for Adam Wayne— not for him to possess, but as decoration for his home."[31] The city of heaven illuminates Adam's earth, and the oak tree graces his home (the city of Notting Hill) as a backyard tree graces a garden. The tree becomes representative of home and country, and of patriotic loyalty nearing worship (implicating nationalism with religion). Themes of sacramentalism and the sovereignty of God who judges the nations are also suggested in Chesterton's portrayal of the tree as the cross of salvation.

The Ball and the Cross (serialized 1905-1906)

The historical debate between Blatchford and Chesterton, which occurred in 1903 and 1904, showed the solidifying of Chesterton's public expression of his beliefs and prepared him for the writing of his next novel, with its explicitly religious meanings. So far, his employment of the tree image to illustrate his fiction has been eclectic; from the earliest juvenilia through this period of spiritual and literary formation, he has painted the tree in many landscapes. The tree has mediated light and provided food and shelter for the adventuring journeyman far from home, becoming home itself. It has been a weapon, a gibbet, and a means of transportation across serpentine rivers and up towards the skies. Forests have pictured the corporate flesh of humanity, a symbol of

---

[29] Dan. 4.

[30] See, e.g., Job 14:6-8; Job 19:9-11; Isa. 6:12-14.

[31] Wills, *Chesterton: Man and Mask*, 106.

the fallen creation and at the same time a symbol of the meeting place between heaven and earth. The tree has been identified with the nation, the city, and the church—hiding a puzzle that has to do with life and death. In *The Ball and the Cross*, Chesterton continued to build meaning into his tree emblem.

The Ball and the Cross is "a mixture of fantasy, farce, and theology" in which two men of opposing philosophical persuasions are convinced that they must defend their beliefs by fighting a duel.[32] On his visit to London, an earnest young Catholic Highlander, Evan MacIan, sees an insult to the Virgin Mary in a bookshop window. The shopkeeper, James Turnbull—a sincere atheist—accepts MacIan's challenge to a duel, and the two travel widely, seeking a place for their fight but always frustrated in their endeavours by well-meaning interveners. They end up in the garden of a mental asylum, the picture of the fallen Eden. MacIan explains, "This garden is not a dream but an apocalyptic vision. This garden is the world gone mad."[33] Turnbull and MacIan, along with everyone who has had a part in their wild fight, are imprisoned by Professor Lucifer, who is attempting to erase any memory of the duel of religious expression from the face of the earth. This Professor Lucifer first appears before the novel's main action begins, in a prologue that describes the continuing heavenly conflict, for the most part unseen by the inhabitants of the earth—a celestial battle for the soul of earthly

---

[32] Martin Gardner, "Levels of Allegory in *The Ball and the Cross*," *Chesterton Review* 18, no. 1 (1992): 37. *The Ball and the Cross* was serialized in *The Commonwealth* in 1905-6, then published in 1909 (New York) and 1910 (Britain).

[33] Chesterton, *Ball and the Cross*, 168. For a treatment of Chesterton's themes of sanity and insanity in *The Ball and the Cross*, see Adam Schwartz, "G. K. C.'s Methodical Madness: Sanity and Social Control in Chesterton," *Renascence: Essays on Values in Literature* 49, no. 1 (1996): 23-40.

man.[34] The dreamlike prologue tells of the scientist Lucifer in a flying airship setting down his passenger, Michael—a monk—onto the peak St. Paul's Cathedral.[35]
Michael makes his way to the street, ending up himself
in the mental institute and, as *inclusio* at the story's
end, he miraculously parades all the inmates to freedom
and safety from the fire that demolishes the asylum.

The dense, brown fog of London in the opening
scene bespeaks the confusion in the celestial orders, im-
aging "chaos in a diabolic heaven," and is symbolic of
the "abandonment of clear outlines" that the modern,
scientific society has undergone in rejecting Christianity.[36] But the fog that engulfs the city is surmounted by
the ball-and-cross ornament on the dome of St. Paul's,
standing for the relationship between the world and the
church. The theme of the novel is the same as in *Orthodoxy*, according to a contemporary review of the book in
the *Pall Mall Gazette*: "There he contrasted the Cross
with its symbolism of four arms stretching away infinite-
ly and the circle with its narrow completeness, and here

---

[34] This introduction (in the prologue) of the devilish villain presents one of the many images that the story shares with the book of Job. As Satan roams the
earth in Job 1:7, so Professor Lucifer has free reign over
the world in this novel.

[35] Note that 1903, two years before this novel
was written, marks the date of the first successful air
flight by the Wright brothers.

[36] According to Stephan Medcalf, "The Achievement of G. K. Chesterton," in *G. K. Chesterton: A Centenary Appraisal*, ed. John Sullivan (London: Paul Elek,
1974), 87, 107. Chesterton regularly used cloud and fog
to intimate confusion or the loss of an objective understanding of truth, often connecting the wicked fog to ur-
ban modernization; see, e.g., Chesterton, *Manalive*,
129-32. Clouds settle on the day of Job's birth and hide
God's face; see Job 3:5 and 22:14.

he develops the contrast."[37] For his part, the satanic Lucifer prefers the ball:

> So fat. So satisfied. Not at all like that scraggy individual stretching his arms in stark weariness. . . . This globe is reasonable; that cross is unreasonable. . . . The very shape of it is a contradiction in terms.[38]

Monk Michael piously points out that the cross, which is on top of the ball and not the other way around, proves the supremacy and primacy of the religion of Christianity over the worldly philosophy of rationalism.[39] The ball represents the rationalism of the world in "its completeness and self-sufficiency," but the very shape of the cross depicts the collision of the paradoxical religion of Christianity.[40] Indeed, Chesterton described his allegory of the war between earth and heaven as a "collision of

---

[37] As quoted by Pearce, *Wisdom and Innocence*, 153.

[38] Chesterton, *Ball and the Cross*, 4, 5. In *Orthodoxy*, Chesterton said, "But the cross, though it has at its heart a collision and a contradiction, can extend its four arms for ever without altering its shape. Because it has a paradox in its centre it can grow without changing. The circle returns upon itself and is bound. The cross opens its arms to the four winds; it is a signpost for free travellers"; Chesterton, *Orthodoxy*, 231.

[39] Chesterton, *Ball and the Cross*, 6.

[40] Clipper, *G. K. Chesterton*, 132. The relevance of the shape of the cross is further developed in *The Flying Inn*, where the wooden signpost of the travelling characters fighting for personal and religious freedom becomes a symbol of the cross. It is strongly contrasted with the curve of the Islamic crescent, with the threat that the cross of St. Paul's Cathedral is to be replaced by the "croscent"—a syncretistic symbol blending two world views of East and West; Chesterton, *Flying Inn*, 446-9.

blasphemy and worship."[41] The novel presents the ball of the world pierced by the root of the cross of Christ, which rises like a triumphant tree above it. Greenhill substantiated this archetypal interpretation, which sees the cross as a planted tree: "In the organic connection thought to exist between that portion of the Cross hidden in the earth and the visible portion above the earth, there lies an immediate analogy with a root and a tree."[42] Chesterton's illustration of the tree in this novel is subtle, and it lies in this visual shape of the cross.

The structure of the novel has been unravelled by John Coates, whose article begins with a reproach levied against the work, seeing *The Ball and the Cross* more as a "phantasmagoria" than a novel and almost "critically impregnable."[43] Critiquing the work presents a daunting challenge because, as Coates pointed out, "Chesterton has broken recognized aesthetic rules" leading to charges of disorder and carelessness.[44] Part of Coates's key to the novel, which furthers understanding of its tree symbolism, is his recognition of the symmetry within the narrative. Opposing pairs of characters, for example, are seen in Lucifer and Michael, in Turnbull and MacIan, and in the pagan idol worshipper and the peacemaker who are met on the duellists' travels. This symmetry is also seen in the parallel actions of the "spiritual" entities warring while the "humans" also fight. That is, the action between Lucifer and Michael broached in the puzzling prologue is parallel to the action in the body of the text (in which the same metaphysical questions are physically contested between atheist and Christian). The symmetry is again seen in the links Chesterton made between symbols. "The prologue, under its air of casual comedy, offers a close-knit system of cross-references and references to the material outside the text but

[41] Chesterton, *Autobiography*, 297.

[42] Greenhill, "The Child in the Tree," 363.

[43] John Coates, "*The Ball and the Cross* and the Edwardian Novel of Ideas," *Chesterton Review* 18, no. 1 (1992): 49.

[44] Ibid., 50.

known to the reader," Coates noted.[45] In other words, a pattern exists within the novel: the lessons of the spiritual realm introduced in the prologue are repeated over and over at the physical level of description and story action, both in the repetitive behavior of the men seeking a place to complete their duel and in the repetition of symbols (with their intra- and extra-textual reference) associated to the tree.

Chesterton made subtle but important connections between the shapes of the sword, the man, the cross, the tree, and the ladder. Because his abstract thinking indicated "an almost mystical absorption in shapes and designs," it is crucial to pay attention to his visual cues in this significant novel.[46] For example, several critics have puzzled over the unexplained presence of a peg on the wall of each of the asylum's cells.[47] Perhaps a clue to the peg mystery lies in Chesterton's fascination with symbolic shapes in general. He said of his hero Robert Louis Stevenson,

> He loved things to stand out; we might say he loved them to stick out; as does the hilt of a sword or the feather in a cap. He loved the pattern of the crossed swords; he almost loved the pattern of the gallows because it is a clear shape like the cross.[48]

---

[45] Ibid., 64.

[46] Wilfred Sheed, "On Chesterton," in *G. K. Chesterton: A Half Century of Views*, ed. Denis J. Conlon (Oxford: Oxford University Press, 1987), 164.

[47] See e.g., Gardner, "Levels of Allegory in *The Ball and the Cross*."

[48] Quoted by Gardner, "Levels of Allegory in *The Ball and the Cross*," 44. Note the very early comparison of the gibbet to the Tree of Life in "The Wild Goose Chase," above. See also Esther 7 for the gallows as an ironic instrument of death intended for the innocent Mordechai, who victoriously lives. In Deut. 21:22 the Hebrew for "tree" carries the meaning of the gallows.

Chesterton's artistic eye was always focused for a glimpse of the cross. Yet it was not simply the silhouettes (of peg, of tree) that attracted him but rather their relationship to one another and to the larger story. He saw the "pattern behind the pattern, the spiritual reality . . . that exists behind the shape of the world he inhabits, analyzes, and diagnoses."[49] Chesterton's artistic attention to shapes had, as its goal, a focus on the truth beneath the external sign, for his concern was always "to move beyond the constraints of Realism, avoiding on the way the illusory, and ultimately enlarging our sense of what is real."[50] He favoured pictures over repetitious and empty designs, and expressed his disgust against the tendency to reduce religious symbols, such as the cross, to mere decoration—as if it were the Islamic crescent, or the Greek key, or the wheel of Buddha that he said "moves round but never moves on."[51] In contrast, to him the symbol of the cross represented the Tree of Life.[52] The Christian faith stands

> alone upon the earth, and lifted and liberated from all the wheels and whirlpools of the earth . . . weighted and balanced indeed with more than Oriental metaphysics and more than Pagan pomp and pageantry. . . . rooted in the primeval joy of God and finding its fruition in the final happiness of humanity.[53]

The ball-and-cross standard on the apex of St. Paul's Cathedral, which dominated Chesterton's physical vision

---

[49] As has been said about Chesterton's mouthpiece, Father Brown; see Andre P. Gushurst-Moore, "Reality, Illusion and Art in the *Father Brown* Stories," *Chesterton Review* 24, no. 3 (1998): 322.

[50] Ibid.

[51] Chesterton, *Saint Thomas Aquinas*, 84.

[52] Ibid., 114.

[53] Ibid., 115-6.

of London and expressed his spiritual vision of orthodox Christianity, also directed his theme within this novel.

The suggestive use of the symbols relevant to the tree image (that show the affiliation between the shapes of the sword, the man, the cross, the tree, and the ladder) begins in an early scene. MacIan plants the steel point of his sword "into the soil like a man planting a tree" to drive home the truth that religion is worth fighting over, especially with the cross-shaped weapon. [54] Later, he plants this same sword-point in the ground "like one who plants his tent-pole for the night," and both he and Turnbull instinctively and reverently stand still "before the sign of the fixed and standing sword," a figure of the cross before which they speak of God. [55] In this way, the sword is emblematic of the tree and the cross. [56] Another image is added to this sword/tree/cross hybrid when MacIan stands "in the road for an instant as if rooted like a tree." [57] To further add the person to the mix of sword and cross and tree, Chesterton described one match between the duelling MacIan and Turnbull:

> The two bright, bloodthirsty weapons made the sign of the cross in horrible parody upon each other. . . . [And] upon the hill, above the crucifix, there appeared another horrible parody of its shape; the figure of a man who appeared for an instant waving his outspread arms . . . like a comic repetition of the cross. [58]

---

[54] Chesterton, *Ball and the Cross*, 34.

[55] Ibid., 68.

[56] Note the secondary association of the tree and home, a theme developed in other stories such as "My Uncle the Professor," above.

[57] Chesterton, *Ball and the Cross*, 73.

[58] Ibid., 90-91. Elsewhere Chesterton more fully developed the tree of the cross as a person; see e.g., *The Trees of Pride*, below. As well, for a man who stood "rigidly with his arms stretched out like the shadow of

In a single story, Chesterton managed to graft the sword, the cross, and the human with the tree—but he was not yet finished. He would add the image of the tree as a ladder, which has ample precedent in literature as a mythological, biblical, and folkloric motif, as "all ancient peoples imagined the link between heaven and earth."[59]

MacIan and Turnbull pass through several London gardens in their search for a suitable spot to carry out their swordfight to the death—a shopkeeper's garden, an obscure kitchen garden, and the garden of an idol-worshipper who welcomes the possibility of sacrificial bloodletting in front of his god.[60] When MacIan gazes over the edge of a cliff at the sea below, he believes they have finally found the perfect spot for the duel. He hears "the cool voice of his companion . . . calling to him from a little farther along the cliff, to tell him that he had found the ladder of descent"—a deeply forested path leading downwards.[61] "All the time that the two travellers sank from stage to stage of this downward journey, there closed over their heads living bridges and

---

the crucifix," see "The Tower of Treason" in *The Man Who Knew Too Much*, Chesterton, *Collected Works*, vol. 8, 716.

[59] Greenhill, "The Child in the Tree," 337, n. 63. Chesterton's use of the tree as ladder is seen also in "The Singular Speculation of the House-Agent," a story in *The Club of Queer Trades* and published in 1905, as serialization of *The Ball and the Cross* began. The short story features a suspected criminal and vagrant who leads the detective in a search for his home, which turns out to be a treehouse hung in the tops of two great elms. The branches of the trees form "a rude natural ladder" like "a giant's staircase going somewhere, perhaps to the stars"; Chesterton, *Club of Queer Trades*, 61. A meeting of men takes place amidst the leaves, stars, and wind, halfway to heaven, and suggests humanity's spiritual nature and yearning to communicate with deity.

[60] Chesterton, *Ball and the Cross*, 23, 47, 51-52.

[61] Ibid., 84.

caverns of the most varied foliage," alive with forest animals and birds.[62] "It was down this clamorous ladder of life that they went . . . to die."[63] Finally they find themselves on the firm sand of the beach, "enclosed on three sides by white walls of rock, and on the fourth by the green wall of the advancing sea."[64] The three phases of the universe surround the pair, with the rocky cliffs and forest thicket of earth, the "victorious sun" of the sky, and the wide, wild sea.[65] Within this theatre, the "huge framework of their folly," Turnbull and MacIan once again strike the duelling pose, only to realize that the advancing tide has cut them off and threatens to drown them. [66] The converting atheist, Turnbull, comments, "There is something fine about fighting in a place where even the conqueror must die."[67] Chesterton has depicted the Christological story of the dying victor who descends by means of a leafy path to the lower regions of creation; it heralds his later comparison between creation and the incarnation:

> Once Heaven came upon the earth with a power or seal called the image of God, whereby man took command of Nature; and once again (when in empire after empire men had been found wanting) Heaven

---

[62] Ibid.

[63] Ibid.

[64] Ibid., 85.

[65] Ibid. Roger Cook noted that, on a mythopoeic level, the "elementary forms of sacred place constitute a cosmos in miniature. . . . [and] consist of a landscape of trees, stone and water"; Roger Cook, *The Tree of Life: Symbols of the Centre* (London: Thames and Hudson, 1974), 21. Also note Calvin's traditional cosmology representing the creation as a theatre in which God manifests Himself in nature, in Calvin *Institutes of the Christian Religion* 1.5.1-10. The three-tiered universe is pictured in Job 11:8-9, Ps. 135:6, and Rev. 14:7.

[66] Chesterton, *The Ball and the Cross*, 85.

[67] Ibid., 86.

came to save mankind in the awful shape of a man.[68]

His fictive device having served his purposes, Chesterton now allowed Turnbull and MacIan to live, taking to the road again in search of the garden in which to finish their quarrel. Still pursued by the police, MacIan and Turnbull dodge them by climbing into a large tree and "crouching in crucial silence in the cloud of leaves."[69] They inch along the top of a tall garden wall, which encloses the asylum and imprisons all who enter.[70] Suddenly,

> the green and crooked branches of a big apple-tree came crawling at them out of the mist, like the tentacles of some green cuttlefish. Anything would serve, however, that was likely to confuse their trail, so they both decided . . . to use this tree also as a ladder—a ladder of descent.[71]

The theme of descent by means of the forest path to the shore is now relocated in an apple tree used as a ladder of descent into the great garden of the fallen world.[72]

---

[68] Chesterton, *Orthodoxy*, 350.

[69] Chesterton, *Ball and the Cross*, 113.

[70] Chesterton's garden walls are often coupled with tree imagery, sometimes taking the form of bushes or hedges; here, the wall brings to mind Job's hedges of protection (1:10) and turmoil (3:23).

[71] Chesterton, *Ball and the Cross*, 113.

[72] The apple tree has long symbolized the evil fruit of Eden, possibly due to a mix-up in the Latin declension of the words for "apple" and "evil." One thinks of the choice offered both Snow White and Eve; see, e.g., Gen. 3; see further *Paradise Lost* 7.542-7. Free will is pictured also in Augustine's pear tree; see *Confessions* 2.4 in Augustine, *Saint Augustine: Confessions*, trans. R. S. Pine-Coffin, ed. Betty Radice (London: Penguin Books, 1961); subsequent references are to this edition.

Chesterton strongly hinted at the picture of the incarnation attained through the instrument of the tree (which also delivers death). He would have been aware of this theme in the poetry he read; Pope, for example, expressed creation as the medium between the two realms:

> Slave to no sect, who takes no private road,
> But looks through Nature up to Nature's God:
> Pursues that chain which links th'immense
>   design,
> Joins Heaven and earth, and mortal and divine.[73]

Perhaps Chesterton was also aware of the cosmological tree as a ladder between heaven and earth, which is figured in the non-biblical Jewish legend of the Midrash Konen. Here the Tree of Life links Eden "with a holier realm directly above; it is like a ladder on which the souls of the righteous may ascend and descend."[74] The motif is known to many mythologies, and the tree linking heaven and earth "provides in its branches a kind of ladder by means of which ascent from one to the other is possible."[75] For example, a common subject of medieval art arising out of the biblical and traditional literature figured the tree of Jesse as closely related to the ladder of Jacob. In his substantial work on this subject, Arthur

---

See further *De Civitate Dei* 14.27. See also the love scene in the tree of Chaucer's *Merchant's Tale*. Calvin, too, saw the tree serving to prove and exercise one's choice, in Calvin, *Institutes of the Christian Religion* 2.1.4. See also Blake, "A Poison Tree" from *Songs of Experience* in Allison and others, *Norton*, 505.

[73] Alexander Pope, "Epistle IV.7.23-26" from *Essay on Man*, in *Works*, 226. Pope sees God through the order in nature rather than through special Christian revelation, according to Peter Milward, *Christian Themes in English Literature* (N.P.: Folcroft Press, 1967), 14.

[74] Greenhill, "The Child in the Tree," 337.

[75] Ibid., 329. For Dante's cosmological tree, see also *Paradise* 18.28-33.

Watson explained, "There are a number of passages in the Fathers in which the Virgin is regarded as, or addressed as, a ladder. . . . In other passages Jacob is regarded as seeing the Lord, the ladder being the Virgin."[76] The tree of Jesse is associated (as early as the sixth century) with the heavenly ladder of Jacob, and both Jesse's tree and Jacob's ladder denote "passage between the earthly and the heavenly,"[77] the "eschatological journey of the soul to heaven."[78] Dante added, to his cosmological tree of the heavens, a picture of Jacob's golden ladder, signifying the contemplation of God.[79] Biblically, the promise of salvation through Isaiah's reference to the tree of Jesse attains its end through the tree of the cross.[80] One can see the connection made in European art between the root of Jesse (Jesus) and the ladder as the cross, and it appears to have been understood also by Chesterton in writing *The Ball and the Cross*.

The novel ends with a hellish forest, the antithesis of the tree-as-cathedral picture, when the asylum keepers under the direction of Professor Lucifer "set fire to the building in accordance with the strict principles of the social contract."[81] The flame "shot out and spread above [the prisoners] like the fiery cloisters of some infernal cathedral, or like a grove of red tropical trees in

---

[76] Arthur Watson, *The Early Iconography of the Tree of Jesse* (London: Oxford University Press, 1934), 50.

[77] Ibid., 52.

[78] Greenhill, "The Child in the Tree," 340.

[79] Dante *Paradise* 18.28-33; 21.28-30. Note also that the ornate west front of Bath's church, certainly known to Chesterton, is famous for its bas-relief sculpture of Jacob's ladder.

[80] See Isa. 11:1-3; Deut. 21:22-23; Acts 5:30; 1 Pet. 2:24; Rom. 15:12.

[81] Chesterton, *Ball and the Cross*, 174. The blaze brings to mind Job 1:16, in which fire falls from the sky in judgement.

the garden of the devil."[82] Turnbull, locked in his cell next to MacIan's, finally converts from his self-sufficient unbelief as he "calls out . . . in what words, heaven knows."[83] Salvation comes through the gracious and miraculous intervention of the old monk, whose face "was so wrinkled that it was like parchment loaded with hieroglyphics . . . [which] seemed like a scripture older than the gods."[84] This forest of fire, like the Red Sea, is suddenly split by a great and invisible wind, and "down this little path was walking a little old man singing as if he were alone in a wood in spring."[85] Turnbull's rationalism is conquered by MacIan's supernaturalism, so that Boyd finds in the novel "something like a theology of grace" in which "grace finds its meaning in the nature which it complements and perfects."[86]

The general influence of foregoing literature upon Chesterton's writing of *The Ball and the Cross* is more apparent than any specific references to the tree in the novel. Chesterton did not foreground the tree; nevertheless, his literary allusions affect the reader's understanding of that symbol. He repeatedly quoted Swinburne, mentioned the gigantic Brobdingnagians of Swift's *Gulliver's Travels*, remarked upon a chamber in *The Arabian Nights*, gave Turnbull a "Robinson Crusoe feeling," and

---

[82] Chesterton, *Ball and the Cross*, 176. Cf. Isa. 9:18.

[83] Again, the novel parallels the biblical story: Job, too, calls out for an arbitrator and living redeemer, in Job 5:1, 9:33, and 19:25.

[84] Chesterton, *Ball and the Cross*, 152; cf. pages 111-2. Note that the face of the "Saviour," Michael, is written upon with hieroglyphics (like the face of the creation pictured in "Apotheosis" above), and that MacIan "looked at the high tree-tops that caught the last light and at the birds going heavily homeward, just as if all these things were written advice that he could read." Nature, as well as the face of the Christ-figure, is inscribed with a message.

[85] Chesterton, *Ball and the Cross*, 117.

[86] Boyd, *Novels of G. K. Chesterton*, 38.

referred to "a vigorous phrase of Bunyan"; these stories all carry tree imagery of their own.[87] Further to the scattered literary allusions that alert the reader to allegorical polysemeity, the structure of the novel shows the use of a prologue that has prior instance in works such as Goethe's *Faust* and the book of Job, emphasizing "an inner meaning or permanent dimension underlying the events which are to follow."[88] Indeed, *The Ball and the Cross* begins with such theologically "loaded" language and setting that a metaphorical reading seems necessary. Chesterton's tree as sword, person, ladder, and cross assumes scriptural intonations of the incarnation and salvation.

The Man Who Was Thursday (1908)

This fantastical spy novel—perhaps Chesterton's "most perplexing" (as Joseph Pearce claimed)—was written at a time when Edwardian London was experiencing anarchist conspiracies and bomb threats.[89] Subtitled "A Nightmare," it has the curious atmosphere of *A Midsummer Night's Dream*, with the main character pursuing someone he cannot catch as he flees from someone he cannot see in a confusion of identities familiar to all dreamers. The novel is a "fictional autobiography," the narrative of Chesterton's pursuit of God through the

---

[87] *The Ball and the Cross*, 33, 89; 33; 50; 108; 93.

[88] Coates, "Edwardian Novel of Ideas," 64. *The Ball and the Cross* shares many images with the book of Job—satanic antagonist, wall or hedge, fire falling from the sky, clouds obstructing truth, the cry for a redeemer. This abundance of images common to both books adds great significance to the appearance of tree imagery in the fiction story, even though the Old Testament story only prophesies the yet-absent tree of the cross.

[89] Pearce, *Wisdom and Innocence*, 107; see also Stephen Medcalf in introduction to Chesterton, *The Man Who Was Thursday*, ix.

chaos of a fallen universe that yet retains traces of the Creator.[90] Chesterton himself described *The Man Who Was Thursday* as an autobiographical perspective on nature as it might appear to a pantheist "whose pantheism is struggling out of pessimism."[91] Twenty years after the book appeared, and upon the adaptation of the story for the stage, Chesterton admitted in an interview that, although he might still have been a bit "foggy about ethical and theological matters" at the novel's writing, he was clear on the issue of good and evil, and that nature was distinguished from God.[92] The colourful narration has been criticized as merely scene painting with brilliant and meaningless word pictures. Boyd dismissed that analysis of his descriptive passages: "Far from being irrelevant digressions, they have an obvious relation to the main action and present important emblems of what the action means."[93] The tree, with its connections to light, is one important emblem in this work.

Gabriel Syme, a poet who clings to law and order, enters into a conspiracy to infiltrate an anarchist society—a council of six disguised men named after the days of the week and run by Sunday. The President's notion of "concealing by not concealing" is applied to the members who, for the duration of the subterfuge, are given suggestive disguises to hide but hint at their identities.[94] Sunday guards his own identity by showing only

---

[90] Boyd, "The Legendary Chesterton," 58.

[91] Chesterton, *Autobiography*, 98.

[92] Ward, *Gilbert Keith Chesterton*, 168-9. Dates are conflicting; Chesterton's novel came out the same year as his *Orthodoxy*, in which he displayed no theological fogginess. Perhaps his own notoriously poor memory is to blame for the time conflict; perhaps Ward misinterpreted a comment dealing with idea conception and not publication. At any rate, the novel has been seen as important mostly for its sacramentally expressed themes of good versus evil, the point Chesterton maintained.

[93] Boyd, *Novels of G. K. Chesterton*, 43.

[94] Chesterton, *The Man Who Was Thursday*, 46.

his back until the conclusion.[95] While the others are un-masked, one by one, the only true anarchist is revealed to be Lucian Gregory, a "walking blasphemy," a "blend of the angel and the ape."[96] The story opens and closes in the Eden-like suburb of Saffron Park (a caricature of Frances's Bedford Park), in which "the little gardens were often illuminated, and the big Chinese lanterns glowed in the dwarfish trees like some fierce and monstrous fruit."[97] Its action, however, takes place in cloud-fogged London, much as it had in *The Napoleon of Notting Hill*. The sunset at the opening scene suggests that the world—the garden—is in anarchy. London (likened by Chesterton to Bunyan's Mansoul in the poem that introduces this novel) is a maze of streets under a sky loaded with heavy clouds, which turns the afternoon into "a queer kind of green twilight."[98] The heavens are troubled throughout the book, with darkness falling in midafternoon, and snow swirling on a warm spring day. The elements are out of order. In reference to Satan's glory after his fall, Chesterton described the novel's setting: "Over the whole landscape lay a luminous and unnatural discoloration, as of that disastrous twilight which

---

[95] As Moses was sheltered from the glory of God; Exod. 33:23.

[96] Chesterton, *The Man Who Was Thursday*, 8, 161. This phrase illustrates in fiction the well-publicized views of Chesterton regarding evolution and also serves, on the biblical level, to introduce the character of Satan—who appears in Job 1:6.

[97] Ibid., 8. The lamps as jewelled fruits reminiscent of Aladdin's enchanted tree appear also in "The Flying Stars" and "The Mirror of the Magistrate" in Chesterton, *The Complete Father Brown*, 54-64, 467-82.

[98] Chesterton, *The Man Who Was Thursday*, 67. Chesterton's setting is further reminiscent of Bunyan's "Vanity Fair," of the cities of Dante's journey, and of Shakespeare's *A Midsummer Night's Dream,* which is set in a wood near the city of Athens.

Milton spoke of as shed by the sun in eclipse."[99] But even beneath this dismal sky, hints of light are everywhere. In a picture of God's reflection in nature, puddles in the streets "reflected the flaming lamps irregularly, and by accident, like fragments of some other and fallen world."[100] Nature in its fallenness is reflecting the light of the lamps, which Chesterton here established as a symbol of divinity.

Then Chesterton tied this symbol of light to the tree. In an initial nighttime scene in a park, anarchist Lucian Gregory and poet Gabriel Syme fix the images of lamppost and tree as paradoxical comment on order and anarchy. Striking first one object then the other with his sword, Gregory says,

> "There is your precious order, that lean, iron lamp, ugly and barren; and there is anarchy, rich, living, reproducing itself—there is anarchy, splendid in green and gold.
> "All the same," replied Syme patiently, "just at present you only see the tree by the light of the lamp. I wonder when you would see the lamp by the light of the tree."[101]

Philosophical expression, in other words, is subject to the limitations placed on it by the truth of reality.

---

[99] Ibid., 43; see also Milton *Paradise Lost* 1.591-600.

[100] Chesterton, *The Man Who Was Thursday*, 76. Chesterton's use of the word "accident" might be referring to the medieval philosophy regarding property and substance, which was theologically applied (by Aquinas and others) to the doctrine of the eucharist.

[101] Ibid., 14. The tree/lamppost connection is made also in many later stories; see, e.g., "The Fad of the Fisherman" in *The Man Who Knew Too Much*, in *Collected Works,* vol. 8, 518.

This early passage in the novel deals with the relationship between God and nature (between the light and the tree), Chesterton associating the lamppost with the tree so that later references to one will revive thought of the other. At one point in the story, for example, Syme is captivated by the sight of an almond tree against the skyline: "He had the feeling that if by some miracle he escaped he would be ready to sit for ever before that almond tree, desiring nothing else in the world."[102] Chesterton's understated reference to the almond capitalizes on the strong symbolism of traditional literature. The almond tree is noted throughout mythic and biblical writings as Israel's most sacred tree because of its use as a pattern for the lampstand of the Jewish tabernacle and as a picture of the Christian church.[103] The seven-branched menorah candlestick is the Jewish symbol related to the cosmic tree; according to Zechariah, its flames stand for the "eyes of the Lord, which run to and fro upon the earth."[104] The candelabra, shown to Moses on the mountain, has been regarded as "the inner spiritual form of the cosmos," a picture arising from the platonism of Philo of Alexandria that saw the lampstand's branched arcs as a map of the paths of the planets about the sun.[105] The lamppost and tree of the fictive Saffron Park (that is, the order and chaos of a fallen creation) showcase Chesterton's strongly sacramental and literary view of life.

Syme leaves the streets of London during his adventure of espionage in seeking to curtail the anarchist plot; the testimony of God as light follows him to the location of his planned duel. A forest scene illustrates

---

[102] Chesterton, *The Man Who Was Thursday*, 101-2.

[103] Exod. 25:31-40; Rev. 1:20. The tree/lampstand imagery of the Tabernacle also pictures the Tree of Life in the Garden of Eden, and so is linked to themes of creation.

[104] Zech. 4:10. See also Milton *Paradise Lost* 3.648-51; 12.255-6 for the seven eyes of God.

[105] Cook, *Symbols of the Centre*, 20.

the confusion that results from mixing the darkness of error with the light of truth. The "wood of witchery" into which Syme and his fellows plunge, so full of "shattered sunlight and shaken shadow," is "a chaos of chiaroscuro . . . after the clear daylight outside."[106] The shifting shadows that obscure the others' faces from Syme (so that people are not what they seem to be) is "a perfect symbol for the world in which he had been moving for three days."[107] The scene signifies the confusion of the identities of Syme's fellow "anarchists" who are seeking the elusive President, and it symbolizes Chesterton's search for a concealing-but-revealing God. In this forest, the poor quality of light is equated with wrong-headed belief systems epitomized (in real life) by the school of art against which Chesterton had so violently reacted while at Slade:

> For Gabriel Syme had found in the heart of that sun-splashed wood what many modern painters had found there. He had found what the modern people call Impressionism, which is another name for that final scepticism which can find no floor to the universe.[108]

This is a turning point in the novel, the peak of Syme's confusion between truth and illusion, and is immediately followed by another forest scene in which Syme comes "to an open space of sunlight. . . the final return of his own good senses."[109] He meets "an allegoric figure of labour" in a "heavy French peasant . . . cutting wood

---

[106] Chesterton, *The Man Who Was Thursday*, 112.
[107] Ibid.
[108] Ibid., 113. A humorous scene in *The Flying Inn* pits the meaninglessness of Impressionism against the representation of the cross, seen in the emblem of the wooden sign of the "Old Ship Inn"; Chesterton, *Flying Inn*, 622, 658-9.
[109] Chesterton, *The Man Who Was Thursday*, 114.

with a hatchet," who reminds the reader of an earlier Chestertonian, messianic woodcutter.[110]

Chesterton has equated light with truth, and darkness with confusion or wrong philosophy. He next employed the lamp picture (which is now connected to the tree image in the mind of the reader) as the symbol suggesting the incarnation. Chesterton drew a scene in which a God-figure provides for the fugitives a way of escape out of the dark anarchy of sin surrounding them by placing his own possession (an ecclesiastical lamp, shining the "substance" of light) into the body of a vehicle of escape (a car, providing the "flesh"). Syme and his companions are trying to avert a general uprising of anarchy and must get to the police station before they are caught by their pursuers. They are fleeing under an unexplainable, preternatural darkness (the pessimism of "the earth in anarchy") in a car that has no headlights.[111] One character

> fished up a heavy, old-fashioned, carved iron lantern with a light inside it. It was obviously an antique, and it would seem as if its original use had been in some way semi-religious, for there was a rude moulding of a cross upon one of its sides.[112]

The lighted lamp (symbolizing the traditions of Christianity, or truth, or Christ Himself) comes from the home of the fictional French friend Dr. Renard, a "mild man with monstrous wealth," whose house (symbolizing the church) resembles the Musée de Cluny in Paris—full of religious, medieval art.[113] When the fugitives ask for

---

[110] Ibid.; see also "Apotheosis" in Chesterton, *Collected Works*, vol. 14, 624.

[111] Chesterton, *The Man Who Was Thursday*, 120-33.

[112] Ibid., 122.

[113] Ibid., 121. Chesterton features other religious *objets d'art* in, for example, "The Blue Cross" and "The

help, he "looked up, blinking amiably at the beautiful arched ceiling of his own front hall," representing heaven.[114]

> From this was suspended, by chains of exquisite ironwork, this lantern, one of the hundred treasures of his treasure house. By sheer force he tore the lamp out of his own ceiling, shattering the painted panels, and bringing down two blue vases with his violence.[115]

He hands the iron lamp to one of the passengers of the car (also provided by Renard). Syme finds "a certain allegory of their whole position in the contrast between the modern automobile and its strange, ecclesiastical

---

Insoluble Problem," in Chesterton, *The Complete Father Brown*.

[114] "Ciel" is French for "heaven" and has been argued to relate etymologically to the word "ceiling."

[115] Chesterton, *The Man Who Was Thursday*, 123. The symbolism of the cup is extensive: Chesterton might have been referring to the Grail legends or to the cups of salvation and judgement; see Ps. 116:13, 75:8, Jer. 51:7. Earthen vessels denote God's choice and use of humans to further his glorious purposes and to carry the gospel; see Jer. 18:1-12; 2 Cor. 4:4, 7. Moreover, blue is the heavenly colour worn by the Jewish temple high priest, perhaps further intimating Chesterton's theme of the incarnation. For Paul as a chosen vessel, see Acts 9:15; see further Dante *Hell* 2.28. St. Paul in 2 Tim. 2:20-21 calls Christians to be vessels of honour—of precious metal rather than of earth, significant considering Chesterton's use of the lamp of iron. For a further use of the vessel image by Chesterton, see "The Fool of the Family" in *The Man Who Knew Too Much*, 535-59, in which two classical urns of an ornamental Greek shrine (set in a forest of twinkling trees) symbolize the lost hope of the ageless mythologies.

lamp."[116] What is this allegory? In the council members' search for Sunday, they had received the light that afforded escape from the enemy just as Chesterton, in his search for God, had received the truth through the sacrifice of the cross. That the light can be seen as religious truth becomes more evident as the lamplit car moves through the darkened town, for "the windows in the houses began one by one to be lit up, giving a greater sense of habitation and humanity."[117] In other words, as the gospel shines into the darkness of a sin-filled world, the civilizing effect of Christianity illumines society.

The anarchy mounts until chaos takes over, when Syme cries, "The morning star has fallen!"[118] At this point, the car smashes into a street lamppost, causing the post to be "bent and twisted, like the branch of a broken tree," a type of the crucifixion.[119] Christ's death on the tree (lamppost) broke his body (car)—but in a foreshadowing of the eventual breaking of the power of death itself, the tree in its turn is broken. In this dark time for the fugitives who, like the disciples, have suffered the loss of their Saviour (car), Syme quotes a poem by Pope:

> Nor public flame, nor private, dares to shine;
> Nor human light is left, nor glimpse divine!
> Lo! thy dread Empire, Chaos, is restored;
> Light dies before thine uncreating word;
> Thy hand, great Anarch, lets the curtain fall;

---

[116] Chesterton, *The Man Who Was Thursday*, 123.
[117] Ibid.
[118] Ibid., 128; cf. Isa. 14:12; Rev. 8:10.
[119] Chesterton, *The Man Who Was Thursday*, 128. Note the similarity of story elements to Dante's incarnation scene of the Gryphon in the forest (e.g., Chesterton's automobile paralleling the chariot or triumph-car in *Purgatory* 29.107; this lamppost and Dante's pole/tree in 32.51 representing the cross), detailed in *The Trees of Pride* and "The Garden of Smoke," both below.

And universal darkness buries all.[120]

The lantern is still intact and throwing its light, just as the light of the gospel (protected and preserved by the church) has not been destroyed by Christ's death upon the cross. Syme holds it high before his enemies, crying in a terrible voice,

> Do you see this lantern? . . . Do you see the cross carved on it, and the flame inside? You did not make it. You did not light it. Better men than you, men who could believe and obey, twisted the entrails of iron and preserved the legend of fire. . . . You will destroy mankind; you will destroy the world. . . . Yet this one old Christian lantern you shall not destroy.[121]

Meaning is added to the theme of the tree as light in this novel, The Man Who Was Thursday, when one considers Chesterton's earlier novel, The Napoleon of Notting Hill. There, the light of London's earthbound street lamps is compared with the light of the heavenly stars; the gas lamps are "things quite as eternal as the stars; the two fires were mingled."[122] Chesterton was portraying divinity shining through humanity. In the great Battle of the Lamps, set in the maze of Adam Wayne's streets of Notting Hill (that is, the city of man's soul), the enemies acknowledge that even they are dependent upon the light, for "there is no such thing as night in London. You have only to follow the line of the street lamps."[123] Wayne's forces, retaining sovereignty over the Gas Company, cut all the power to these lamps and blind the enemy forces that, "unacquainted with the

---

[120] Chesterton, The Man Who Was Thursday, 130. Chesterton was quoting Pope's poem, The Dunciad, Bk. 4, lines 651-6; cf. Pope, Works, 189.
[121] Chesterton, The Man Who Was Thursday, 132.
[122] Chesterton, Napoleon of Notting Hill, 53.
[123] Ibid., 85.

road, lost all their bearings in the black world of blindness," in a pre-creation darkness.[124] The battle is won
by Adam Wayne, and peace ensues for a period. Every
"sacred lamp-post that saved Notting Hill"—by its
judgement, its withdrawal of light, from the unrepent-
ant—is later decorated in tribute to the victory, that "no
child in Notting Hill could play about the streets without
the very lamp-posts reminding him of the salvation of
his country in the dreadful year."[125] The coupling of the
images of the lamppost and tree pictures the light of
God administered through the flesh of humanity. Thus
the tree, by way of the lamp symbolism in both *The Napoleon of Notting Hill* and *The Man Who Was Thursday*,
suggests Christ's incarnation. The tree-as-light scheme
underscores Christian ritual, which is founded in Old
Testament creation and tabernacle imagery, and is reiterated in John's gospel with its theme of Christ as the
light of the world.[126]

To return again to *The Man Who Was Thursday*,
the main mystery of the plot is the identity of Sunday,
even after he has turned to face his committee near the
end of the novel. The unmasked anarchists are con-
sumed with the necessity to understand Sunday. Syme
asks, "What are you?"

> "I? What am I?" roared the Presi-
> dent. . . . "Grub in the roots of those trees
> and find out the truth about them. Stare

---

[124] Ibid., 88.

[125] Ibid., 94, 112. Chesterton's theme of salvation is strengthened by his description of the gaslights
as "an orchard of fiery trees, the beginnings of the
woods of elf-land" (that is, mystical belief), followed by
his use of these same lamps as the means of victory in
the Battle of the Lamps; Chesterton, *Napoleon of Notting Hill*, 54, 79-88.

[126] For the tree as Edenic imagery, see 1 Kings
6:34-36, Exod. 25:32-34; see also Milton *Paradise Lost*
12.474 and John 1:4-5 for light shining out of the darkness.

at those morning clouds. But I tell you
this, that you will have found out the truth
of the last tree and the topmost cloud before the truth about me. You will understand the sea, and I shall still be a riddle;
you shall know what the stars are, and
not know what I am. Since the beginning
of the world all men have been hunting
me like a wolf."[127]

Some have argued that Sunday represents God Himself.
Chesterton, however, wrote that one "can take Sunday
to stand for Nature. . . . Tear off the mask of Nature and
you find God."[128] Sacramentalism is his way of seeing
God "from behind" and experiencing Him through creation. The trees are representative of nature and become
a part of nature's mask.

"Listen to me," cried Syme, with
extraordinary emphasis. "Shall I tell you
the secret of the whole world? We see
everything from behind, and it looks bru-
tal. That is not a tree, but the back of a
tree. That is not a cloud, but the back of a
cloud. Cannot you see that everything is
stooping and hiding a face? If we could
only get round in front."[129]

The Man Who Was Thursday illustrates the major
themes of chaos/order and pessimism/optimism through
the picture of the tree, with the fallen creation retaining
vestiges of the Creator. The tree intimates spiritual light
and the incarnation through its implications with the
lamp of the tabernacle, which in turn recalls the creation

---

[127] Chesterton, *The Man Who Was Thursday*, 137.
For Dante's wolf, see *Hell* 1.49-60.
[128] From an interview, noted by Stephen Medcalf
in Chesterton, *The Man Who Was Thursday*, xxvi; see
also Ward, *Gilbert Keith Chesterton*, 168-9.
[129] Chesterton, *The Man Who Was Thursday*, 150.

of the world. Chesterton's reading of Genesis is evident; he was, according to Wills, "drawn back, constantly, to the Book of Genesis because of its beginnings in chaos."[130] This biblical understanding of personal chaos in himself and the world surrounding him led Chesterton to consider each human life "a re-enactment, day by day, of the first verses of Genesis."[131] That is, the creation is constantly being re-created—the person is renewed over and again.

Chesterton's association of the tree with light imagery (experienced in his childhood "fairy lamps" and expressed in his adolescent "Queen of the Evening Star") was founded in his reading of Scripture, and is substantiated by other literary sources. Jewish Scripture and legend echo the Ancient Near Eastern image of the Tree of Life as a cosmological tree, which had its roots in the underworld and its branches "reaching to the heavens and supporting the constellations."[132] This imagery was readily identified by early Christians with the cross, Christ, and the eucharist—and also with the figure of the lamp, which shows up, for example, in a sixth-century San Clemente mosaic (based on an early Christian assimilation of the image of the Tree of Life) in which two liturgical lamps flank a cosmological tree.[133] The theme of light in the trees appears again in Dante's wood, where that writer described the "thick and leafy tent" to have "tempered the new sun's rays."[134] Blake, also, combined the images of the light of the stars with the trees of Eden.[135] Chesterton reapplied this old illustration of the tree as light throughout the duration of his "sapling" literature.

---

[130] Garry Wills, "The Man Who Was Thursday," in *G. K. Chesterton: A Half Century of Views*, ed. Denis J. Conlon (Oxford: Oxford University Press, 1987), 341.

[131] Ibid., 340.

[132] O'Reilly, "Trees of Eden," 170.

[133] Ibid., 171.

[134] Dante *Purgatory* 28.1-3.

[135] See, e.g., Blake, "Introduction" from *Songs of Experience*, in Allison and others, *Norton*, 503.

Tremendous Trifles (1909)

By the end of the first decade of the new century, as Chesterton and Frances prepared to move from London to their country home in Beaconsfield, his fictional tree was deeply imbued with recurrent metaphysical and literary themes. His eclectic applications of the motif were beginning to cluster under fewer, more specific functions, portraying particular meanings relating to humankind in relationship with the creation and the Creator. For example, two articles written around this time and collected with other *Daily News* essays into a volume entitled *Tremendous Trifles* made use of the tree to explain Chesterton's philosophy regarding humanity. Although an exposition of essays might seem out of place in a book regarding fiction, Chesterton himself freely used the fictional tool of analogy regardless of his genre. As Boyd noted, "His novels are full of propaganda, and his journalism is full of story."[136] A glance at the analogy in his essays is warranted.

The descriptive language in "The Wind and the Trees" portrays Chesterton's surroundings during the writing and clarifies his meaning of the tree picture. He was "sitting under tall trees, with a great wind boiling like surf about the tops of them" so that he felt as though he were at the bottom of the sea "among mere anchors and ropes," while overhead "the green twilight of water" crashed in rushing waves. [137] "The wind [tugged] at the trees as if it might pluck them root and all out of the earth like tufts of grass."[138] While watching

---

[136] Boyd, "Philosophy in Fiction," 44.

[137] G. K. Chesterton, "The Wind and the Trees," in *Tremendous Trifles* (London: Methuen, 1909), 69. For another underwater forest, see the 1925 story "The Paradise of Human Fishes," below.

[138] Chesterton, "The Wind and the Trees," 69. Note the tugging/uprooting theme as in "The Honest Quack" and *Napoleon of Notting Hill,* above—suggesting the presence of an external authority or judge; cf. Ezek. 17:24.

the colossal display of energy between the wind and the trees, he recalled the comment of a little boy walking beneath such a violently tossed grove in Battersea Park: "Why don't you take away the trees, and then it wouldn't wind."[139] Chesterton found the naive comment very natural, typical of the confused way in which people often view reality. He wrote, "Any one looking for the first time at the trees might fancy that they were indeed vast and titanic fans, which by their mere waving agitated the air around them for miles."[140] Chesterton identified the meaning of the parable for us:

> The trees stand for all visible things and the wind for the invisible. The wind is the spirit which bloweth where it listeth; the trees are the material things of the world which are blown where the spirit lists. The wind is philosophy, religion, revolution; the trees are cities and civilizations.[141]

Chesterton's point was that the wind or belief systems of the human race activate the physical effects of the world; moral circumstances determine material circumstances and not the other way around. "Mind precedes matter," as he said elsewhere. [142] "The great human dogma, then, is that the wind moves the trees. The great human heresy is that the trees move the wind."[143]

This heresy, that the visible (flesh) has power over the invisible (soul), is further exposed in a subsequent essay entitled "In Topsy-Turvy Land," in which Chesterton more clearly applied the illustration of the tree to humanity. Now home from his outing in the woods and back on Fleet Street, Chesterton recalled the setting of the former essay and was strangely haunted

---

[139] Chesterton, "The Wind and the Trees," 70.
[140] Ibid.
[141] Ibid., 70-71. For the wind of the Spirit blowing "where it listeth," see John 3:8.
[142] Chesterton, *Orthodoxy*, 346.
[143] Chesterton, "The Wind and the Trees," 72.

by this accidental comparison. The people's figures seem a forest and their soul a wind. All the human personalities which speak or signal to me seem to have this fantastic character of the fringe of the forest against the sky. That man that talks to me, what is he but an articulate tree?[144]

The question echoes words by Blaise Pascal:

> Man's greatness lies in his capacity to recognize his wretchedness. A tree does not recognize its wretchedness. So it is wretched to know one is wretched, but there is greatness in the knowledge of one's wretchedness.[145]

Chesterton, too, highlighted the tree to say something about humanity: the physical body, like an insensate tree, is activated by the Spirit of God. He wrote elsewhere,

> Man is not a balloon going up into the sky, nor a mole burrowing merely in the earth; but rather a thing like a tree, whose roots are fed from the earth, while its highest branches seem to rise almost to the stars.[146]

Chesterton's comparison of the human to a tree is consistent with the seventeenth-century poetry of George Herbert. Consider, for example, Herbert's simile of "a

---

[144] G. K. Chesterton, "In Topsy-Turvy Land," in *Tremendous Trifles* (London: Methuen, 1909), 81. Chesterton's comparison brings to mind the biblical description of the person as "a tree planted by the rivers of water" (Ps. 1:3) that "spreadeth out her roots" (Jer. 17:8).

[145] Blaise Pascal, *Pensées and Other Writings*, trans. Honor Levi, The World's Classics (Oxford: Oxford University Press, 1995), 36-37.

[146] Chesterton, *Saint Thomas Aquinas*, 164.

sweet and vertuous soul, like season'd timber" or of himself as growing among the trees of Paradise. [147] Again, he wrote, "For Man is ev'rything, / And more: he is a tree, yet bears more fruit."[148]

The tree, one sees, has taken on the identity of the nation and of the individual. These essays showing humankind as a forest, or the person as a tree, indicate Chesterton's developing and narrowing of one of the several tree themes that find further stability in the last period of his fiction. His stories continue to reflect the importance he placed in his personal life on social and political issues, spiritual expressions of joy and wonder in creation, and the love of adventure as well as of home. His ethics and politics, focusing on the rights of the individual (seen, for example, in *The Napoleon of Notting Hill*), are linked to nationalism and patriotism. Religiously, he struggled through the early pantheism into a surer orthodoxy (seen in *The Man Who Was Thursday*), and he pit good against evil in his story as he had in his life (as in *The Ball and the Cross*). The tree illustrates Chesterton's life history and the literature he read, and bears meanings related to the lamp, the ladder, the person, and the cross. The fiction of his maturity continues these trends.

---

[147] George Herbert, "Vertue," lines 13-14; "Paradise" in *The Temple*, in George Herbert, *The Works of George Herbert* (Hertfordshire, U.K.: Wordsworth Editions, 1994), 78, 122. All subsequent references regarding Herbert's work are to this edition.
[148] George Herbert, "Man," lines 7-8 in *The Temple*, in *Works*, 81.

FIVE

SPREADING TREE: FICTION OF MATURITY (1911-1935)

Manalive (1912)

Within a few years of his 1909 "return to the real England," as Chesterton said of his move out of London, he wrote a novel that parades his love of home and country. His own "lost wandering" of youth and early marriage, and Frances's gentle shepherding of his sense of adventure, bizarre behaviour, and appearance can be seen in *Manalive* (1912), in which the tree motif plays a significant part. The novel's journey theme of the global wanderer, now stretching beyond the limits of a city's streets, coincides with Chesterton's attention on the pastoral and his increase in foreign travel, and speaks of his own homecomings—physical and spiritual.[1]

One day, as Chesterton was packing for an out-of-town trip, a friend visited his flat in Battersea and asked where he was going. "I am going to Battersea," answered Chesterton in a riddle.[2] He meant that the

---

[1] The journeys of great literature have been metaphysical exposition. In distinguishing between the literary themes of the "empire" and the "city," Dorothy L. Sayers explained that Dante's whole allegory might be interpreted "as representing the way of salvation, not only for the individual man, but for Man-in-community"; see her commentary in Dante, *Hell*, page 69. Chesterton himself explicitly described the *via crucis* (way of the cross) as a journey through "a woodland," "a wild thicket," and "a wild garden" of trees; "The Tower of Treason" in *Collected Works*, vol. 8, 713-4.

[2] G. K. Chesterton, *The Riddle of the Ivy* (London: Methuen, 1909), 203.

purpose of a vacation is to see one's own home in a new light and to appreciate the ordinary things of life.

> The only way to get back to them is to go somewhere else; and that is the real object of travel and the real pleasure of holidays. Do you suppose I go to France in order to see France? . . . I am seeking Battersea. . . [and] the only way to go to England is to go away from it.[3]

Perhaps this anecdote was the inspiration behind *Manalive*, in which the image of the tree (and its related lamppost and wooden garden rake) helps to illustrate the ideas of journey, re-creation, and the home.[4] It opens with a standard Chestertonian "weather report":

> A wind sprang up in the west, like a wave of unreasonable happiness, and tore eastward across England, trailing with it the frosty scent of forests and the cold intoxication of the sea. In a million holes and corners it refreshed a man like a flagon and astonished him like a blow. . . . There was in it something more inspired and authoritative even than the old wind of the proverb; for this was the good wind that blows nobody harm.[5]

---

[3] Ibid., 204.

[4] Although this novel was begun fifteen years before its publication, it did not appear until three years after the Chestertons moved from Battersea to the country town of Beaconsfield, a noteworthy point considering the name of the boarding house in note below. Rolland Hein, "G. K. Chesterton: Myth, Paradox, and the Commonplace," *Seven* 13 (1996): 15.

[5] Chesterton, *Manalive*, 9-10. Perhaps Chesterton had in the mind the "harmful" east wind of God's judgement found, for example, in Ezek. 17: 10 or Isa.

This "oddly romantic" wind blows only good fortune into the lives of the listless boarders in Beacon House, London.[6] Over the garden wall, in search of his windblown Panama hat, tumbles Innocent Smith, a globetrotter on a journey around the world, whose zestful creativity stimulates the pessimists peopling the story.[7] A tree, which "swung and swept and thrashed to and fro in the thundering wind like a thistle, and flamed in the full sunshine like a bonfire," snags the hat.[8] Innocent springs up into its branches, muttering a string of odd, disjointed phrases: "Tree of Life . . . Ygdrasil [sic] . . . climb for centuries perhaps . . . gone to heaven. . . ."[9] Chesterton's understated reference behind Innocent's words (ignored by the three onlookers in the Beacon House garden) was to the cosmological tree of a primitive Scandinavian legend. This tree is said to stand at the centre of the universe with its roots descending to the underworld, its trunk rising upwards through the plane

---

27: 8. At any rate, Chesterton's wind speaks of change and of the will of God.

[6] Chesterton, *Manalive*, 10-11. "Beacon House" sounds like Beaconsfield, which was named after the beech forest that surrounded it, as has been noted in the biography, above. This connection is not frivolous, for later in this novel a character claims that names should match the named, "that people named after colours should always dress in those colours, and that people named after trees or plants (such as Beech or Rose) ought to surround and decorate themselves with these vegetables"; Chesterton, *Manalive*, 175.

[7] Hunter described Innocent Smith as "the fusion of religion, morality and expression"; Hunter, *Explorations in Allegory*, 101.

[8] Chesterton, *Manalive*, 19. Chesterton made several such gentle allusions to Moses' burning bush of Exod. 3; note also the tree-as-fire theme in *The Ball and the Cross*.

[9] Chesterton, *Manalive*, 19.

of mortals, and its branches ascending to the heavens.[10] In the legend, the destruction of the world is achieved through the shaking of the tree, but concealed within its trunk are the seeds of a new race in the shape of a man and woman who repopulate the earth.[11] The theme of the legend becomes one of the themes of *Manalive*: damaged creation is re-created through the homely union of husband and wife.

Innocent (who is unable to remember whether his is "a formal Christian name or a moral description") joins the boarders, and his apparently insane games and practical jokes breathe new life into the Beacon House relationships.[12] One of these is his own whirlwind courtship of Mary, a quiet woman who wears "a small silver cross" and who agrees immediately to Innocent's proposal of marriage, despite the horror of her friends who label him a seducer.[13] But Innocent's mind is on the home, and when one tenant criticizes the fairytale quality of happiness in *The Swiss Family Robinson*, Innocent champions the tree-dwellers' "dead accurate philosophy."[14] This is consistent with one of Chesterton's favourite beliefs, that the family is "the most important

---

[10] Cook, *Symbols of the Centre*, 11-12. Cook identified the Yggdrasil tree as in the Scandinavian Eddas (prose and poetry).

[11] The shaking of the tree is a motif in Chesterton's fiction. A later example in this story has the gale shaking "every shrub in the garden," with "the moving limbs of the fugitive [melting in] the multitudinous moving limbs of the tree." Chesterton, *Manalive*, 84.

[12] Ibid., 28.

[13] Ibid., 24. Mary sounds like his own Frances, who "brought the cross" to him. There was never a hint in Chesterton's life of any philandering, of course.

[14] Ibid., 40. *The Swiss Family Robinson* was written by the Wyss family in Switzerland in the mid-eighteenth century, in imitation of Defoe's *Robinson Crusoe*.

unit to the health of society."[15] Innocent makes a playful announcement to his fellow boarders:

> Let's issue a Declaration of Independence from Beacon House. . . . Let us begin the League of the Free Families! Away with Local Government! A fig for Local Patriotism! Let every house be a sovereign state as this is, and judge its own children by its own law.[16]

However, the seeming irrationality of Innocent's actions brings accusations against his sanity and ultimately leads him to criminal trial, charged with attempted murder, burglary, and polygamy.[17] In truth, he is guilty only of threatening to murder pessimists (which awakens each to the joy of life), of breaking and entering his own house (to become more appreciative of his possessions), and of repeatedly wooing and "remarrying" the same woman (to keep their love fresh and alive). His guilt is only that he "distinguished between custom and creed."[18] For Mary is indeed already Innocent's wife and the mother of their two children, all of whom he "deserted" to go "plodding around the whole planet [in order] to get back to his own home."[19] At intervals along his

---

[15] Hein, "Myth, Paradox, and the Commonplace," 16. See also Clipper, *G. K. Chesterton*, 72; Boyd, *Novels of G. K. Chesterton*, 64. Chesterton fully developed his view of the family in G. K. Chesterton, *What's Wrong with the World* (London: Cassell and Company, 1912).

[16] Chesterton, *Manalive*, 40. Chesterton's strong patriotism of *Napoleon of Notting Hill* is in this story tempered, subjugated to the primacy of the family. See also a collection of his sociological essays, Chesterton, *What's Wrong with the World*.

[17] The greater part of the novel is devoted to a trial of the innocent person, who sounds like Job before his "friends."

[18] Chesterton, *Manalive*, 183.

[19] Ibid., 181.

journey, Innocent reunites with an incognito Mary to re-play their courtship and "repeated and irregular nup-tials" in order to "recover her again and again with a raid and a romantic elopement . . . a perpetual recap-ture of his bride to keep alive the sense of her perpetual value, and the perils that should be run for her sake."[20]

At the novel's close, and like the "Adam and Eve" within the mythic tree Yggdrasil, Innocent and Mary rec-reate their home once again. [21] Chesterton modelled marriage as an allegory of the spiritual journey and the home as a re-creation of Eden for, as Innocent says to a revolutionary Russian at one stop along his route:

> This round road I am treading is an un-trodden path. I do believe in breaking out; I am a revolutionist. But don't you see that all these real leaps and destructions and escapes are only attempts to get back to Eden—to something we have had, to something we have at least heard of? Don't you see one only breaks the fence or shoots the moon in order to get home?[22]

The garden tree, tied now to the cosmological tree of myth, has come to symbolize the story of marriage and of the greater journey suggestive of Everyman's soul.[23]

---

[20] Ibid., 171, 182. For biblical bride/church im-agery, see Isa. 62:5; Rev. 19:7. See also the nuptial bower in Milton's garden of marriage, Milton *Paradise Lost* 4.690-775.

[21] As the home is reinstated in Job 42:10-12; cf. Gen. 3:23 and Rev. 21:1-4 for the re-creation of home seen in Eden and the New Jerusalem.

[22] Chesterton, *Manalive*, 155-6.

[23] A later story continues the romantic love/spiritual journey/incarnation connection; in "The End of Wisdom" (1931), a hard-nosed American busi-nessman is reformed by the love of his wife, learning that "it is he who has really gone round the whole world

111

Before the novel's happy conclusion, episodes of Innocent's travels are replayed in the courtroom through testimonial letters, which show that the picture of the tree is not limited to the allusion earlier in the tale. Besides the hat-grabbing tree in the garden of Beacon House, the image plays a repetitive role in Innocent Smith's journey, begun in his own garden, which

> hung very high above the lane, and its end was steep and sharp, like a fortress. Beyond was a roll of real country, with a white path sprawling across it, and the roots, boles, and branches of great grey trees writhing and twisting against the sky. But as if to assert that the lane itself was suburban, . . . sharply relieved against that grey and tossing upland [was] a lamp-post painted a peculiar yellow-green . . . [standing] exactly at the corner.[24]

---

who is anxious to come home; and that the end of wisdom is the beginning of life; and that God Himself bowed down to enter a narrow door, in the hour when the Word was made flesh." Chesterton, *Collected Works*, vol. 14, 385. See also "The Insoluble Problem," below.

[24] Chesterton, *Manalive*, 146. Often in Chesterton's fiction tree branches appear in silhouette as the gnarled, snaking characters of some mysterious alphabet, intimating a secret message that can be read upon the tablet of nature, if one knows the code. For example, earlier in this novel the shadows of garden tree branches are "arabesque written in ink on some page"; Chesterton, *Manalive*, 42. Gerhart Ladner noted that Renaissance arabesques, usually enjoyed as purely ornamental architectural designs, do sometimes carry spiritual meanings, in Gerhart B. Ladner, "Vegetation Symbolism and the Concept of Renaissance," in *De Artibus Opuscula XL: Essays in Honor of Erwin Panofsky*, ed. Millard Meiss (New York: New York University Press,

The garden of home is defined against the background of the wild natural woods of England and identified with the tree-inspired lamppost that becomes the signature of home throughout the plot.[25] Late in his journey, for example, Innocent hints at the depths of spiritual reality behind the physical symbols when he says that

> if there be a house for me in heaven it will either have a green lamp-post and a hedge, or something quite as positive and personal as a green lamp-post and a hedge. . . . God bade me love one spot and serve it . . . [for] Paradise is some-where and not anywhere, is something and not anything. And I would not be so very much surprised if the house in heav-en had a real green lamp-post after all.[26]

1961), 321. *Manalive* continues Chesterton's subtle theme of the sacramental nature of the creation.

[25] See, e.g., Chesterton, *Manalive*, 150. See tree/lamppost connection in *The Man Who Was Thursday*, above.

[26] Chesterton, *Manalive*, 163. The Tree of Life in the midst of the Garden of Eden reappears in Paradise; see Gen. 2:9; Rev. 2:7; Rev. 22:2. The hedge around his home, which Innocent clears at a leap in crossing the border at the beginning of his spiritual journey, is mean-ingful in other Chesterton stories. For example, trees and bushes act as the border between good and evil, hiding bandits from discovery in "The Paradise of Thieves" in Chesterton, *The Complete Father Brown*, 182-96. The biblical theme of the hedge of protection against turmoil has its source in the book of Job, as not-ed in *The Ball and the Cross*, above. In *Orthodoxy*, Chesterton spoke of his taking notice of the natural world (after his childhood immersion in the land of fair-ytales) as putting his "head over the hedge of the elves"; Chesterton, *Orthodoxy*, 254.

The tree symbolism extends not only to the lamppost but also to the emblem of the ordinary garden rake, which accompanies Innocent on his trip around the world. The wooden rake is repeatedly described as a pole, which is another title commonly used for the cross of Christ.[27] One October morning, in his garden with his children, "Innocent began to play around with his rake, as he often did," his gardener testifies. But this particular morning, he strikes out from home, for home, heading east and carrying his rake along. In France, he is seen leaning like a mythic god "on a long rake or forked pole, which looked like a trident, and made him look like a Triton."[28] In Russia, his hand rests "on a huge pole such as peasants rake in weeds with to burn them."[29] On his next stop, carrying his "pole with a row of teeth on it like the teeth of a dragon," he rejects the Eastern religion by saying to the Asian mystic, "This is only a temple; I am trying to find a house."[30] Innocent has come to resemble a divine being—a fisher-god or a heavenly harvester grasping his tree of deliverance and desiring not the empty customs of a religion but the creeds of a Christian faith.

Innocent reaches the Sierras of California, where an isolated hermit describes his mountains as the foundations of the world using the biblical imagery of Judaism and Christianity, reviving Chesterton's allusion to the tree/lamp as a source of light: "We could almost fancy the mountain branching out above us like a tree of

---

[27] The Greek word for the "tree" of Christ's suffering in Acts 5:30 and 1 Pet. 2:24 carries the meaning of pole, wooden beam, club, stick, timber, and so on; the Hebrew "tree" of Deut. 21:22-23 implies gallows or wooden handle. See pole imagery with its link to the Christological figure in "The Garden of Smoke," below. The cross symbolism of the wooden sign used in *The Flying Inn* has been noted above.

[28] Chesterton, *Manalive*, 149.

[29] Ibid., 152. For the parable of the burning of weeds, see Matt. 13:24-30.

[30] Chesterton, *Manalive*, 157.

stone, and carrying all those cosmic lights like a cande-labrum."[31] The Californian, who almost worships nature, describes meeting Innocent Smith struggling up the path:

> He carried . . . a long, dilapidated garden rake, all bearded and bedraggled with grasses, so that it looked like the ensign of some barbarian tribe. . . . The rake or pitchfork, or whatever it was, he used sometimes as an alpenstock, sometimes . . . as a weapon.[32]

Leaning on his "grassy pole," Innocent explains himself to the mountain dweller: "I have become a pilgrim to cure myself of being an exile."[33] As Rolland Hein wrote, Chesterton assumed Bunyan's vision of "the commonplace and everyday life of ordinary people who confess they are pilgrims and strangers in this world" and who are struggling upon the narrow path leading to "that better country whose builder and maker is God."[34] Chesterton himself stated, "Man has always lost his way. He has been a tramp ever since Eden."[35] In *Manalive*, the tree (and its related lamppost and wooden garden rake) again illustrates these ideas of journey, re-creation, and the home, involving the human who looks like God.

---

[31] Ibid., 160. Again, the tree is likened to the menorah, as discussed above.

[32] Ibid., 160-1. Note Chesterton's own pilgrim's staff in the biography, and his use of a wooden pole as a weapon in his early story "The Human Club," above. Note the use of the pitchfork as a crucifixion-related weapon in "The Crime of Gabriel Gale," below.

[33] Chesterton, *Manalive*, 162. One is reminded also of the exile and journey theme in Exodus.

[34] Hein, "Myth, Paradox, and the Commonplace," 15.

[35] Chesterton, *What's Wrong with the World*, 65.

Father Brown Stories (1910-1935)

By 1910, when the first of the Father Brown detective stories began appearing in the magazines of England, Chesterton had fully converted to Christianity. Ronald Knox called the Father Brown tales "mystery stories with a difference," for, "as usual, the box has been so tightly packed that the clasps will not fasten; there is too much meat in the sandwich."[36] The five collections are worthy of an in-depth analysis (much beyond the scope of this paper); the more than four-dozen stories trace a fictional timeline of Chesterton's own spiritual progression.[37] A brief introduction now to one mystery written at the beginning of his period of maturity infers the "complete created order" he proposed through Father Brown—a substitute for the partial philosophies he rejected.[38]

"The Secret Garden" (1911) chronicles the murder of an American philanthropist intent on pouring his money into the church in France. Suspicion is fixed upon the Chief of Paris Police: Valentin is an atheist who "would do anything, *anything,* to break what he called the superstition of the Cross."[39] The act of bloodshed is a beheading of an American who looks "Mephistophelean," and the clever replacement by the policeman of a

---

[36] Ronald Knox, "Chesterton's Father Brown," in *G. K. Chesterton: A Half Century of Views*, ed. Denis J. Conlon (Oxford: Oxford University Press, 1987), 133.

[37] According to Hollis, *The Mind of Chesterton*, 180; see further Gertrude M. White, "Mirror and Microcosm: Chesterton's Father Brown Stories," *Chesterton Review* 10, no. 2 (1984): 183-97.

[38] Gushurst-Moore, "Reality, Illusion and Art," Several additional Father Brown stories are mentioned throughout this book; see especially "Final Stories," below.

[39] In *The Innocence of Father Brown,* Chesterton, *The Complete Father Brown*, 38. On page 924, Valentin is described as "one of the great French freethinkers," referring probably to Descartes, whose philosophy Chesterton criticized elsewhere.

guillotined criminal's head confuses the corpse's identi-ty.[40] The crime is set in Valentin's own garden, which has no doors to the street, with access to be gained only through the villain's house. One physical clue to the cul-prit's identity is the presence of many chopped up tree twigs lying on the lawn far from the tree; Valentin has accomplished the murder by occupying his victim with sabre tricks before striking. The allegory sees Valentin's garden crime scene as an Eden in which the tree be-comes a means of deadly distraction. One Irish charac-ter feels the mythic quality of the crime:

> A voice older than his first fathers seemed to be saying in his ear: "Keep out of the monstrous garden where grows the tree with double fruit. Avoid the evil garden where died the man with two heads."[41]

The implication is that the godless Valentin is like the tempter, Satan, with the treed garden standing for his domain of activity. The fallen Garden of Eden, with its tree of choice for good or evil, is left to humanity's dual nature.

Chesterton's reference to one tree having double fruit appears contrary to the biblical depiction of the two trees in the Garden of Eden and is somewhat at odds with his own declaration that the cross is the Tree of Life.[42] However, the image of a single tree bearing the fruit of eternal life as well as of death through knowledge of good and evil has precedent in traditional Christian literature; Chesterton's staging of a beheading beneath this double-fruited tree stirs up primordial pic-tures. A legend dating from the time of Julius Africanus holds that Adam's skull lies buried at Golgotha; this re-sulted in many paintings of the Byzantine era depicting a

---

[40] Ibid., 25. Again we see Chesterton's referral to Marlowe's or Goethe's character, Faust.

[41] Ibid., 37.

[42] Gen. 2:9, 17; 3:22-23; Chesterton, *Saint Thomas Aquinas*, 114.

skull at the foot of the Tree of Life/cross of Christ.[43] A later, fifteenth-century painting by Berthold Furtmeyer shows a single tree of both life and knowledge, upon which hangs both a crucifix and a skull and from which Mary administers life to the church and Eve administers death to the faithless.[44] The medieval, two-fold tree is unlike Milton's two separate trees in *Paradise Lost* (one delivering life and the other death) but might be the source of Chesterton's story idea.[45] The highly ambiguous symbolism of the fruit borne of the Tree of Knowledge and the Tree of Life has produced too vast a literature regarding the fall to be dealt with at this time, but in light of Chesterton's focus on the doctrine, his use of one tree with two fruits is noteworthy. It brings to mind the line of George Herbert's poem, "The Sacrifice," in which Christ says of the results of the fall, "Man stole the fruit, but I must climbe the tree."[46]

The Trees of Pride (pre-1919)

The influence of Chesterton's encyclopedic reading is especially obvious in his novella, *The Trees of Pride*,

---

[43] O'Reilly, "Trees of Eden," 180.

[44] See reproduction of Furtmeyer's 1481 "Tree of Death and Life" in Cook, *Symbols of the Centre*, plate 44.

[45] Milton *Paradise Lost* 4.218-23. Cf. Lord Byron *Manfred* 1.1.12, which declares the "fatal truth": the Tree of Knowledge is not the Tree of Life.

[46] George Herbert, "The Sacrifice," line 202 in *The Temple* in *Works*, 26. This, in its turn, sounds like the poem of the Holy Rood (dating back to eighth-century Britain), in which the tree of the Saviour tells its story of being cut down in the grove, set on a hill, and embraced by the hero—God Almighty—in crucifixion. See further "Tree of Knowledge" in Jeffrey, *Dictionary of Biblical Tradition*, 781-3.

written before 1919.[47] Wills noted Chesterton's attraction to "myth, biblical grandeur and prophecy, moral parable and allegory."[48] That attraction might be nowhere as noticeable as in this story, which examines the identity of a particular tree, tying it through literary themes to both humanity and deity. The tree, in this incarnational parable, becomes both mortal and god.

The plot of *The Trees of Pride* deals with original sin and the fall. According to Clipper, Chesterton understood the original sin to be pride, especially the "pride of reason, the failure of man to recognize his limits" that are to be defined "by dogma and the authority of the Church."[49] This sin of idolizing reason is the motivation behind an aristocratic ploy by characters in *The Trees of Pride* to disarm the power of local peasant folklore in order to promote "the cause of progress and common sense, and the killing of such silly superstitions everywhere."[50] Chesterton again positioned reason and science against religious belief in a tale set on the wooded estate of Squire Vane, tenants are the commoners of

---

[47] Chesterton, *The Trees of Pride* in *Collected Works*, vol. 8. Published in 1922, this story, along with three others, appeared as an appendix to the unrelated collection, *The Man Who Knew Too Much*. In assembling his short story collections, Chesterton usually built around a central character, moral, or theme that he illustrated with six or eight discreet stories (previously published individually), with the first and last tales often forming a framework; see Barr's introduction to *Collected Works*, vol. 8, 20-21. For example, each story in *The Paradoxes of Mr. Pond* begins with a casual remark that seems silly or contradictory—until the characters have played out the action; G. K. Chesterton, *The Paradoxes of Mr. Pond* (New York: Dover Publications, 1990). *The Trees of Pride* and "The Garden of Smoke" are two exceptions to his habit.

[48] Wills, *Chesterton: Man and Mask*, 73.

[49] Clipper, *G. K. Chesterton*, 86.

[50] Chesterton, *Manalive*, 635.

Cornwall.[51] The main story, replete as usual with death and intrigue, frames a shorter tale that echoes the lesson that pride, unrestrained by both reason and respect for external authority, always leads to the fall into sin. This shorter story-within-a-story takes the form of an ancient legend explaining the presence of three massive, foreign trees on the squire's estate, blamed by Vane's fearful tenants for the mysterious illnesses and disappearances of some villagers.

> Out of the middle of [the] low and more or less level wood rose three separate stems that shot up and soared into the sky like a lighthouse out of the waves or a church spire out of the village roofs. They formed a clump of three columns close together, which might well be the mere bifurcation, or rather trifurcation, of one tree, the lower part being lost or sunken in the wood around.[52]

Chesterton drew immediate attention to the triune presentation of the trees and only later revealed the mystery that they "branched from one great root, like a candelabrum."[53] He heightened the sense of mythic enigma by describing the weird, blue-green colour of its leaves straining high above the forest like "the scales of some three-headed dragon towering over a herd of huddled and fleeing cattle."[54]

---

[51] Some of the Arthurian legends are connected to this southwest corner of England; Chesterton set the story's mood right away by mentioning the Cornish traditions, "as old as Merlin." Ibid., 580.

[52] Ibid., 582. For a description of the proud nation of Assyria, like a towering cedar shooting up in the garden of God and the envy of all the trees of Eden, whose "heart is lifted up in his height," see Ezek. 31.

[53] Chesterton, *Collected Works*, vol. 8, 607.

[54] Chesterton, *Manalive*, 582. Job 20:6 pictures the pride of the wicked as mounting to the heavens and

The legend has it that, long ago, a pirate boat home from Barbary floated to the Cornish shore with the foreign trees as freight and dead sailors as crew. Death has ever since attended the trees—those "towers of pestilence."[55] They had come from an enchanted forest inhabited by a hermit saint who loved trees "like companions" and whose desire effected their animation.[56] The trees, the "mildest and most blameless of creatures," were "loosened from time to time to walk like other

---

touching the clouds. See also Isa. 27:1 for a marine symbol of the enemies of God in the crooked serpent and dragon, Leviathan. The mythic dragon is tucked into many of Chesterton's tales, symbolizing Satan in Eden and recalling the apocalyptic dragon of Rev. 12; e.g., the "evolution" of the serpent into a dragon pictured in the "Half-Hours in Hades" sketch. Note also the murder in the garden of the Green Dragon Inn, in "The Insoluble Problem," below. Again, tree roots are "limbs of a dragon lifting itself from sleep"; Chesterton, *The Flying Inn*, 431. Elsewhere Chesterton described "straggling roots of pine like the tails of dying dragons"; Chesterton, "The Five of Swords" in *Collected Works,* vol. 8, 672. Cf. Edmund Spenser *The Faerie Queene* 1.11.46, in which the Tree of Life grows where the evil dragon dies; Edmund Spenser, *The Works of Edmund Spenser* (Hertfordshire, U.K.: Wordsworth Editions, 1995). (All subsequent references are to this edition.) See also Dante *Purgatory* 32.131; see further Milton *Paradise Lost* 4.3-5. Two of Chesterton's famous drinking songs feature the dragon as the enemy of England: the first is of the valiant dragon-slayer, St. George, and the second ("The Song of the Oak" previously mentioned, reproduced below) portrays the dragon as a symbol of the creeping syncretism of Lord Ivywood; see further Chesterton, *Flying Inn*, 587-8, 702-3.

[55] Chesterton, *Collected Works*, vol. 8, 640.

[56] Ibid., 589. God breathed life into the mud of Adam, made in His image to walk with Him; see Gen. 2:7; 1:26; 3:8-9. The story of Pinocchio is a corollary.

things."[57] But the strict condition of their freedom was that they were to destroy and devour nothing. One summer's eve, one of the trees

> heard a voice that was not the saint's . . . [and] became conscious of something sitting and speaking in its branches in the guise of a great bird, and it was that which once spoke from a tree in the guise of a great serpent.[58]

The tempter filled the forest with a "starry pageant of peacocks," and the tree succumbed to its "great desire to stretch out and snatch" at them, devouring them.[59] "The spirit of the brute overcame the spirit of the tree and the saint's judgement condemned it to be rooted to the earth with a curse."[60] The curse followed the trees from pagan Africa to Squire Vane's woods, where for generations their presence has oppressed the villagers. The trees are finally removed by Squire Vane's daughter and heir, in an effort to pull down the high places "where a wicked god has been worshiped, to destroy his altar and cut down his grove."[61] Barbara, who comes to

---

[57] Chesterton, *Collected Works*, vol. 8, 589. The trees mimic the first humans who were sinless and able to walk with their God.

[58] Ibid., 590. Milton's serpent first took the form of a cormorant perched in the Tree of Life; Milton *Paradise Lost* 4.194-6. See also Gen. 3:4-5. The bird is not always evil; see Chesterton's reference to the pelican as the medieval symbol for charity and for Christ crucified, in *The Man Who Was Thursday*, 142.

[59] Chesterton, *Collected Works*, vol. 8, 590; cf. Gen. 3:6.

[60] Chesterton, *Collected Works*, vol. 8, 590.

[61] Ibid., 621. Cf. I Kings 19:4; cf. II Kings 18:4. See also Chesterton, *The Ball and the Cross*, 52, in which MacIan tips over the South Sea idol. See further *Paradise Lost* 9.776-838, where Milton's Eve worships the Tree of Knowledge.

see the peasants' (and her own) fear of the trees as a form of idolatry, has undergone a sort of conversion when the narration of the legend awakened her to the reality of the spiritual realm. "I was born then," she says. "I had walked in this garden like a somnambulist in the sun. . . . I came alive somehow. . . . I began to take notice."[62]

The identity of the trees is never fully disclosed. The common peasants, who mix up truth and fancy (as the atheistic village doctor patronizingly observes), have "that nightmare feeling that you don't know whether the hero is a plant or a man or a devil."[63] This mystery of the tree as mortal or devil is maintained, allowing the characters to quote myth and Scripture almost in the same breath—alluding to the folktales of Uncle Remus and to Jesus' healing of the blind person who saw "men as trees walking."[64] Chesterton's repeated reference to the three-in-one nature of the peacock trees, likened to "some unholy great seaweed that don't belong to the land at all," catches our attention.[65] For example, in the "evil trinity of the trees" there seems something "faintly serpentine and even spiral," so that one character fancies "he saw them slowly revolving as in some cyclical dance."[66] Again, "Only the triple centrepiece of the peacock trees rose clear of the sky-line; and these stood up in tranquil sunlight as things almost classical, a triangular temple of the winds. They seemed pagan."[67] The temple-like columns of the tree invite worship, but is it

---

[62] Chesterton, *Collected Works*, vol. 8, 620. Barbara sounds like Chesterton, who "woke up" after his "period of lunacy" with demonic obsession.

[63] Ibid., 590.

[64] Chesterton, *The Trees of Pride* in *Collected Works*, vol. 8 590-1; cf. Mark 8:22-25.

[65] Chesterton, *Collected Works*, vol. 8, 584-5.

[66] Ibid., 601. For Milton's "unholy trinity," see *Paradise Lost* 2.727-30.

[67] Chesterton, *Collected Works*, vol. 8, 606.

of God or of Pan?[68] Death is found beneath the forest trees, for a tunnel holds human bones in a picture similar to Chaucer's "Deethe," waiting as a horde of treasure beneath an oak tree in a forest grove.[69]

Within such an abundance of imagery alluding to the tree as human and as devil, the story provokes thought upon the nature of humanity, its similarity to spiritual entities, the vivification of one's spirit, and the person's creation in the image of God. Chesterton's Trinitarian language broaches the subject of the incarnation, although he does not enlarge that theme—as has been noted, often "his imagery is stated but not developed."[70] Perhaps Chesterton assumes his readership will understand his allusions to the mythopoeic, incarnational literature that formed his outlook. The childhood influence of Robert Louis Stevenson's *Treasure Island*, for example, can be seen in *The Trees of Pride*. Stevenson's "grey, melancholy woods" form a background replicated in Chesterton's "veil of grey woods."[71] Three tall trees tower in Stevenson's forest, and from the midst of them comes a "thin, high, trembling" voice that frightens the pirates, much as Chesterton's characters are unnerved by the ghostly wailing of the peacock trees, "the voices

---

[68] The tree as temple appears in "Le Jongleur de Dieu," written a quarter of a century before *The Trees of Pride*.

[69] Geoffrey Chaucer, *The Pardoner's Tale* in *Canterbury Tales*, lines 472-83 in Allison and others, *Norton*, 33. Thomas Gray's "Elegy Written in a Country Churchyard" describes graves beneath rugged elms and yew-trees.

[70] Maurice B. Reckitt, *G. K. Chesterton: A Christian Prophet for England To-day* (London: S. P. C. K., 1950), 25.

[71] Robert Louis Stevenson, *The Best Known Works of Robert Louis Stevenson* (New York: The Book League of America, n.d.), 43; Chesterton, *Collected Works*, vol. 8, 582.

of the three trees talking together."[72] *The Trees of Pride* shows how, more and more, Chesterton leaned upon the English classics, which in their turn depended upon scriptural themes.[73] Chesterton, as a medievalist, would have comprehended the twelfth-century motif of the virtuous tree, with its root of humility (and its anti-type, the corrupted tree) that, Greenhill noted, the Christian can choose (or not) to ascend, as Jesus chose to ascend the tree of the cross.[74]

Other antecedent literature echoes throughout this story. The legend of Seth (which runs pervasively through the medieval *Cursor Mundi* much as the legend of the African saint's trees runs through *The Trees of Pride*) balances the story of the fall into sin with the good news of the redemption.[75] It begins with a vision of

---

[72] Stevenson, *Best Known Works*, 111-2; Chesterton, *Collected Works*, vol. 8, 626. For Milton's celestial voices heard from the thicket, see *Paradise Lost* 4.681-2.

[73] In one of his own poems, Chesterton continued the flesh/God synonym by describing the mightiest and best of "Earth's lovers" as a tree standing "stiller than a stone" in a field and swarming with the life of birds, insects, and worms. "The Human Tree" hears from below the "great sea of grass / Roar towards the stars" in worship—crying for their God to save them by blood and so prove His existence. "The Human Tree" in *The Works of G. K. Chesterton*, Wordsworth ed., 260-1; first published in his 1900 collection, *The Wild Knight, and Other Poems*. Cf. Hosea 14:8, where God says, "I am like a green fir tree. From me is thy fruit found."

[74] Greenhill, "The Child in the Tree," 364.

[75] *Cursor Mundi* was written about A.D. 1300 and consists of thirty thousand lines of rhyming couplets braiding together biblical narrative and legend. A seven-part poem paralleling the seven ages of man, it incorporates the legend of Seth, which runs through it as an important and influential myth that affected much of the following literature. For example, Chaucer picked up the depiction of the burning bush of Moses as green, leafy,

a great, dead tree in the midst of a garden, the roots of which extend to hell, its topmost branches cradling the swaddled Christ-child. Seth, Adam's son who took Abel's place, is the spokesman. He is given three tree seeds— cedar, cypress, and palm—signifying the Father, the Son, and the Holy Ghost. He plants them, and the trunks of the three trees grow together, although they retain their three separate identities. The wood of the peculiar trees is used throughout the redemption history—by Moses to sweeten the waters at Marah, by Solomon in building the temple, and by the angels to stir the waters of Shiloah. Eventually the tree is fashioned into the cross of Christ. This legend of Seth, which ties together the Old and New Testaments, was very popular in medieval art. The literary tradition that saw the wood of the forbidden tree in Eden becoming the cross of Christ also used the biblical picture of the ingrafted branches to formulate an analogy for the incarnation.[76]

Furthermore, in Dante's *Purgatory*, the hypostatic union of divine and human is seen in the Gryphon, a

---

and blossoming to be a foreshadowing of the Virgin. Subsequently, the Virgin is seen in connection with the tree and in Aaron's flowering rod of Num. 17:8, her blossoms giving way to the fruit of Christ; David C. Fowler, *The Bible in Early English Literature* (London: Sheldon Press, 1977), pp. 165-76.

[76] See, e.g., William Langland's *Piers Plowman*, which employs the grafting imagery, as noted by Jeffrey, *Dictionary of Biblical Tradition*, 780; cf. Rom. 11:17-24. Of course, Christian literature far predating the medieval period indicates the yoke between wood as the body of the human and as the Spirit of God. For example, Hippolytus, a third-century bishop of Rome, said, "But the Lord was without sin, made of imperishable wood, as regards His humanity; that is, of the Virgin and the Holy Ghost inwardly, and outwardly of the word of God, like an ark overlaid with the purest gold." Hippolytus of Rome, "The Lord is my Shepherd," *Fragment of Discourses or Homilies* 6, n.d., accessed 25 October 2014, http://www.newadvent.org/fathers/0502.htm.

creature wholly lion and wholly eagle, who is "the beast in whom two natures met."[77] The Gryphon (Christ) applies the gracious action of the grafting of trees by tying the pole (the cross) of his chariot (the church) to the Tree of Knowledge (referring to the fall) in the act of redemption—both the first and second Adams represented by his particular tree, according to Dorothy Sayers.[78] Chesterton drew upon this plethora of traditional imagery to illustrate his *Trees of Pride*, as well as a shorter work of the same time period, "The Garden of Smoke" (1919). This second story actively engages the character of the Gryphon, for the hero, Captain Fonblanque, with his aquiline face and a feline figure, is portrayed as a "griffin."[79] That Chesterton intended the reader to make connections between Dante's religious themes and his own becomes even more obvious in this murder-suicide mystery set in a rose garden that is enclosed by laurel hedges.[80] The short story is full of sensory description centring on aromas: the "rich and reeking" smoke of cigars, the elemental scent of earth and fresh air, the heavy vapours of the poisonous spray by which the murderer kills his opium-smoking wife—all mingling with the sweet perfume of the garden's roses.[81] The evocative imagery of fragrance in "The Garden of Smoke" recalls Chesterton's contrasting phrase of "a bad smell in the mind," depicting the horrid feeling that attended his

---

[77] Dante *Purgatory* 32.47; 29.108-14.

[78] Dante *Purgatory* Cantos 28-32; note especially Sayers's comments on the Gryphon in Dante, *Purgatory*, on pages 305 and 327. Recall the automobile accident of *The Man Who Was Thursday*, above.

[79] "The Garden of Smoke" in Chesterton, *Collected Works*, vol. 8, 644.

[80] Note the allusion to the laurel as an object of worship in Chesterton, *Collected Works*, vol. 8, 647. See also the laurels as "immortal shrubs" forming a cloister in "The Flying Stars" in Chesterton, *The Complete Father Brown*, 56.

[81] Chesterton, *Collected Works*, vol. 8, 649; 645; 650; 652.

boyhood sprees with spiritualism.[82] He shares this coupling of scent and spirit with Dante and others, who often spoke of the "ambrosial odours" associated with heaven or Eden.[83] For example, in Dante's Sacred Wood, "All the soil breathed out a fragrant scent," and Spenser wrote in *Faerie Queene* that "ambrosiall odours" emanated from the "goodly Ladie" who stepped through the forest glade.[84] In this way, Chesterton focused reader

---

[82] O'Connor, *Father Brown on Chesterton*, 25. Earlier, Gabriel Syme has a poetic inspiration of truth, which he likens to "that sudden smell of the sea which may be found in the lush woods," in Chesterton, *The Man Who Was Thursday*, 89. Chesterton used the sea as a symbol for the separation from earth.

[83] "The cup of the sacred tree is the elixir of immortality, the ambrosia [food or drink] of the gods," according to Cook, *Symbols of the Centre*, 101. Indeed, in the vision of the Holy Grail recounted in the story of King Arthur, all the knights of the Round Table smell the fragrance of its celestial sweetness. Cf. Gen. 8:21; Exod. 29:18; Song of Sol. 4:11; 2. Cor. 2:14; Eph. 5:2.

[84] Dante *Purgatory* 25.6; Spenser *Faerie Queene* 2.3.22. Note the Rose of Sharon as the bride in Song of Sol. 2:1, and also that the Greek for "tree" (*dendron*) in certain passages (e.g., Matt. 12:33, speaking of a tree known by the fruit it produces) led to the English word "rose-tree." The archetypal medieval rose garden of sexual love is represented by the allegorical *Roman de la Rose* (written by Guillaume de Lorris early in the thirteenth century), where Passion is contradicted by Reason, who is "the image of God in man, a link between earthly and heavenly life," according to Helen Phillips, "Gardens of Love and the Garden of the Fall," in *A Walk in the Garden: Biblical, Iconographical and Literary Images of Eden*, ed. Paul Morris and Deborah Sawyer, Journal for the Study of the Old Testament: Supplement Series 136 (Sheffield, U.K.: JSOT Press, Sheffield Academic Press, 1992), 110. Gerhardt Ladner further explored the theme of pruning (that Chesterton introduced in "The Garden of Smoke") as a Renaissance picture of

attention on the theme of the incarnation and the tree as the *imago Dei*, flesh of humanity for the Person and Spirit of God.

The tree as both human and God became a prevalent theme in Puritan literature, especially notable in Edward Taylor's *Meditations*.[85] That poet's tree had God at its heart, with its branches "hung with celestial groupings of lesser spirits, the saints and the angels."[86] The tree symbolizes God and all of creation, with the person an in-grafted twig. Cecelia Halbert summed up Taylor's idea:

> God grafts into man, and man is implanted into God. God is a tree, as is man. Yet just as man is the whole tree, so is he the meanest part of the tree, a twig. Likewise, Christ as a man-God on earth becomes a mean twig.[87]

This fully mirrored metaphor of Taylor comes out of the common Christian knowledge of the image of grafting, with the Tree of Life a type for Christ symbolic of His body, the church.[88] In both *The Trees of Pride* and "The

---

regrowth or spiritual rebirth. He noted that the early Romans viewed the act of pruning or cutting as "comparable to a wounding," symbolism that he tied to the Gryphon passage in *Purgatory*; Ladner, "Vegetation Symbolism," 304.

[85] Taylor's poetic imagery, echoing earlier writings, was dealt with by Cecelia L. Halbert, "Tree of Life Imagery in the Poetry of Edward Taylor," *American Literature* 38 (1966): 22-34. See also Ursula Brumm, "The 'Tree of Life' in Edward Taylor's *Meditations*," *Early American Literature* 3 (1968): 72-87.

[86] Halbert, "Tree of Life Imagery," 26. Perhaps the Puritan Taylor was influenced, in his turn, by Dante's picture of heaven; Dante *Paradise* 18; 21.

[87] Halbert, "Tree of Life Imagery," 34.

[88] According to Brumm, "Tree of Life," 75, 73. She noted also Augustine's interpretation of the Tree of

Garden of Smoke," Chesterton repeated the image of grafting to further illustrate his correlation between humanity and divinity.

The Poet and the Lunatics (1929)

The 1929 publication of a short story collection entitled *The Poet and the Lunatics: Episodes in the Life of Gabriel Gale* afforded Chesterton further scope for utilizing the tree as a religious device. "The Crime of Gabriel Gale" is one of the comedies in the collection, and it applies the images of a pitchfork and an apple tree, symbols of death that bring about spiritual life. Gabriel Gale—painter, poet, and amateur psychologist—has a theory about how to cure insanity. In the setting of a stormy garden party, he recognizes in another character, Saunders, the sure signs of madness—by which Chesterton meant spiritual sickness—that have gone unnoticed by others.

Saunders is a theological student whose brooding on religious doubts and prophecies has led him to the brink of believing himself to be God. For example, upon the comment of the hostess, he believes he himself has indeed "brought the bad weather."[89] In an explanation of Chesterton's own "period of lunacy" in his youth, Gale

---

Life as Christ in *De Civitate Dei* 13, 21. The ancient poem entitled *De Pascha* (variously dated, likely fourth century), often copied among the works of St. Cyprian, also draws the Tree of Life as synonymous with Christ and with the church; see, e.g., Greenhill, "The Child in the Tree," 338-43.

[89] G. K. Chesterton, *The Poet and the Lunatics*, 108. In several stories, Chesterton linked his descriptions of the weather to the internal temperature of a person's soul. In one, a character stares at the stormy sky and comments, "It does sometimes happen that meteorological conditions make men more conscious of moral conditions." Chesterton, "Ring of Lovers" in *Paradoxes of Mr. Pond*, 90. See also *The Flying Inn*, 519.

describes the disintegration of the emotional state of the young Saunders:

> You might almost say it's normal to have an abnormal period. It comes when there's a lack of adjustment in the scale of things outside and within. . . . In this young man it was rather symbolically expressed even in the look of him. It was like his growing out of his clothes, or being too big for his boots. The inside gets too big for the outside. . . . Now in that dangerous time, there's a dreadfully dangerous moment; when the first connexion is made between the subjective and the objective: the first real bridge between the brain and real things.[90]

At this moment in Saunders's tenuous state, Gale challenges him to command the garden apple tree to move—to dance—being certain that "unless he learnt his human limitations sharply and instantly, something illimitable and inhuman would take hold of him."[91] But Saunders takes no notice of Gale's challenge, dashing off in an emotional frenzy, so that Gale knows he has had a break with reality. He ropes Saunders to the apple tree and snatches up a hay fork, brandishing it "like the fabulous fork of a demon."[92] Gale drives the prongs of the pitchfork into the tree on either side of Saunders's neck, holding him pinned like a prisoner in an iron ring. Saunders struggles futilely against his bonds. At dawn,

---

[90] Chesterton, *Poet and the Lunatics*, 120-21. See further Chesterton, *Autobiography*, chapter four, "How to be a Lunatic." Note that, in *The Man Who Was Thursday*, the shifting shadows in the forest of Impressionism also contrast the subjective with the objective.

[91] Chesterton, *Poet and the Lunatics*, 125. Notice the reference to Jesus' statement in Luke 17:6 regarding faith causing a tree to move.

[92] Chesterton, *Poet and the Lunatics*, 113.

after wrestling for dark hours in vain, the megalomaniac captive "nailed to the tree" finally expresses a "huge tide of healthy relief and thanks, like a hymn of praise from all nature," over "the great and glorious news; the news that he was only a man."[93] He sounds like George Herbert, who wrote:

> But as I rav'd and grew more fierce and wilde
> At every word,
> Methought I heard one calling, "Childe";
> And I reply'd, "My Lord."[94]

Like Herbert, Saunders's escape comes through his admission that he is incapable of achieving his own salvation, giving voice to Chesterton's reminder of the only Man who ever freed Himself from the bonds of death and sin.[95]

In a quirky (but typically Chestertonian) paradox, Gale is both the figure of Satan and the deliverer himself, teaching Saunders that he cannot control matter or the elements of nature, "that he could not move trees or remove pitchforks."[96] In other words, the creature is not the Creator, the sinner is not the Saviour. Saunders could not liberate himself from his captivity under sin and his desire to be God for, as Gale says,

---

[93] Ibid., 132.

[94] George Herbert, "The Collar," lines 33-36 in *The Temple*, in *Works,* 142. Saunders perhaps also expresses Chesterton's reading of Donne, who likewise cries to God, "[I] am betrothed unto Your enemy. / Divorce me, 'untie or break that knot again; / Take me to You, imprison me, for I, / Except You enthrall me, never shall be free. . . ." Donne, lines 10-13, "Sonnet 14" in *Holy Sonnets*, in Allison and others, *Norton*, 222.

[95] Chesterton's scriptural theme of spiritual bondage and freedom is based, for example, in John 8:31-36, Rom. 6:14-23, and Gal.5:1.

[96] Chesterton, *Poet and the Lunatics*, 125-6.

> There is no cure for that nightmare of
> omnipotence except pain; because that is
> the thing a man knows he would not tol-
> erate if he could really control it. A man
> must be in some place from which he
> would certainly escape if he could, if he is
> really to realize that all things do not
> come from within. . . . There was a man
> who saw himself sitting in the sky. . . .
> And, God forgive me for blasphemy, but I
> nailed him to a tree.[97]

Gale understands the tale in which he figured in that
stormy night garden (that was to him "one purple patch
of Paradise—and of Paradise Lost") to be parabolic of a
greater story. That is, he is reminded of Eden and of
Gethsemane—of the enslaving sin and of its horrible solution. Gale "spoke indeed in parables," and

> the things of which he was thinking were
> far away from that garden or even from
> that tale. There swelled up darkly and
> mountainously in his memory the slopes
> of another garden against another
> storm.[98]

The tree is Saunders's cross, where he learns
that he is human and not divine—incapable of delivering
himself. The tree, Gale explains, is everyone's cross, for
"we are all tied to trees and pinned with pitchforks. And
as long as these are solid we know the stars will stand
and the hills will not melt at our word."[99] In this story,

---

[97] Ibid., 130.
[98] Ibid., 131. See Christ's spiritual inner storm of
Gethsemane in Matt. 26:36-42.
[99] Chesterton, *Poet and the Lunatics*, 132. According to Jeffrey, the stars in their courses (cf. Judg.
5:20) came in literature to represent the futility of striking out against "fate"—as expressed by "star-crossed

the tree of crucifixion is the standard against which Chesterton measured human mortality, defining the difference between the subjective belief that self is at the "centre of the cosmos" and the objective truth that "man is a creature" who cannot "control the skies and uproot trees and call up the thunder."[100] In "The Crime of Gabriel Gale," the picture of the tree as the cross comes into clear focus. The historical truth of the crucifixion of Christ is an allegory; indeed, Gale doubts "whether any of our actions is really anything but an allegory . . . whether any truth can be told except in a parable."[101]

The integrated and mature parables of Chesterton employ the tree as a symbol of the God-like nature bestowed upon man in creation, and the man-like nature taken up by God in the re-creating incarnation and the death on the cross of salvation.

Final Stories (1930-1936)

After the 1929 publication of *The Poet and the Lunatics*, Chesterton was to have only seven years more of parable telling before his death at Top Meadow, Beaconsfield. They were not as productive for fiction as the preceding years had been, but several parables in this period of his waning health contain notable imagery expressing his

---

lovers" Romeo and Juliet; Jeffrey, *Dictionary of Biblical Tradition*, 735.

[100] Ibid., 130, 129, 127. Only Jesus could "call up the thunder" of God's voice, as when he prayed, "Father, glorify thy name"; John 12:28-30. Recall again the Christ-figure of Adam Wayne, who *could* uproot the tree that stood at the centre of the cosmos; see discussion in *Napoleon of Notting Hill*, above.

[101] Chesterton, *Poet and the Lunatics*, 130. Ps. 90:9 declares with Chesterton's Gale: "We spend our years as a tale that is told." An early historical example of the parabolic, typological link between the tree and the cross of Christ is seen in John Chrysostom *Homily on Romans* 10.13-14.

sacramental world view. For all his youthful, joyous humour, G. K. Chesterton did not take the subject of death lightly. This early theme of death, introduced through tree imagery in childhood and continued especially in the Father Brown detective mysteries, had by this time been securely identified with the violence of murder or suicide. For example, "The Miracle of Moon Crescent" (1926) tells of travellers in the shadows of the forest who find a body hung, like a broken branch, in the trees—a scene sounding eerily like that of the journeying poets in Dante's pathless wood, who come upon withered, bleeding trees enclosing the souls of suicides "cramped" in the "knotty form."[102] "The Ghost of Gideon Wise" shows another victim's body hanging "huge and horrible, amid the broken forks and branches of the little wood into which its weight had crashed."[103] The splintered wood of that story recalls an earlier tale; in "The Sins of Prince Saradine," a bushy rose-tree is smashed by a falling body, shaking up into the sky "a cloud of red earth—like the smoke of some heathen sacrifice."[104] There is nothing new in finding death among Chesterton's trees.

But, in the final collection published before Chesterton's own demise (*The Secret of Father Brown*, 1935), the deathly tree also bears a message of love. In "The Point of a Pin," a man is murdered and his body hidden, but a suicide note is left scratched into the smooth bark of a tree near the river, claiming he drowned himself. Meanwhile, the deceased man's wife is found to have been carrying on an affair, with the

---

[102] Dante *Hell* 13.88; cf. "The Miracle of Moon Crescent" in Chesterton, *The Complete Father Brown*, 377.

[103] Chesterton, *The Complete Father Brown*, 449.

[104] "The Sins of Prince Saradine" in *The Innocence of Father Brown*, Chesterton, *The Complete Father Brown*, 113-4. Job 24:20 states that "wickedness shall be broken like a tree." Note the earlier reference to the rose as a picture of Christ and the church in "The Garden of Smoke," above.

sweethearts' initials carved as "vows upon the trysting-tree," a love confession inscribed above the death notice.[105] These notices are red herrings to the actual murder that Father Brown eventually solves, but parts of the priest's commentary marry themes of love and self-inflicted death via the messages cut into the tree. Chesterton took advantage of a diversion in a detective mystery to remind the reader allegorically of the communication from the Creator, whose love and self-sacrifice are also written upon one tree. The suicide note of the story is carved at eye level, but Father Brown "glanced upward once at the darker and more hidden hieroglyph"—the record of romance in the incriminating initials.[106] Father Brown says,

> We've all heard of love-messages written on trees; and I suppose there might be death-messages written on trees too, . . . sort of arboreal correspondence . . . [from one who would] write on a tree, as the song says, if all the world were paper and all the sea were ink or all these woods were a forest of quills and fountain pens.[107]

---

[105] Chesterton, *The Complete Father Brown*, 684.

[106] Ibid., 685.

[107] Ibid., 683. The song Chesterton alluded to sounds like the 1917 hymn called "The Love of God," by American Fredrick Martin Lehman (Church of the Nazarene). The origin of the third stanza (beginning "Could we with ink the oceans fill") has been attributed to an Aramaic acrostic poem written by a twelfth-century rabbi in Germany and still chanted as part of the conservative Jewish liturgy in the Torah service; see Meir Ben Isaac, "Akdamut," in *Or Hadash: A Commentary on Siddur Sim Shalom for Shabbat and Festivals,* by Reuven Hammar (New York: The Rabbinical Assembly, 2003), accessed 25 October 2014, http://www.rabbinical assembly.org/sites/default/files/public/jewish-law/holidays/shavuot/akdamut-from-or-hadash.pdf.

His words sound like the *Confessions* of St. Augustine to
God:

> You have spread out the heavens like a
> canopy of skins, and these heavens are
> our Book. . . . There in the heavens, in
> your Book, we read your unchallengable
> decrees. . . . Now we see your Word, not
> as he is, but dimly, through the clouds,
> like a confused reflection in the mirror of
> the firmament.[108]

Thus, love and death serve Chesterton's sacramental
outlook by providing motive and means for the message
that the transcendent God is also immanent in His creation.

A second episode in Chesterton's final collection
is the convoluted "Insoluble Problem" (1935), featuring
a staunchly religious man who appears to have been
murdered in the garden of the Green Dragon Inn.[109] He
is hung (already dead by natural agency) from the
branch of a Judas tree and pinioned to its trunk through
the torso with a rusty, antiquated sword.[110] This clever

---

[108] Augustine, *Confessions* 13.15. Recall similar
themes in "Apotheosis," above. In *The Flying Inn*,
Ivywood comments about art: "Surely we can read its
alphabet as easily as the red hieroglyphics of sunrise
and sunset, which are on the fringes of the robe of
God"; Chesterton, *Flying Inn*, 518.

[109] Chesterton, "The Insoluble Problem" in *The
Complete Father Brown*, 690-704. For dragon imagery,
see *The Trees of Pride*, above.

[110] Accounts of human sacrifices made to Odin,
which demanded first hanging upon a tree and then
piercing, were answered by eighth-century poem,
"Dream of the Rood," which strove to address the paradox of the shame and splendour of the crucifixion. Jeffrey, *People of the Book*, 117-24. Absalom, hanging
"between heaven and earth" from an oak tree by his
hair, was also pierced as recounted in 2 Sam. 18:9-14.

arrangement of the body is a trick played by a thief whose devoted wife helps stage the "murder" scene to detract from the real crime—the theft of a precious religious reliquary. Here the tree is again implicated in death, but more important than the plot is one of FatherBrown's revealing "preachments."[111] The mystery focuses on a marriage that has an atmosphere (unlike the Smiths' in *Manalive*) that Father Brown finds "dreadful and passionate and oppressive."[112] The priest moralizes upon the strength of the "ghastly" form of love that "filled the house with terror"—a distorted love (once holy) that caused the lovers to sin:

> Do you think I don't know that the love of a man and a woman was the first command of God and is glorious forever? . . . Do I need to be told of the Garden of Eden or the Wine of Cana? It is just because the strength in the thing was the strength of God, that it rages with that awful energy even when it breaks loose from God.[113]

This powerful Edenic love, originally pure and now perverted, provokes the fall of mankind and of the world itself ("when the garden becomes the jungle, but still a glorious jungle"), and leads eventually to the cross ("when the second fermentation turns the wine of Cana

---

[111] Clipper dubbed the priest's frequent sermonettes as "preachments," noting their integral function in the structure of the stories, in Clipper, *G. K. Chesterton*, 124. John Peterson, on the other hand, described them as "emotional tirades" in John Peterson, "Father Brown's War on the Impermanent Things," in *Permanent Things*: *Towards the Recovery of a More Human Scale at the End of the Twentieth Century*, ed. Andrew A. Tadie and Michael H. Macdonald (Grand Rapids: Eerdmans, 1995), 17.

[112] Chesterton, *The Complete Father Brown*, 700.

[113] Ibid., 701.

into the vinegar of Calvary").[114] The Judas tree is utilized as a framework for themes of creation, marriage, the wine of communion, and Christ's crucifixion.

"The Insoluble Problem" discloses Chesterton's view of the world as a fallen Eden in which a married love gone awry has overgrown the garden, sin transferring it into a (yet glorious) jungle. In repetition of the theme he broached a quarter-century earlier in *Manalive* (years before his 1922 reception into the Roman Catholic Church), Chesterton now espoused the institution of Christian marriage as an expression of Christ's redemption. Peter Milward explained the holy love of man and woman as "a deeper symbolism of divine grace," with Christian marriage as the "culminating point" of every Shakespearean comedy.[115] Catholic theologians use the term "sacrament of nature" for marriage, and Milward noted that the same phrase is used by English writers when referring to nature as "a sacrament of divine presence" in seeing the world "charged with the active presence of God, the Creator, the Redeemer and the Sanctifier."[116] The sacraments bespeaking the presence of God in marriage, in the last supper, and in the sacrifice of the cross are themes that meet in Chesterton's image of the tree—the tree Yggdrasil, the Judas tree, the trysting-tree.

For Chesterton, wine carried a strong metaphysical significance, its colour symbolic of Christ's redeeming omnipresence—often in reference to the tree. For example, in "The Secret of Father Brown" (1927), a cryptic vision experienced by the priest holds glimpses of the writer's own childhood garden lamps within the spectacle of the larger universe. Chesterton pours his character a glass of wine, upon which

> Father Brown also lifted his glass, and the
> glow of the fire turned the red wine

---

[114] Ibid.

[115] Milward, *Christian Themes in English Literature*, 233-4.

[116] Ibid., 235, 236.

transparent, like the glorious blood-red glass of a martyr's window. The red flame seemed to hold his eyes and absorb his gaze that sank deeper and deeper into it, as if that single cup held a red sea of the blood of all men, and his soul were a div-er, ever plunging in dark humility and in-verted imagination, lower than its lowest monsters and its most ancient slime. In that cup, as in a red mirror, he saw many things. . . . Then the sunset seemed to break up into patches: red lanterns swing-ing from garden trees and a pond gleam-ing red with reflection; and then all the colour seemed to cluster again into a great rose of red crystal, a jewel that irra-diated the world like a red sun . . . .[117]

If, as Lynette Hunter proposed, Father Brown's cup is an analogy for "the cup of all men,"[118] then the wine into which he plunges baptizes him into communion with the rest of creation. Adam Wayne's eschatological promise of the wine to be poured at "the inn at the end of the world" is already tasted in the present cup of communi-ty.[119] Chesterton's overarching analogy is of a wine-washed world, the re-creation of the earth as "an earthly paradise."[120] He believed that the real person of God in-tentionally communicates His real presence to humanity; as Janet Knedlik pointed out, Chesterton sought truth and found it in the Creator's immanent yet transcendent

---

[117] "The Secret of Father Brown" in Chesterton, *The Complete Father Brown*, 466. Father Brown's epiph-any, like Dante's, incorporates tree imagery; see, e.g., Dante *Paradise* 12.100-5; 15.90; 16.22.

[118] Hunter, *Explorations in Allegory*, 153-4.

[119] Chesterton, *Napoleon of Notting Hill*, 124.

[120] Chesterton, *Flying Inn*, 464. See also Chester-ton's 1922 story "The Vengeance of the Statue" in *The Man Who Knew Too Much, Collected Works* vol. 8, 578.

presence in nature and the creation.[121] This sacramental viewpoint gives us a clue as to how to read Chesterton's stories and understand his symbolic use of the tree, which (in creation as well as in Chesterton's creative fiction) is a piece of nature embodying the trace of God's handiwork—the *"visibilia"* into which his allegory pours its meaning (as David Lyle Jeffrey put it).[122] The tree stands as one of Chesterton's "signs" pointing to a greater thing in eternity being "signified" (to use Augustinian terms).[123] He said in Thomist terms:

> If things deceive us, it is by being more real than they seem. As ends in themselves they always deceive us; but as things tending to a greater end, they are even more real than we think them. . . . They are potential and not actual; they are unfulfilled, like packets of seeds or boxes of fireworks. And there is an upper world of what the Schoolman called Fruition, or Fulfillment, in which all this relative relativity becomes actuality; in which the trees burst into flowers or the rockets into flame.[124]

The objective "reality" of the tree is not as real as the eternal referent that the tree symbolizes. Nature is the symbol, heaven the actuality. Years earlier, Chesterton poetically expressed this perspective of divine presence within creation:

---

[121] Janet Blumberg Knedlik, "Derrida Meets Father Brown: Chestertonian 'Deconstructionism' and that Harlequin 'Joy'," in *G. K. Chesterton and C. S. Lewis: The Riddle of Joy*, ed. Michael H. Macdonald and Andrew A. Tadie (Grand Rapids: Eerdmans, 1989), 273-89.

[122] Jeffrey, *Dictionary of Biblical Tradition*, 29.

[123] Augustine, *On Christian Doctrine* 1.2.

[124] Chesterton, *Saint Thomas Aquinas*, 179-80; written in 1933.

Speller of the stones and weeds,
Skilled in Nature's crafts and creeds,
Tell me what is in the heart
Of the smallest seeds.

God Almighty, and with Him
Cherubim and Seraphim,
Filling all eternity—
Adonai Elohim.[125]

The sacramental themes introduced in earlier writing have, by Chesterton's maturity, been refined and the tree imagery advanced. The Garden of Eden, fallen into wildness, becomes the glorious jungle of the world, inhabited now by both evil and good, and still offering humanity a choice. The tree is the cause of, and the escape from, sin. It becomes the instrument of violent, sacrificial death climbed because of love, and figures not only the crucifixion but also the incarnation, the church, and the light of Christian truth. Chesterton connects the tree to the gracious vestige of God in marriage and nature. God has written a message to his people that Chesterton, immersed in his cohesive and unified world view, illustrates with the picture of the tree.

---

[125] Chesterton, "The Holy of Holies," in *The Works of G. K. Chesterton*, Wordsworth ed., 264; first published in *The Wild Knight*, 1900. Medieval Jewish mystics, the Kabbalists, extensively used the image of the tree in similar language: "For, just as the seed contains the tree, and the tree the seed, so the hidden world of God contains all Creation, and Creation is, in turn, a revelation of the hidden world of God"; Cook, *Symbols of the Centre*, 18. See further Paul Morris, "Exiled from Eden: Jewish Interpretation of Genesis," in *A Walk in the Garden: Biblical, Iconographical and Literary Images of Eden*, ed. Paul Morris and Deborah Sawyer, Journal for the Study of the Old Testament: Supplement Series 136 (Sheffield, U.K.: JSOT Press, Sheffield Academic Press, 1992), 21-38.

SIX

CONCLUSION

Chesterton once said that the art of biographical and literary criticism could be undertaken in two ways. The first is a chronological approach, "as one cuts a currant cake or a Gruyère cheese, taking the currants (or the holes) as they come."[1] The second, in carpentry metaphor, dissects the literature "as one cuts wood—along the grain."[2] We have so far sliced through Chesterton's cake from front to back, encountering pictures of the tree like currants scattered throughout his life and work, and we can agree with him that there is difficulty "in keeping moral order parallel with chronological order."[3] Now, using Chesterton's second approach, a concluding overview follows each of six themes that arise within his fiction: home and journey, the person and God, light, the church, the ladder, and the cross. Associated with these themes, the tree becomes an allegory for salvation. It acts as Chesterton's "visual aid" or wholistic model of the spiritual process by picturing the incarnational, redeeming work of Christ and the continuing, sacramental presence of God in the world. It evolved along with (and analogizes) Chesterton's own understanding of the basic convictions of Christianity: God's image in the created human, free will leading to the fall into sin, the yearning of the banished exile for a return to Paradise, and the promise of deliverance through the light of the gospel, the institution of the church, and the hope of the cross as a passage between heaven and earth.

Chesterton's forest portrays the **home** of humanity, an illustration of the world or the fallen Garden of Eden, which becomes Father Brown's "glorious jungle." Through this forest the traveller journeys on a quest for

---

[1] Chesterton, "The Victorian Age in Literature," 7.
[2] Ibid.
[3] Ibid., 25.

true identity, seeking courage, wisdom and truth on a "Wild Goose Chase," fleeing death in escaping his own funeral through the woods of "Flickerflash," pushing from home towards home as the fallen creation is re-created through the sacrament of marriage in *Manalive*. The forest, though, is not the eternal home, for the woodcutter of "Apotheosis" calls his people out as he harvests the woods, laying an axe at the roots in judgement. Not only the collective forest but also the individual tree becomes a symbol of home; a fruit or shade tree affords a choice between good and evil as in "The Secret Garden" or inspires "The Honest Quack" to stop and make rest. Treehouses provide a view of the universe from the ground up. The centrality of the great oak on Notting Hill speaks of nationalism and patriotic love of home, trees even identified by Chesterton as cities and civilizations in "The Wind and the Trees." The forest is truly a place of meeting, as the children met the "Queen of the Evening Star"; it is truly a place of spiritual communion, as the fugitives found companionship and a poet found God in the woods of *The Flying Inn*.[4]

Not simply background filler, the fringe of forests comes to bear the meaning of the flesh of corporate humanity "In Topsy-Turvy Land." The tree becomes a **person**, the person an articulate tree. The tree expresses one's innermost beliefs and essence, its genus unveiling belief systems in "A Picture of Tuesday." Chesterton tied the shape of the human to the shape of the tree in *The Ball and the Cross*. Later, he literally tied a man to a tree in crucifixion imagery through *The Poet and the Lunatics*. His hiding of the corpse in Mr. Windrush's tree trunk emphasizes the likeness between flesh and wood, preparing the reader for the theme of grafting between the earthly, physical body and the heavenly, spiritual

---

[4] For an in-depth handling of Chesterton's conversion narrative told allegorically through *The Flying Inn*, see Elkink, "The Seven Moods of Gilbert: Conversion Narrative in *The Flying Inn*," bound within this volume as Part II, below.

being in "The Garden of Smoke." The personification of Squire Vane's peacock trees further identifies the plant with humanity and divinity through the introduction of themes of tree worship and spiritual embodiment. This hint of the incarnation is furthered by Chesterton's parallel between the tree and the lamp.

The tree bearing **light** is a strong picture in the stories. Stars tangled in Notting Hill's branches produce visions in another story of a heavenly queen; glittering flashes of stolen gems fallen from boughs in "The Flying Stars" become a starry pageant of peacocks fluttering throughout the living forests in the legend within *The Trees of Pride*. The tree is a torch—a flaming brand bringing light to civilization in "The Human Club" or judgemental destruction through the fire set by the asylum Master with the cleft chin. The light-infused *Man Who Was Thursday* depicts empty philosophies through the shifting shadows in the wood of witchery; its tree-like lampposts contrast order and anarchy, truth and error, light and darkness. The sunrise and sunset over the garden in that novel are balanced against the tempestuous skies above the tree of Gabriel Gale, full of weather mirroring internal moral conditions. Tree-based Jewish temple imagery implied by Symes's fascination with the almond is seen again on Innocent Smith's journey through the Sierra Mountains of California and in the garden tree flaming like Moses' holy bush. Christ as the light of the world, indwelling the wood of the menorah, is reflected in fallen humanity, the shining puddles in Notting Hill's streets picturing fragments of divinity.

The theme of living wood as Christ's incarnation, extended to the lamp of His **church**, shines forth the light of Christian doctrine and ritual. Chesterton's forested landscapes comprise places of veneration, both idolatrous and virtuous. The Tree of Knowledge, diabolically sketched in "Half-Hours in Hades," offers again the original sin; the temple-like columns of *The Trees of Pride*— looking like the altar of a wicked god—confer death. On the other hand, the landscape of the wild lonely moors in "The White Cockade" provides a monastic setting for solitary contemplation of the heavens. Trees render a hiding place or refuge for Turnbull and MacIan, and for *The Flying Inn* characters. Like the church, the grove is a corporeal meeting place—a devotional playground in the early stories and, later, a duelling arena in "The Paradise of Thieves" or trysting spot in "The Point of a Pin." Chesterton used tree imagery to describe his cathedrals (in "A Nightmare" and "Le Jongleur de Dieu"); conversely, he used cathedral imagery to describe his forests (in the underwater "Paradise of Human Fishes"). The church, although distinct, is not removed from the world; Chesterton pictured the universe itself as the tree of "My Uncle the Professor" that must be climbed in order to reach eternity.

The tree as a **ladder** emerges in the boyhood tales, with characters scaling trees for escape, protection, and sanctuary from enemies. The ladder of the tree grants entry, in "The Singular Speculation of the House-Agent," to a treehouse that acts as a home halfway to heaven on a journey from the City of Man to the City of God. As ascent up the ladder of the tree typifies human exaltation towards the divine and immortal as well as Christ's climbing of the tree of the cross, so descent down the ladder intimates again the incarnation of Christ. MacIan and Turnbull's plunge down the leafy forest path to struggle for religious expression is repeated in their climb down the apple tree into the garden of the mental asylum ("the world gone mad") towards a salvific re-creation of the ruined creation. Chesterton's imagery associating Christ (the root springing forth from the tree of Jesse) with the ladder of Jacob makes the link between the tree and the cross—the passage between heaven and earth.

The **cross** is intimated even in Chesterton's childhood expression of death, both physical and spiritual, through the verbal picture of a tree of vultures and the notebook sketch of the Tree of Knowledge. The violence of murder and suicide is linked to the trees in "The Ghost of Gideon Wise" and "The Insoluble Problem"; as an instrument of self-inflicted wounding, it carries messianic overtones. This crucifixion theme is furthered by Adam Wayne's embracing of his tree of death and his subsequent resurrection. The felling of the "Apotheosis" tree in judgement is balanced by the triumphal replanting of the cross of St. Paul's tree upon the summit of the earth's ball. The Tree of Knowledge bringing choice and death in Valentin's "Secret Garden" is answered by the Tree of Life that gives its climber a closer look at heaven (in "My Uncle the Professor"). The wooden pole that pierces becomes the wooden rake that gathers for the burning and acts as a pilgrim's walking stick of guidance and support (*Manalive*) as well as the wooden cross-shaped sign announcing freedom (*The Flying Inn*). The divisive shape that offends, seen in "The Human Club" member's ritualistic sign of crossing himself, is modelled by the sharp outlines of duelling sword and person. Hero Gabriel Gale binds Saunders to the apple tree, which becomes his cross of crucifixion—that tree of double fruit that decrees spiritual condemnation or heavenly escape.

As "the leading spokesman of a sacramental view of the world,"[5] Chesterton wrote in a time influenced by the biblical symbolism of Victorian English writers whose doctrines of analogy and reserve held that, although God "so created the world that its very physical nature contains signs of His creation," yet religion is "a veiled and secret matter, not immediately revealed to the profane."[6] Chesterton's own writing exposes his themes (of home and journey, man and God, light, the church, the ladder, and the cross) with expanding metaphorical and revelatory implication. For example, the young Chesterton's wine of Cana, poured out at the last supper beneath the gibbet-tree, is poured again at "the inn at the end of the world." The oak gracing the city of Notting

---

[5] Clipper, *G. K. Chesterton*, 37.

[6] G. B. Tennyson, "'So Careful of the Type?'—Victorian Biblical Typology: Sources and Applications," *Essays and Studies: New Series* 37 (1984): 36-37. This article, which decries the "Evangelical mistake" of divorcing allegory and symbolism from the more accepted typology, uses the "tree of Jesse" windows of European cathedrals as an example of the continued witness of the church to the long-living allegorical/typological tradition.

Hill becomes the transcendent tree of St. Paul's, casting a long shadow over the earth. The concealed-but-revealed message of God is written upon the fallen creation in the woodcutter's forest and upon the cathedral-like columns of autumn groves and underwater gardens. The trees are part of nature's chaotic mask that, torn away, unveils the Creator. Spiritual truth shines as festive lanterns hung fruit-like in trees, as celestial lights snarled up in branches, and as flames atop lampposts. The sun's rays wash the world in wine and the wooded hills in blood-red glory. Chesterton's polysemous language is itself sacramental.

Although Chesterton's fiction is thick with imagery, it must be conceded that his story descriptions are not restricted to the tree motif. In fact, his writing "suffers from an imaginative excess," according to some, and even indicates "a sense of imagination working out of control."[7] His lavish employment of concrete objects as unrelated as a glass of milk, a piece of chalk, and a red necktie (however great a store of symbolism they provide for future exploration) must not detract from the importance of the tree as a powerful illustration of Chesterton's world view—an illustration deeply established in the literary tradition that he inherited. The cosmic tree in literature and art is considered by some critics, such as Roger Cook, to be the central image of creation, the "point of 'absolute beginning' . . . 'Divine Egg,' 'Hidden Seed' or 'Root of Roots.' "[8] The literature that resulted, read by Chesterton, awoke in him a train of associations regarding the image of the tree that he incorporates into his fiction.

Chesterton's imagination was not created *ex nihilo*. A cursory review follows of the pattern within the great body of Christian writing preceding Chesterton that was so influential in shaping his aesthetic and so present in his own stories.

---

[7] Boyd, "In Search of the Essential Chesterton," 31.

[8] Cook, *Symbols of the Centre*, 9.

Among the many applications of the tree within Scripture itself, the most impressive is the unifying illustration of a salvation history. It begins with the sin incurred through the eating of the fruit of the Tree of Knowledge in the Garden of Eden and the resulting banishment of Adam and Eve from their home and from the Tree of Life, with a promise by God to restore to the wilderness of Zion the lushness of the garden.[9] The tree becomes analogous to the temporary Old Testament sacrificial system. The incarnation of Christ ("the man that stood among the myrtle trees"), and His death on the tree of the cross, finally reinstate humanity's access to Paradise with its trees of eternal life and healing.[10] Genealogical relationships are also pictured, with the root of Jesse appropriated by Paul and applied to Christ.[11] The destiny of the individual and of the nation, as well as the progress of a person's life, are synonymous with a tree's growth.[12] Wisdom is figured by the Tree of Life.[13] The theme of hopelessness as a dried-up stump is balanced by the robust tree of happiness and longevity.[14] The person is a flourishing green olive or cedar if godly, or else a mere thistle—with God Himself "like a green fir tree," the source of all blessing and the ground of all fertility.[15] Creation is renewed in the joy and praise of the wooded fields; judgement is drawn as a fruitless tree hewn down and cast into the fire.[16] The burning tree, alight with positive symbolism, is seen in Moses' bush, in the almond pattern of the tabernacle candlestick, and in the lampstands of the church.[17] The

---

[9] Gen. 2-3; Isa 51:3.

[10] Zech. 1:10; Acts 5:30; 1 Pet. 2:24; Rom. 11:17-24; Rev. 2:7; 22:2.

[11] Isa. 11:1-2; Rom. 15:12.

[12] Dan. 4; Judg. 9:15; Ezek. 31; Isa. 10:34; Rom. 11:17-25; Ps. 1; Jer. 17:8.

[13] Prov. 3:18; 11:30; 13:12; 15:5.

[14] Job 14:7-10; Isa. 65:22.

[15] Ps. 52:8; 2 Kings 14:9; Hos. 14:5-8.

[16] Ps. 96:12; Isa. 55:12; Matt. 3:10; Luke 3:9.

[17] Exod. 3; Exod. 25; Rev.1:12, 20.

biblical literature provides a sound base for the construction of the tree themes appearing in ensuing works.

Extensive commentary by the patristic writers
gave rise to a cosmological tree that embodied major
doctrines and mysteries of the Christian faith, as pointed
out by Roger Cook. For example, the third-century East-
er sermon by Hippolytus of Rome portrays the transcendent cross of Christ as a tree "wide as the heavens
itself," an immortal growth towering between heaven
and earth, the "fulcrum of all things and the place where
they are all at rest."[18] In language that sounds like
Chesterton's, Hippolytus continued to describe this tree:

> It is the foundation of the round world,
> and the centre of the cosmos. In it all the
> diversities in our human nature are
> formed into a unity. It is held together by
> the invisible nails of the spirit so that it
> may not break loose from the divine. It
> touches the highest summits of heaven
> and makes the earth firm beneath its foot,
> and it grasps the middle regions between
> them with immeasurable arms.[19]

The fourth-century poem, *De Pascha*, allegorizes the
Tree of Life as the cross and the church, a theme repeated, for example, by Chrysostom, Jerome, and others.[20] Augustine applied the element of free choice to
the picture of the tree in his famous confession of his
theft of pears.[21] Legends flourished; the Holy Rood of
the eighth century made way for the later Holy Grail stories (both utilizing bountiful tree imagery) as well as the

---

[18] Cook, *Symbols of the Centre*, 21.
[19] Hippolytus, quoted in Cook, *Symbols of the Centre*, 21.
[20] See, e.g., John Chrysostom *Homily on Romans* 10.13-14.
[21] Augustine *Confessions* 2.4; cf. Augustine *De Civitate Dei* 13.21.

influential *Cursor Mundi*, with its legend of Seth that reverberates in *The Trees of Pride.*

Medieval writers followed the example of their fathers, developing the allegory to include the Tree of Knowledge as producing the wood of the cross. In addition to the genealogy of Christ, the tree of Jesse came to bear implications to the virginity of Mary and illustrated the figurative relationship between the Old and New Testaments. A cohesive redemption history ensued, producing a great deal of visual art (such as the stained glass "Jesse windows" and ladder motif of European cathedrals, in Chesterton's own backyard), and an elaborate scheme grew up around the trees of vices and virtues (with their roots of pride and humility).[22] Dante, applying Aquinas's four-fold exegetical system, substantially contributed to the literary pool of allegory dealing with the tree through his allusions to grafting, the Trinity, the incarnation, and the church. Langland's *Piers Plowman* and the tales of Chaucer similarly connect the tree to themes of life and death, hope and illicit passion and Christ's own Passion. Although the Reformation stunted the further progress of allegorical excgesis of Scripture, both Luther and Calvin still utilized the symbol to their ends, concentrating on the typological reading.[23] Spenser's *Faerie Queene* and Shakespeare's work reinforced the biblical readings by this time so established in the literature. Scripture was further sustained in the Puritan fiction of Milton (*Paradise Lost*) and Bunyan (*The Pilgrim's Progress*), as well as in the writings of the epoch of Romanticism. There is no doubt that, as Chesterton made his way through the writings of his predecessors, the motif of the tree as a Christian emblem took root in his own imagination.

The stimulation of Chesterton's symbolic imagination was accomplished not only through literature but also through life experiences in his childhood home and

---

[22] See, e.g., Adolf Katzenellenbogen, *Allegories of the Virtues and Vices in Mediaeval Art* (London: The Warburg Institute, 1939).

[23] See, e.g., Calvin *Institutes* 2.1.4.

the home of his marriage, through the cultural milieu of Victorian London, and by way of his own religious curiosity as a traveller on a spiritual journey. Real trees decorated with fairy lamps in his walled garden in Kensington, Baring's courtyard fig shading the entrance of the underground passage to Westminster, and the timber girders of Chesterton's final home of Top Meadow all excited his artistic vision. His progress through the visual and literary arts clarified his philosophies and allowed him to seek a meaning not realized by the rationalism and subjectivism then being introduced. Chesterton's discovery of orthodox Christianity expressed itself in theme-laden fiction, as the roots of his aesthetic and spiritual formation gave way to the branches of his aesthetic and spiritual expression. The accumulation of tree imagery in his life and fiction is not gratuitous but adds to his larger declaration of God's presence in creation. The theme unifies his life, emerging out of his allegorical imagination as a sacramental motif that becomes encompassing.

Have we been presumptuous by reading too much meaning into Chesterton's image of the tree? It is indisputable that the Christian literary and artistic tradition engages the cosmological tree. Chesterton's own themes are so evidently influenced by this larger literature that, although each instance of the tree in his own stories might not have been conscious and deliberate, yet his overall symbolic purpose is patent. Moreover, the literature that so absorbed him demanded a reading in accordance with the intentions of the author. For example, Chesterton would have understood that *Robinson Crusoe* was not simply an adventure but "a morality of the Christian life."[24] He imparted no less to his own readership. Our mistake would not be one of inappropriate conjecture in looking for metaphysical meaning. George Landow, in describing the loss to our generation

---

[24] Milward, *Christian Themes in English Literature*, 49. Milward specifically mentioned this favourite book of Chesterton as an example of a story that *requires* a Christian reading.

of the intimate biblical knowledge that informed the writers of Chesterton's era, contended that our ignorance of typology causes us rather to "under-read and misread many Victorian works," resulting in the distortion and reduction of the meanings proposed by these authors.[25] Chesterton would certainly have hoped for a boldly symbolic approach by his readers.

It is to be expected that some will reject a reading of Chesterton's fiction that seeks a lucid rendering of his symbolism. Jeffrey suggested that modern critics dislike allegory, which is presently not fashionable, because of its directive nature that disallows the reader to exercise her own interpretation. In the wake of Romanticism, moderns "have tended to be averse to the intellectuality, didacticism, universalized significance, a-temporality, and hierarchically conservative tendency of allegory," preferring to find multiple meanings rather than one unified thought or significance beneath the nuanced symbol.[26] Chesterton himself did not claim a global meaning for the tree. He used it not only as a cohesive and unified religious ensign but sometimes as just scenery, sometimes as an illustration, an exclamation, or a throwaway not obviously developed in the text. But he acknowledged his strong urge to look for meaning beneath symbols, for "every true artist does feel, consciously or unconsciously, that he is touching transcendental truths; that his images are shadows of things seen through the veil."[27] He insisted that "there is something *there*; something behind the clouds or within the trees" that cannot be found through the artistic pursuit of beauty alone.[28] It is only Christian conviction that can perceive the underlying truth, for "religion is revelation,

---

[25] George P. Landow, "Moses Striking the Rock: Typological Symbolism in Victorian Poetry," in *Literary Uses of Typology from the Late Middle Ages to the Present*, ed. Earl Miner (Princeton: Princeton University Press, 1977), 315.

[26] Jeffrey, *Dictionary of Biblical Tradition*, 30.

[27] Chesterton, *Everlasting Man*, 105.

[28] Ibid.

it is a vision, and a vision received by faith; but it is a vision of reality."[29] The discernment of Chesterton's biblical and literary symbolism is linked to a religious revelation of scriptural and traditional truth. Ian Boyd wrote, "It would not be an exaggeration to say that all his writings may be read as an extended commentary on Sacred Scripture."[30]

Lest his reader still be tempted to digest the fiction on a purely artistic basis without reference to an underlying belief system, we must remember Chesterton's own declaration:

> All art is religious. . . . Whatever is [an artist's] conception of the cosmos and the consciousness, that will be in his art, even when his practical private morality is not particularly noticeable in it. . . . I do not say that the pattern of a wall-paper will necessarily teach a moral lesson by examples, or be a woven tracery of the Ten Commandments. But I know a wall-paper pattern of Christendom from a pattern made by Moslems or Hindus.[31]

The creedal doctrines of Chesterton, always the didactic artist, interpenetrated even his purely fictional work in which he felt "compelled to state and re-state the world view of Catholic Christianity."[32] He noted that a casual critic will always ask, "Do you mean that a poet cannot be thankful for grass and wild flowers without connecting it with theology?"[33] To this he answered, "Yes . . . , unless he can do it without connecting it with thought," for artists "can only directly believe in Nature if they

---

[29] Ibid., 243-4.
[30] Boyd, "Chesterton and the Bible," 22.
[31] G. K. Chesterton, *Come To Think Of It*, Essay Index Reprint Series (Freeport, N. Y.: Books for Libraries Press, 1931), 72-73.
[32] Crowther, *G. K. Chesterton*, 49-50.
[33] Chesterton, *Autobiography*, 348.

indirectly believe in God."[34] The universe is not a "blind and indifferent growth," but "a great design," he insisted, warning his readers that when they stop seeking the purpose beneath the beauty, then "the many-coloured forest really is a rag-ball and all the pageant of the dust only a dustbin."[35]

Chesterton's sacramental conception of life, based on a biblical and essentially mystical spirituality, unifies both his impression of God's creation and his literary expression of its meaningful beauty. Whatever Chesterton's genre or topic, "his underlying subject is always the same: the presence of God in created being."[36] In a descriptive passage of the forest that sheltered the fugitives in *The Flying Inn*, for example, Chesterton alluded to this overarching, parental attendance, hinting at the age-old yearning of humanity for divinity, which was sought in the ancient myths and found in the church:

> The hill like a cluster of domes, though smooth and even bare in its lower contours, was topped with a tangle of spreading trees like a bird brooding over its nest. . . . The emerald twilight between the stems, combined with the dragon-like contortions of the great grey roots of the beeches, had a suggestion of monsters and the deep sea . . . . And yet, contradictorily enough, [the travellers] had also a strong sense of being up high; and even near to heaven; and the brilliant summer stars that stared through the chinks of the leafy roof, might almost have been white starry blossoms on the trees of the wood.[37]

---

[34] Ibid, 348-9.

[35] Ibid., 349.

[36] Boyd, "Chesterton and the Bible," 31.

[37] Chesterton, *Flying Inn*, 671. For God/bird imagery, see, e.g., Ps. 91:4; Luke 13:34.

Along with his story characters, Chesterton saw the branching tree as "a friend with arms open for the man."[38] For him:

> When the voice spoke from between the outstretched arms of the Crucified, those arms were truly opened wide, and opening most gloriously the gates of all the worlds; they were arms pointing to the east and to the west, to the ends of the earth and the very extremes of existence. They were truly spread out with a gesture of omnipotent generosity; the Creator himself offering Creation itself.[39]

Chesterton's was "a religious imagination which seeks to interpret the many signs of a sacramental universe through which God speaks to man."[40] His conviction of the thumbprint of God upon the primary creation stimulated his own creative response of religious allegory as an expression of worship, which is in itself sacramental in nature. Chesterton's telling of the story is the pouring of his wine, the growing of his tree. In his fiction, the tree is a joyful re-creation of God's message to His beloved creature through nature—a mirror image of the truth of His presence. As he said through Adam Wayne, "I am doing what I have done all my life, what is the only happiness, what is the only universality. I am clinging to something."[41]

In this way G. K. Chesterton has administered the rich literary symbolism of the tree as an invocation—an outward and visible symbol of an inward and spiritual grace.

---

[38] Chesterton, *Flying Inn*, 725.

[39] Chesterton, *Saint Thomas Aquinas*, 135. Chesterton was here describing St. Thomas but could just as easily have been speaking about his own beliefs.

[40] Boyd, "In Search of the Essential Chesterton," 44.

[41] Chesterton, *Napoleon of Notting Hill*, 124.

BIBLIOGRAPHY

Primary Sources
(Arranged in alphabetical order)

Chesterton, Gilbert Keith. *The Autobiography of G. K. Chesterton*. New York: Sheed and Ward, 1936.

_____. *The Ball and the Cross*. Dover Publications: New York, 1995.

_____. *The Club of Queer Trades*. Hertfordshire: Wordsworth Editions, 1995.

_____. *The Collected Works of G. K. Chesterton*. Edited by David Dooley. Volume 1, *Orthodoxy, Heretics, Blatchford Controversy*. San Francisco: Ignatius, 1986.

_____. *The Collected Works of G. K. Chesterton*. Edited by George J. Marlin and Richard P. Rabatin. Volume 8, *The Return of Don Quixote, Tales of the Long Bow, The Man Who Knew Too Much*. San Francisco: Ignatius Press, 1999.

_____. *The Collected Works of G. K. Chesterton*. Edited by George J. Marlin, Richard P. Rabatin, and John L. Swan. Volume 14, *Short Stories, Fairy Tales, Mystery Stories, Illustrations*. San Francisco: Ignatius Press, 1993.

_____. *The Coloured Lands*. New York: Sheed and Ward, 1938.

_____. *Come To Think Of It*. Essay Index Reprint Series. Freeport, N.Y.: Books for Libraries Press, 1931.

_____. *The Complete Father Brown*. London: Penguin Books, 1981.

_____. *The Everlasting Man*. San Francisco: Ignatius Press, 1993.

_____. *The Flying Inn*. In *A G. K. Chesterton Omnibus*. London: Methuen, 1947.

_____. *Four Faultless Felons*. New York: Dover Publications, 1989.

_____. *G. F. Watts*. London: Duckworth, 1904.

_____. "In Topsy-Turvy Land." In *Tremendous Trifles*, 81-86. London: Methuen, 1909.

_____. *Manalive*. G. K. Chesterton Reprint Series. Beaconsfield: Darwen Finlayson, 1962.

_____. *The Man Who Was Thursday: A Nightmare*. Edited by Stephen Medcalf. Oxford: Oxford University Press, 1996.

_____. *The Outline of Sanity*. London: Methuen, 1926.

_____. *The Napoleon of Notting Hill*. Ware, U.K.: Wordsworth Editions, 1996.

_____. *The Paradoxes of Mr. Pond*. New York: Dover Publications, 1990.

_____. *The Poet and the Lunatics: Episodes in the Life of Gabriel Gale*. London: Cassell and Company, 1929.

_____. "The Protection of the Bible." *Chesterton Review* 22, no. 3 (1996): 289-91.

_____. "Puritan and Anglican." *Chesterton Review* 9, no. 4 (1983): 304-7.

_____. *The Riddle of the Ivy*. London: Methuen, 1909.

_____. *Saint Thomas Aquinas: The Dumb Ox*. New York: Doubleday, 1956.

_____. *The Victorian Age in Literature*. London: Oxford University Press, 1955.

_____. *What's Wrong with the World*. London: Cassell and Company, 1912.

_____. "The Wind and the Trees." In *Tremendous Trifles*, 69-80. London: Methuen, 1909.

_____. *The Works of G. K. Chesterton*. The Wordsworth Poetry Library. Hertfordshire: Wordsworth Editions, 1995.

Secondary Sources

Allison, Alexander W., Herbert Barrows, Caesar R. Blake, Arthur J. Carr, Arthur M. Eastman, and Hubert M. English Jr., eds. *The Norton Anthology of Poetry*, 3rd ed. New York: W. W. Norton and Company, 1983.

Asquith, Michael. "G. K. Chesterton: Prophet and Jester." In *G. K. Chesterton: A Half Century of Views*, ed. Denis J. Conlon, 118-23. Oxford: Oxford University Press, 1987.

Augustine. *Saint Augustine: Confessions*. Translated by R. S. Pine-Coffin. London: Penguin Books, 1961.

Avni, Abraham Albert. *The Bible and Romanticism: The Old Testament in German and French Romantic Poetry*. Studies in General and Comparative Literature 6. The Hague, Paris: Mouton, 1969.

160

_____. "The Influence of the Bible on European Literatures: A Review of Research from 1955-1965." *Yearbook of Comparative and General Literature* 19 (1970): 39-57.

Barker, Dudley. *G. K. Chesterton*. London: Constable Publishing, 1973.

Belloc, Hilaire. *On the Place of Gilbert Chesterton in English Letters*. New York: Sheed and Ward, 1940.

Blake, William. In Alexander W. Allison and others, eds. *The Norton Anthology of Poetry*, 3 ed. New York: Norton, 1983, 496-510, passim.

Boyd, Ian. "Chesterton and the Bible." *Chesterton Review* 11, no. 1 (1985): 21-31.

_____. "In Search of the Essential Chesterton." *Seven* 1 (1980): 28-45.

_____. "The Legendary Chesterton." In *G. K. Chesterton and C. S. Lewis: The Riddle of Joy*, ed. Michael H. Macdonald and Andrew A. Tadie, 53-68. Grand Rapids: Eerdmans, 1989.

_____. *Novels of G. K. Chesterton: A Study in Art and Propaganda*. London: Paul Elek, 1975.

_____. "Philosophy in Fiction." In *G. K. Chesterton: A Centenary Appraisal*, ed. John Sullivan, 40-57. London: Paul Elek, 1974.

Braybrooke, Patrick. *The Wisdom of G. K. Chesterton*. London: Cecil Palmer, 1929.

Brumm, Ursula. "The 'Tree of Life' in Edward Taylor's *Meditations*." *Early American Literature* 3 (1968): 72-87.

Calvin, Jean. *Institutes of the Christian Religion*. 2 Volumes. Edited by John T. McNeill. Philadelphia: The Westminster Press, 1960.

Chaucer, Geoffrey. From *The Canterbury Tales*. In Alexander W. Allison and others, eds. *The Norton Anthology of Poetry*, 3 ed. New York: Norton, 1983, 6-52.

[Chesterton, Cecil]. *G. K. Chesterton: A Criticism*. American ed. New York: John Lane Company, 1909.

Clemens, Cyril. *Chesterton As Seen by His Contemporaries*. New York: Haskell House Publishers, 1969.

Clipper, Lawrence J. *G. K. Chesterton*. Twayne's English Authors Series, ed. Sylvia E. Bowman. New York: Twayne Publishers, 1974.

Coates, John. "*The Ball and the Cross* and the Edwardian Novel of Ideas." *Chesterton Review* 18, no. 1 (1992): 19-81.

_____. "Symbol and Structure in *The Flying Inn*." *Chesterton Review* 4, no. 2 (1978): 246-59.

Cock, Douglas J. "Chesterton in Fiction." *Chesterton Review* 18, no. 3 (1992): 385-9.

_____. "A Protestant View of Chesterton." *Chesterton Review* 17, no. 1 (1991): 25-31.

Colebatch, Hal G. P. "The Meanings of *The Napoleon of Notting Hill*." *Chesterton Review* 25, no. 4 (1999): 437-49.

Collette, Carolyn P. "'*Ubi Peccaverant, Ibi Punirentur*': The Oak Tree and the Pardoner's Tale." *Chaucer Review* 19 (1984): 39-45.

Cook, Roger. *The Tree of Life: Symbols of the Centre*. London: Thames and Hudson, 1974.

Coren, Michael. *Gilbert: The Man Who Was G. K. Chesterton*. London: Jonathan Cape, 1989.

Crowther, Ian. *G. K. Chesterton*. Thinkers of our Time. London: The Claridge Press, 1991.

Dale, Alzina Stone. "G. K. Chesterton, the Disreputable Victorian." In *G. K. Chesterton and C. S. Lewis: The Riddle of Joy*, ed. Michael H. Macdonald and Andrew A. Tadie, 141-59. Grand Rapids: Eerdmans, 1989.

_____. *The Outline of Sanity: A Biography of G. K. Chesterton*. Grand Rapids: Eerdmans, 1982.

_____. "Some Ideas on a Christian Core Curriculum from the Writings of G. K. Chesterton, T. S. Eliot, and Dorothy L. Sayers." In *Permanent Things: Toward the Recovery of a More Human Scale at the End of the Twentieth Century*, ed. Andrew A. Tadie and Michael H. Macdonald, 253-70. Grand Rapids: Eerdmans, 1995.

Dante. *The Comedy of Dante Alighieri the Florentine*. Translated and ed. by Dorothy L. Sayers. 3 volumes. London: Penguin Books, 1949.

Donne, John. "Sonnet 14." In *Holy Sonnets*. In Alexander W. Allison and others, eds. *The Norton Anthology of Poetry*, 3 ed. New York: Norton, 1983, 220-2.

Duncan, Joseph E. *Milton's Earthly Paradise: A Historical Study of Eden*. Minneapolis: University of Minnesota Press, 1972.

Fagerberg, David W. "Chesterton on Ritual." *Worship* 71, (May 1997): 194-205.

163

6

Ffinch, Michael. *G. K. Chesterton*. San Francisco: Harper and Row, 1986.

Fowler, David C. *The Bible in Early English Literature*. London: Sheldon Press, 1977.

Gardner, Martin. "Levels of Allegory in *The Ball and the Cross*." *Chesterton Review* 18, no. 1 (1992): 37.

Greenhill, Eleanor Simmons. "The Child in the Tree: A Study of the Cosmological Tree in Christian Religion." *Traditio* 10 (1954): 323-71.

Gushurst-Moore, Andre P. "Reality, Illusion and Art in the *Father Brown* Stories." *Chesterton Review* 24, no. 3 (1998): 321-7.

Halbert, Cecelia L. "Tree of Life Imagery in the Poetry of Edward Taylor." *American Literature* 38 (1966): 22-34.

Haussy, Christiane d'. "The Symbolism of the Key in Chesterton's Work." *Seven* 4 (1983): 38-44.

Hein, Rolland. "G. K. Chesterton: Myth, Paradox, and the Commonplace." *Seven* 13 (1996): 13-24.

Herbert, George. *The Works of George Herbert*. Hertfordshire, U.K.: Wordsworth Editions, 1994.

Hetzler, Leo A. "Chesterton's Writings in His Teenage Years." In *G. K. Chesterton: A Half Century of Views*, ed. Denis J. Conlon, 291-300. Oxford: Oxford University Press, 1987.

Hippolytus of Rome. "The Lord is my Shepherd." In *Fragment of Discourses or Homilies* 6. No Date. Accessed 25 October 2014. http://www.newadvent.org/fathers/0502.htm.

Hollis, Christopher. *The Mind of Chesterton*. Coral Gables, FL: University of Miami Press, 1970.

Horne, Brian L. "'Art: A Trinitarian Imperative?'." In
Trinitarian Theology Today, ed. Christoph
Schwobel, 80-91. Edinburgh: T. and T. Clark,
1995.

Hunt, Peter R. "Dickens's Influence on Chesterton's Imaginative Writing." *Chesterton Review* 7, no. 1
(1981): 36-49.

Hunter, Lynette. *G. K. Chesterton: Explorations in Allegory*. New York: St. Martin's Press, 1979.

_____. "A Reading of *The Napoleon of Notting Hill*."
Chesterton Review III, no. 1 (1976-77): 119-28.

Jeffrey, David Lyle. *People of the Book: Christian Identity and Literary Culture*. Grand Rapids: Eerdmans,
with The Institute for Advanced Christian Studies,
1996.

_____, ed. *A Dictionary of Biblical Tradition in Eng-
lish Literature*. Grand Rapids: Eerdmans, 1992.

Katzenellenbogen, Adolf. *Allegories of the Virtues and
Vices in Mediaeval Art*. London: The Warburg Institute, 1939.

Knedlik, Janet Blumberg. "Derrida Meets Father Brown:
Chestertonian 'Deconstructionism' and that Har-
lequin 'Joy'." In *G. K. Chesterton and C. S. Lewis:
The Riddle of Joy*, ed. Michael H. Macdonald and
Andrew A. Tadie, 273-89. Grand Rapids: Eerd-
mans, 1989.

Knox, Ronald. "Chesterton's Father Brown." In *G. K.
Chesterton: A Half Century of Views*, ed. Denis J.
Conlon, 133-9. Oxford: Oxford University Press,
1987.

_____. "G. K. Chesterton: The Man and His Work."
In *G. K. Chesterton: A Half Century of Views*, ed.
Denis J. Conlon, 46-49. Oxford: Oxford University
Press, 1987.

Ladner, Gerhart B. "Vegetation Symbolism and the Con-
cept of Renaissance." In *De Artibus Opuscula XL:
Essays in Honor of Erwin Panofsky*, ed. Millard
Meiss, 1, 303-22. New York: New York University
Press, 1961.

Landow, George P. "Moses Striking the Rock: Typological Symbolism in Victorian Poetry." In *Literary
Uses of Typology from the Late Middle Ages to
the Present*, ed. Earl Miner, 315-44. Princeton:
Princeton University Press, 1977.

Leigh, David. "The Psychology of Conversion in Chesterton's and Lewis's Autobiographies." In *G. K.
Chesterton and C. S. Lewis: The Riddle of Joy*,
ed. Michael H. Macdonald and Andrew A. Tadie,
290-304. Grand Rapids: Eerdmans, 1989.

Lodge, David. "Dual Vision: Chesterton as a Novelist." In
G. K. Chesterton: A Half Century of Views, ed.
Denis J. Conlon, 326-35. Oxford: Oxford Univer-
sity Press, 1987.

Manganiello, Dominic. "'Where in Hell Are We?': Chesterton on Dante." *Chesterton Review* 20, no. 1
(1994): 65-81.

McLuhan, H. Marshall. "G. K. Chesterton: A Practical
Mystic." In *G. K. Chesterton: A Half Century of
Views*, ed. Denis J. Conlon, 1-10. Oxford: Oxford
University Press, 1987.

Medcalf, Stephan. "The Achievement of G. K. Chesterton." In *G. K. Chesterton: A Centenary Appraisal*,
ed. John Sullivan, 81-21. London: Paul Elek,
1974.

Meir ben Isaac, "Akdamut." In *Or Hadash: A Commentary on Siddur Sim Shalom for Shabbat and Festivals*, by Reuven Hammar New York: The Rabbinical Assembly, 2003. Accessed 25 October 2014. http://www.rabbinicalassembly.org/sites/default/files/public/jewish-law/holidays/shavuot/akdamut-from-or-hadash.pdf.

Milton, John. *Paradise Lost and Paradise Regained*. Christopher Ricks, ed. Signet Classic Poetry Edition. New York: Penguin Books, 1968.

Milward, Peter. *Christian Themes in English Literature*. N.P.: Folcroft Press, 1967.

Morris, Kevin L. "Chesterton Sees Red: The Metaphysics of a Colour." *Chesterton Review* 21, no. 4 (1995): 505-17.

Morris, Paul. "Exiled from Eden: Jewish Interpretation of Genesis." In *A Walk in the Garden: Biblical, Iconographical and Literary Images of Eden*, ed. Paul Morris and Deborah Sawyer, 21-38. Sheffield, U.K.: JSOT Press, Sheffield Academic Press, 1992.

Nelson, Lawrence E. *Our Roving Bible: Tracking Its Influence Through English And American Life*. New York: Abingdon-Cokesbury Press, 1945.

"Now Go'th Sun Under Wood" in Alexander W. Allison and others, eds. *The Norton Anthology of Poetry*, 3 ed. (New York: Norton, 1983), 3.

O'Connor, John. *Father Brown on Chesterton*. London: Frederick Muller, 1937.

O'Reilly, Jennifer. "The Trees of Eden in Mediaeval Iconography." In *A Walk in the Garden: Biblical, Iconographical and Literary Images of Eden*, ed. Paul Morris and Deborah Sawyer, 167-202.

Sheffield, U.K.: JSOT Press, Sheffield Academic Press, 1992.

Pascal, Blaise. *Pensées and Other Writings*. Translated by Honor Levi. The World's Classics. Oxford: Oxford University Press, 1995.

Pearce, Joseph. *Wisdom and Innocence: A Life of G. K. Chesterton*. London: Hodder and Stoughton, 1996.

Peters, Thomas. *The Christian Imagination: G. K. Chesterton on the Arts*. San Francisco: Ignatius Press, 2000.

Peterson, John. "Father Brown's War on the Impermanent Things." In *Permanent Things: Toward the Recovery of a More Human Scale at the End of the Twentieth Century*, ed. Andrew A. Tadie and Michael H. Macdonald, 17-30. Grand Rapids: Eerdmans, 1995.

_____. "The Nutshell," *Gilbert Magazine*, December 2000, 7.

Phillips, Helen. "Gardens of Love and the Garden of the Fall." In *A Walk in the Garden: Biblical, Iconographical and Literary Images of Eden*, ed. Paul Morris and Deborah Sawyer, 205-19. Sheffield, U.K.: JSOT Press, Sheffield Academic Press, 1992.

Pope, Alexander. *The Works of Alexander Pope*. Hertfordshire, U.K.: Wordsworth Editions, 1995.

Race, Herbert. *Gilbert Keith Chesterton: Essays*. Notes on Chosen English Texts, ed. Norman T. Carrington. London: James Brodie, 1961.

Reckitt, Maurice B. *G. K. Chesterton: A Christian Prophet for England To-day*. London: S. P. C. K., 1950.

168

Sheed, Wilfred. "On Chesterton." In *G. K. Chesterton: A Half Century of Views*, ed. Denis J. Conlon, 162-78. Oxford: Oxford University Press, 1987.

Schwartz, Adam. "G. K. C.'s Methodical Madness: Sanity and Social Control in Chesterton." *Renascence: Essays on Values in Literature* 49, no. 1 (1996): 23-40.

Sparkes, Russell, ed. *Prophet Of Orthodoxy: The Wisdom of G. K. Chesterton*. London: HarperCollins Publishers, 1997.

Spenser, Edmund. *The Works of Edmund Spenser*. Hertfordshire, U.K.: Wordsworth Editions, 1995.

Stevenson, Robert Louis. *The Best Known Works of Robert Louis Stevenson*. New York: The Book League of America, n. d.

Sullivan, John. *G. K. Chesterton: A Bibliography*. London: University of London Press, 1958.

_____, ed. *Chesterton Continued: A Bibliographical Supplement*. London: University of London Press, 1968.

Tennyson, G. B. " 'So Careful of the Type?'—Victorian Biblical Typology: Sources and Applications." *Essays and Studies: New Series* 37 (1984): 31-45.

Ward, Maisie. *Gilbert Keith Chesterton*. London: Sheed and Ward, 1944.

Watson, Arthur. *The Early Iconography of the Tree of Jesse*. London: Oxford University Press, 1934.

White, Gertrude M. "Mirror and Microcosm: Chesterton's Father Brown Stories." *Chesterton Review* 10, no. 2 (1984): 183-97.

Wills, Garry. *Chesterton: Man and Mask*. New York:
     Sheed and Ward, 1961.

_____. "The Man Who Was Thursday." In *G. K.
     Chesterton: A Half Century of Views*, ed. Denis J.
     Conlon, 335-42. Oxford: Oxford University Press,
     1987.

THE SONG OF THE OAK

The Song of the Oak

(G. K. Chesterton, "Pub Poetry" from *The Flying Inn*)

The Druids waved their golden knives
And danced around the Oak
When they had sacrificed a man;
But though the learned search and scan,
No single modern person can
Entirely see the joke.
But though they cut the throats of men
They cut not down the tree,
And from the blood the saplings sprang
Of oak-woods yet to be,

But Ivywood, Lord Ivywood,
He rots the tree as ivy would,
He clings and crawls as ivy would
About the sacred tree.

King Charles he fled from Worcester fight
And hid him in an Oak;
In convent schools no man of tact
Would trace and praise his every act,
Or argue that he was in fact
A strict and sainted bloke,
But not by him the sacred woods
Have lost their fancies free,
And though he was extremely big
He did not break the tree.

But Ivywood, Lord Ivywood,
He breaks the tree as ivy would,
He eats the woods as ivy would
Between us and the sea.

Great Collingwood walked down the glade
And flung the acorns free,
That oaks might still be in the grove
As oaken as the beams above,
When the great Lover sailors love
Was kissed by death at sea.
But though for him the oak-trees fell
To build the oaken ships
The woodman worshipped what he smote
And honoured even the chips.

But Ivywood, Lord Ivywood,
He hates the tree as ivy would,
As the dragon of the ivy would
That has us in its grips.

PART II

THE SEVEN MOODS OF GILBERT: CONVERSION NARRATIVE IN *THE FLYING INN*

The Seven Moods of Gilbert:
Conversion Narrative in *The Flying Inn*

Dorian Wimpole has had a change of heart.

As merely a secondary character in *The Flying Inn*, G. K. Chesterton's exuberant 1914 novel, Dorian's message is easily overlooked. Despite his "singular entrance and exit" in relation to the parlours of the aristocracy, his quiet actions are eclipsed by the woodland adventures of Dalroy and Pump, the parliamentary intrigues of Lord Ivywood, and the religious antics of Misysra Ammon, Prophet of the Moon.[1] With a tongue-in-cheek reproach against such Chestertonian peeves as teetotalism, Impressionism, and corrupt government, *The Flying Inn* offers social and political commentary on Edwardian England, written as it was on the eve of the First World War when American Prohibition and the Temperance movement threatened the existence of British pubs. It was received in its time as "a light diversion" emphasizing "the importance of sheer fun."[2] Indeed, the drinking songs from this book (printed in a separate volume as *Wine, Water and Song*) became a part of Chesterton's own popular culture, finding their way even into meetings of the Fabian society.[3] But more serious criticism followed the early analysis of its puzzling array of themes, plot twists, and emblematic characters; for example, John Coates (who dubbed *The Flying Inn* Chesterton's "most underrated novel") found it to be a coherent political, social, philosophical, and religious

---

[1] G. K. Chesterton, *The Flying Inn*, in *A G. K. Chesterton Omnibus* (London: Metheun and Co., 1947), 608.

[2] John Coates, "Malaise at the Heart of *The Flying Inn*," *Seven: An Anglo-American Review* 8 (1987): 25.

[3] As noted by Christopher Hollis, *The Mind of Chesterton* (Coral Gables, FL: University of Miami Press, 1970), 145.

statement.[4] Yet he demurred from "explaining" the novel, as did Chesterton himself, who described *The Flying Inn* as "a harlequinade" at which he failed, "an extremely promising subject—for somebody else."[5] Despite critical appreciation for the richness of the work and Chesterton's own humble disclaimer, the novel's abundance might be interpreted through the eyes of the forgotten character, Dorian, whose story summarizes perhaps the foremost theme of the book. *The Flying Inn* is a narrative of conversion in which the subplot of Dorian Wimpole stands as an encapsulating example, bearing similarity to Chesterton's own spiritual journey.

Let us briefly review *The Flying Inn*. Lord Philip Ivywood, a diplomatic Member of Parliament and a Nietzschean fatalist of "faultless and hueless face" who misunderstands "the animal side of man," has used his influence to shut down the inns of England, reserving for only the upper classes the right to imbibe spirits.[6] The Turkish Misysra Ammon promotes a syncretistic interpretation of Islam, making his way from a dwindling audience on the beach, via the middle-class Society of Simple Souls, into the elite of England through the patronage of Ivywood. He preaches a restrictive message of alcoholic abstention and vegetarianism in the drawing rooms of the inebriated and gluttonous, who are no longer "oppressed by the passing superstitions of the Galilaeans."[7] Meanwhile, the common man, who has been unwillingly delivered from the "curse of wine" by the closing of the public houses, cheers on two hero rebels: Captain Patrick Dalroy is an Irish revolutionary

---

[4] John Coates, "The Philosophy and Religious Background of *The Flying Inn*," *The Chesterton Review* 12, no. 3 (1986): 326; see also John Coates, "Symbol and Structure in *The Flying Inn*," *The Chesterton Review* 4, no. 2 (1978): 246-59.

[5] G. K. Chesterton, *Autobiography*, ed. David Dooley, in *The Collected Works of G. K. Chesterton*, vol. 16 (San Francisco: Ignatius, 1988), 276.

[6] Chesterton, *The Flying Inn*, 562, 540.

[7] Ibid., 440.

sworn to uphold the British people's personal liberty and right of choice; he enlists dispossessed pub owner Humphrey Pump whose domestic mind is "a rich soil of subconscious memories and traditions."[8] Dalroy and Pump uproot the cross-emblazoned, wooden signpost of The Old Ship Inn and flee with a cask of rum and a wheel of cheese that they freely dispense almost sacramentally, relying on a legal loophole guaranteeing liquor may be served anywhere an inn sign is planted.

Several other characters affect the story line. The sceptical and bored Lady Joan Brett is in love with Captain Dalroy but being wooed into Lord Ivywood's harem—an institution now legalized out of English respect for the Moslem family.[9] The relativistic journalist, Hibbs However, is a higher critic whose subjective interpretation of the news has "scattered the brains of all men."[10] Dorian Wimpole is an aristocrat who begins in the camp of the elite and is drawn away from his academic inactivity towards the revolutionary zeal of the fugitives. For each character, the choice is the same: to passively follow the vague, wandering, and intrusive Eastern teachings (that end in the monomaniacal solipsism of Ivywood, who believes himself to be God) or to join the deliberate forest journey of the loyal Christian British forces beneath the mobilized sign of the inn (that promotes spiritual self-determinism and leads to reclamation of democracy).

The fictional characters of *The Flying Inn* reflect aspects of Chesterton's own life and disposition, as seen in his more overtly autobiographical writings. Like Ivywood, for example, Chesterton as a young man was caught in a nightmare, in danger of becoming "a monomaniac about a notion" merely because it was his own.[11] The ethics and theology of Chesterton's late-Victorian society were "wearing thin," producing a religious hunger in him resembling the curiosity of the "simple souls"

---

[8] Ibid., 430, 434.
[9] Ibid., 426-8.
[10] Ibid., 510.
[11] Chesterton, *Autobiography*, 328.

of *The Flying Inn*'s England.[12] Like Lady Joan, Chesterton attended a "strange club where somebody was lecturing on Nietzsche" in a fashion replayed by his character Misysra; Chesterton's introduction there to the Dalroy-like curate, Conrad Noel, caused "dreadful seeds of doubt" to be sown in his mind concerning his own anti-clerical attitude and spiritual beliefs.[13] As Dorian begins to question the view of the vegetarians because of Dalroy's lusty test of truth and commonsense applied to the current philosophies, so Chesterton began a "serious consideration of the theory of a Church" because of the humorous, idealistic, and eccentric Reverend Noel. [14] Chesterton, then, identified himself almost schizophrenically with many of his characters in *The Flying Inn*. It is not surprising to see such a variety of limited metaphors to his real-life experiences in a single piece of his fictional writing, for (as Dorothy Sayers commented on the relationship between a creative work and its creator) no author is completely revealed in a single work or character.[15] Only a synthesis of all Chesterton's writing would prove that his outlook on life was unified—a redundant task.[16] We must be more specific. Our purpose in focusing on the elected character of Dorian Wimpole in *The Flying Inn* is to seek analogical and autobiographical reflections of Chesterton's own conversion.

To say that Chesterton intended a religious and didactic reading of Dorian's fictional transformation is almost tautological. Hillaire Belloc, for example, early on noted his friend's active teaching through parallelism,

---

[12] Ibid., 36.

[13] Ibid., 154.

[14] Ibid., 155-9.

[15] Dorothy L. Sayers, *The Mind of the Maker* (San Francisco: HarperCollins, 1968), 55.

[16] See, e.g., Alzina Stone Dale, *The Outline of Sanity: A Biography of G. K. Chesterton* (Grand Rapids: William B. Eerdmans Publishing Company, 1982), 130-1.

simile, and metaphor.[17] More recently, Ian Boyd called all Chesterton's novels powerful allegory meant to teach and persuade, meant to "interpret the many signs of a sacramental universe through which God speaks to man."[18] Although Chesterton's socio-political motives through fiction have been discussed, many scholars have also supported a vigorously theological interpretation of his journalism and his fiction. Lynette Hunter, for example, found in *The Flying Inn* a contrast between the creeds of perfectionistic fatalism and catholic Christianity.[19] Ian Crowther maintained that Chesterton stated and re-stated a Christian world view, even in his fiction.[20] Chesterton has been dubbed a "metaphysical moralist,"[21] and Marshall McLuhan encouraged Chesterton's readers to abandon a purely literary and journalistic appraisal in favour of seeking his contemporary moral relevance through his use of analogy.[22] The critics have been convincing in their appraisal of Chesterton's works as primarily religious.

Not only scholarly testimony but also his own attestations indicate that Chesterton himself intended a religious reading of every detail for, as he said, a writer

---

[17] Hilaire Belloc, *On the Place of Gilbert Chesterton in English Letters* (New York: Sheed and Ward, 1940), 15, 39.

[18] See Ian Boyd, *Novels of G. K. Chesterton: A Study in Art and Progaganda* (London: Paul Elek, 1975), preface, xi; Ian Boyd, "In Search of the Essential Chesterton," *Seven: An Anglo-American Review* 1 (1980): 44.

[19] Lynette Hunter, *G. K. Chesterton: Explorations in Allegory* (New York: St. Martin's Press, 1979), 109.

[20] See Ian Crowther, *G. K. Chesterton*, Thinkers of our Time (London: The Claridge Press, 1991), 49-50.

[21] Hugh Kenner, *Paradox in Chesterton* (New York: Sheed and Ward, 1947), xxi.

[22] See H. Marshall McLuhan, "Where Chesterton Comes In," in *G. K. Chesterton: A Half Century of Views*, ed. D. J. Conlon (Oxford: Oxford University Press, 1987), 77.

"cannot be thankful for grass and wild flowers without connecting it with theology."[23] He declared all art to be religious.[24] Chesterton doubted "whether any of our actions is really anything but an allegory . . . whether any truth can be told except in a parable."[25] He employed religious images (familiar from other works) that demand our symbolic interpretation: compare the use of wine in this novel to Father Brown's recurring sacramental metaphor of the wine-washed world.[26] Again, an early scene in *The Flying Inn* pits freedom against tyranny when the hero (angry over the destruction of the vineyards) uproots an olive tree at a diplomatic conference promoting peace at all costs; in the same way, the hero of *The Napoleon of Notting Hill* uproots a great tree when faced with similar military and spiritual battle.[27]

---

[23] Chesterton, *Autobiography*, 325. "Consider the lilies" of Luke 12:27.

[24] G. K. Chesterton, *Come To Think Of It*, Essay Index Reprint Series (Freeport, N. Y.: Books for Libraries Press, 1931), 72-73. Cf. Matthew 7:16, 20 in which the heart of a person is known, as is a tree, by its fruits.

[25] As spoken by his fictional character, Gabriel Gale, in G. K. Chesterton, *The Poet and the Lunatics: Episodes in the Life of Gabriel Gale* (London: Cassell and Company, 1929), 130. In Matthew 13:34, Jesus spoke to the multitudes, "and without a parable spake he not unto them."

[26] See Chesterton, *The Flying Inn*, 464; cf. "The Secret of Father Brown" in G. K. Chesterton, *The Complete Father Brown* (London: Penguin Books Limited, 1981), 466. Cf. Matthew 26:28, where Jesus said of the wine, "This is my blood," and Colossians 1:20, in which Christ's blood reconciles "all things" heavenly and earthly to Himself.

[27] Chesterton, *The Flying Inn*, 428-31; cf. G. K. Chesterton, *The Napoleon of Notting Hill* (Ware, GB: Wordsworth Editions, 1996), 122-4. See also the uprooting of nations and personal hope in Jeremiah 45:4 and Job 19:10; for salvific imagery see Genesis 2:9, 17 for the Tree of Knowledge, Genesis 1:2 and Revelation 2:7,

The Flying Inn repeatedly pictures the moon as a symbol for fatalism, a detached intellectualism that Chesterton described elsewhere as "light without heat . . . secondary light, reflected from a dead world."[28] The creeping syncretism of "Chrislam" (Ivywood's new religion of progress) blends together the symbols of cross and crescent to form the new "Croscent," reminding the reader of Chesterton's earlier synthesis of shapes in *The Ball and the Cross*, which symbolizes as well the battle between rationalism and Christianity.[29] The illustration of sunset and daybreak as spiritual death and re-awakening can be seen also in *The Man Who Was Thursday*, which opens at dusk in the "disastrous twilight" of anarchy and closes at the hopeful sunrise.[30] The wind of free will blowing through *The Flying Inn* likewise animates the traveller in *Manalive,* on a journey seeking his spiritual home, for "Man has always lost his way. He has been a tramp ever since Eden."[31] Others have noted

---

22:2 for the Tree of Life, and Galatians 3:13 for the tree of the cross.

[28] See, e.g., Chesterton, *The Flying Inn*, 519, 524, 720; see also G. K. Chesterton, *Orthodoxy*, ed. David Dooley, in *The Collected Works of G. K. Chesterton*, vol. 1 (San Francisco: Ignatius, 1986), 231-2. Cf. Job 25:5 on the dullness of the moon and the depravity of man.

[29] See Chesterton, *The Flying Inn*, 530, 447; G. K. Chesterton, *The Ball and the Cross* (Dover Publications: New York, 1995), 4-5. Cf. G. K. Chesterton, *Saint Thomas Aquinas: The Dumb Ox* (New York: Doubleday, 1956), 84. See also Ephesians 2:11-22 for reconciliation and triumph through the cross.

[30] G. K. Chesterton, *The Man Who Was Thursday: A Nightmare*, ed. Stephen Medcalf (Oxford: Oxford University Press, 1996), 43. Cf. Romans 13:11-12 for a picture of the works of darkness and the dawn of salvation, John 3:21 for Christ's symbolic figuring of conversion as moving from darkness to light.

[31] G. K. Chesterton, *Manalive*, G. K. Chesterton Reprint Series (Beaconsfield: Darwen Finlayson, 1962),

this emphasis by Chesterton on "the constant journeys, the wandering search," and the *via crucis* is an expedition Chesterton elsewhere set in a fictional forest. [32] These reiterated images of wine and tree and cross, of moon, sun, wind, and the journey home convince us that Chesterton had religious motives in writing *The Flying Inn*. Moreover, even the fictional and antagonistic higher critics of Dorian's day describe the mystery of the vanishing pub sign as "a curious parallel to the Gospel narrative."[33] It is not surprising, then, to find in this novel a chapter entitled "The Seven Moods of Dorian" (in which the character undergoes a "very considerable and rather valuable change") offering a step-by-step guide through the silver fairylands that are the Dantesque wood of personal reformation in Dorian's own dark night of the soul.[34]

9-10, 155-6. Cf. John 3:8 for the wind of the Spirit. See also G. K. Chesterton, *What's Wrong with the World* (London: Cassell and Company, 1912), 65.

[32] See, e.g., Peter R. Hunt, "Dickens's Influence on Chesterton's Imaginative Writing," *Chesterton Review* 7, no. 1 (1981): 39. See further "The Tower of Treason" in G. K. Chesterton, *The Collected Works of G. K. Chesterton: The Return of Don Quixote, Tales of the Long Bow, The Man Who Knew Too Much*, ed. George J. Marlin and Richard P. Rabatin, vol. 8 (San Francisco: Ignatius Press, 1999), 713-4. For the Old Testament journey theme, see T. Desmond Alexander, *From Paradise to the Promised Land: An Introduction to the Main Themes of the Pentateuch* (Grand Rapids: Baker Books, 1995). Cf. Genesis 2:9, 3:22-24, Revelation 21:1-22:5 for the return to Eden, and Hebrews 4:1-11 regarding spiritual journeyers entering rest.

[33] Chesterton, *The Flying Inn*, 510.

[34] Ibid., 594, 580. The occurrence of Dante's dark wood of choice seen in other of Chesterton's work has been noted elsewhere; see Dominic Manganiello, " 'Where in Hell Are We?': Chesterton on Dante," *The Chesterton Review* 20, no. 1 (1994): 65-81.

The evidence endorsing a religious reading of Chesterton's novel does not, however, mandate an autobiographical interpretation. That is, just because Chesterton's fiction is theologically informed does not prove he intended it to describe his own affective conversion. However, others have read his fiction as autobiographical.[35] David Leigh, for example, found that Chesterton's use of allegorical fiction reveals intense convictions about his personal transformation, and that his allegory, apologetical essay, and autobiography all express his conversion to Christianity.[36] If we can demonstrate that Dorian's sojourn in the wood and resulting rejection of Ivywood's principles constitute a type of conversion, and note some similarities to Chesterton's own phases of spiritual enlightenment, we make a case for the thesis that Dorian's philosophical change is Chesterton's spiritual conversion. Before considering the parallels between Dorian's fictional moods and Chesterton's spiritual course, it would be helpful to consider the definition of conversion and its literary genre, the conversion narrative.

Definition of Conversion

In understanding Dorian's tale as a fictional conversion narrative, we are not entering the denominational discussion so thoroughly undertaken by others regarding Chesterton's 1922 reception into the Roman Catholic

---

[35] See, e.g., Hollis, *The Mind of Chesterton*, 59-60; see also Ian Boyd, "The Legendary Chesterton," in *G. K. Chesterton and C. S. Lewis: The Riddle of Joy*, ed. Michael H. Macdonald and Andrew A. Tadie (Grand Rapids: William B. Eerdmans, 1989), 58.

[36] David Leigh, "The Psychology of Conversion in Chesterton's and Lewis's Autobiographies," in *G. K. Chesterton and C. S. Lewis: The Riddle of Joy*, ed. Michael H. Macdonald and Andrew A. Tadie (Grand Rapids: Eerdmans Publishing Company, 1989), 292.

Church.[37] Certainly Chesterton regarded himself as a Christian before he was a Roman Catholic.[38] Neither are we seeking to articulate the doctrines of Islam, even as Chesterton laid them out in *The Flying Inn*, tempting as this subject might be in our times of political and religious turmoil. Rather, we are centring on the dynamic of the soul change itself, and the stages of turning away from personal error and towards the Person of Christ (however allegorical and symbolic the Christocentric goal in this novel). That is, we are holding to the orthodoxy Chesterton himself had achieved by 1908 that, six years before his writing of *The Flying Inn*, he described as "the central Christian theology (sufficiently summarized in the Apostles' Creed) . . . the best root of energy and sound ethics."[39] This theology for Chesterton revolved around the doctrines of creation, the fall into sin, redemption, and the new creation. In its essence and for our discussion, Christian conversion can be defined as a mysterious act initiated by the Creator whereby an individual turns from sin and towards God through faith in Jesus Christ, as first described in Scripture and subsequently repeated innumerable times in countless hearts.

Scripture uses various metaphors in speaking of conversion. The Old Testament sees conversion as God's turning back to Israel or turning His people back towards Himself, but an overview of the New Testament renders a clearer pattern to this process of the spiritual pilgrimage.[40] The synoptic gospels picture the response

---

[37] See, e.g., Joseph Pearce, *Literary Converts: Spiritual Inspiration in an Age of Unbelief* (San Francisco: Ignatius, 2000); Douglas Cock, "A Protestant View of Chesterton," *The Chesterton Review* 17, no. 1 (1991): 25-31; Dale, *Outline of Sanity*, 203-33; Cyril Clemens, *Chesterton As Seen by His Contemporaries* (New York: Haskell House Publishers, 1969), 69; Crowther, *G.K. Chesterton*, 50-55, 124.

[38] Chesterton, *Autobiography*, 85.

[39] Chesterton, *Orthodoxy*, 215.

[40] For three samples of conversion, see Deut. 13:17, Ezekiel 14:6, Acts 9.

that results in a life of faith in the face of danger, where forgiveness and healing, joy and peace are to be found vertically in reconciliation between God and the human, and horizontally in communion among people. In the book of Acts, blindness turns to sight as Jew and Gentile alike are called into fellowship. The gospel of John is radiant with the theme of cosmic light and darkness in the confrontation between good and evil, and shows that active faith results in ethical obedience. Paul's writings emphasize the newness of life in Christ, picturing creation recreated and revealing the doctrine of justification by faith whereby resultant works spring forth in the convert's life. The Christian Scriptures, then, do not suggest one stereotypical conversion experience, for, as Richard Baxter concluded, "God breaketh not all men's hearts alike." [41] Yet, the New Testament uses the words *metanoia* (a change of mind) and *epistrophe* (turning) to convey this central idea of spiritual change as turning from sin and towards God.[42] *The Flying Inn* is saturated with these biblical themes, proving Chesterton's familiarity with the biblical definition of conversion. We see the reluctant pilgrim, Dorian, as he faces danger in the darkness and discovers enlightening, revivifying wonder in his reconciliation with nature and re-energizing fellowship with man.

The findings of current scholarship on the topic of biblical conversion apply, as well, to Dorian's story. For example, in a comprehensive critique of the cultural and social factors of the religious phenomenon, Lewis Rambo described genuine conversion as a total metamorphosis,

[41] Richard Baxter, *The Autobiography of Richard Baxter* (New York, NY: E. P. Dutton, 1931); quoted in Hugh T. Kerr and John M. Mulder, *Famous Conversions* (Grand Rapids, MI: William B. Eerdmans Publishing Company, 1983), 29.

[42] Acts 3:19 (NIV) sums up the consistent New Testament command, "Repent [*metanoeo*], then, and turn [*epistrepho*] to God, so that your sins may be wiped out, that times of refreshing may come from the Lord."

radical in nature, "striking to the root of the human pre-
dicament."[43] Ronald D. Witherup's biblical study empha-
sized the holistic aspect of the transformation, which is
not limited to feelings of remorse or a passionless intellectualism but engages the whole person (intellect, emotion, and volition) and involves a factual and positive
recognition of the truth that is personally appropriated.[44]
For his part, Alan Tippett recognized several stages in
the spiritual route that include God's preparation in the
life of the pre-convert, a Christocentric message, recognition of personal sin, a heart response, and a changed
life.[45] Dorian's conversion is a compendium; his altera-
tion is radical (in keeping with Rambo), holistic (as
Witherup insisted), and allegorically reflective of each of
Tippett's stages. Dorian is prepared by his abandonment
in the forest to receive a sacramentally coded message
of salvation that brings him into an awareness of his
own shortcomings and evokes a joyful metaphysical response resulting in an altered lifestyle.

Conversion Narrative as a Genre

One consequence of conversion within the Christian tradition is the production of stories or testimonies that
stimulate others to convert, acting as paradigms of conversion for the next generation.[46] Early conversion tales
in the form of fictional literature include such works as
Dante's *Vita Nuova* (an allegory of reformation from car-
nal love to spiritual), Chaucer's *Canterbury Tales,* and
Cervantes's *Don Quixote* (the last two even mentioned

---

[43] Lewis R. Rambo, *Understanding Religious Conversion* (London: Yale University Press, 1993), xii.
[44] Ronald D. Witherup, *Conversion in the New
Testament* (Collegeville, MN: The Liturgical Press, 1994).
[45] Alan R. Tippett, "Conversion as a Dynamic Process in Christian Mission," *Missiology* 2 (1977): 203-21.
[46] Rambo, *Understanding Religious Conversion*, p.
158.

by Chesterton in Dorian's quest).[47] Dickens's writings, so formative upon Chesterton's own, include *Little Dorrit* (with its metaphors of birth and rebirth) as well as *A Christmas Carol* (showing the conversion of Scrooge, with the images of the "ghosts of time" taking the place of the Holy Ghost in conviction, and spiritual rebirth allegorized by Scrooge's new spirit of kindness).[48] Chesterton read the Puritans' fiction as well: John Bunyan's allegorical *Pilgrim's Progress* and Daniel Defoe's *Robinson Crusoe* (in which the shipwrecked sailor comes to faith in God after finding and reading a Bible) and George MacDonald's *The Princess and the Goblin* (one of the legends preceding and stimulating Chesterton's "more orthodox Christianity").[49] The Protestant emphasis on conversion accounts produced a fictional literature in keeping with the U-shaped narrative structure of conversion seen in Scripture and, not surprisingly, reproduced in Chesterton's fiction.[50]

Christian conversion sparked the writing not only of allegory but also of autobiography, which is a blend of historically recordable truth and literary artistry.[51] Its post-canonical expression was introduced by Augustine's *Confessions*, which was greatly influential in subsequent

---

[47] See Chesterton, *The Flying Inn*, 601.

[48] See "Conversion" in David Lyle Jeffrey, ed. *A Dictionary of Biblical Tradition in English Literature* (Grand Rapids: William B. Eerdmans Publishing Company, 1992), 159-62.

[49] Dale, *Outline of Sanity*, 15. For the influence of many writers on Chesterton's life, see also his brother's biography: [Cecil Chesterton], *G. K. Chesterton: A Criticism*, American ed. (New York: John Lane Company, 1909).

[50] See, e.g., "Myth II: Narrative" in Northrop Frye, *The Great Code: The Bible and Literature* (San Diego: Harcourt Brace and Company, 1982), 169-98.

[51] See Georges Gusdorf, "Conditions and Limits of Autobiography," in *Autobiography: Essays Theoretical and Critical*, ed. James Olney (Princeton: Princeton University Press, 1980), 28-48.

Christian confessional literature from the writings of Loyola to Luther, from Pascal to Kierkegaard. But it was the seventeenth century—close upon the heels of the Reformation—that saw, according to D. Bruce Hindmarsh, the "autobiographical moment in the history of conversion."[52] The "keen sense of introspective conscience and of individual self-determination" of the modern period popularized the self-conscious writing of retrospective spiritual memoirs, resulting in works like Bunyan's significant *Grace Abounding to the Chief of Sinners* as well as such Methodist publications as Wesley's *Journal*.[53] But Defoe went on to provide a fascinating new hybrid with *Moll Flanders* that dynamically combined criminal biography and spiritual autobiography.[54] Its lesser-known subtitle highlights the intensity with which the genre combined fiction and evangelical conversion in Moll, *Who was Born in Newgate, and during a Life of continu'd Variety for Threescore Years, besides her Childhood, was Twelve Year a Whore, five times a Wife (whereof once to her own Brother), Twelve Year a Thief, Eight Year a Transputed Felon in Virginia, at last grew Rich, liv'd Honest, and died a Penitent, Written from her own Memorandums.*

As a writer of memoir and fiction, Chesterton inherited this autobiographical religious culture so deeply imbued with the Methodist experience and expression of conversion. We can see the generic, U-shaped pattern of these early conversion stories appearing in his life writings as well as his novels. The typical early Methodist narrative, as described by Hindmarsh, begins with childhood as "a state of relative innocence and spiritual

---

[52] D. Bruce Hindmarsh, " 'My chains fell off, my heart was free': Early Methodist Conversion Narrative in New England," *Church History* 68, no. 4 (1999): 913.

[53] Ibid., 914-5.

[54] According to David Lyle Jeffrey, *People of the Book: Christian Identity and Literary Culture* (Grand Rapids: William B. Eerdmans Publishing Company with The Institute for Advanced Christian Studies, 1996), 283.

promise," followed by the rebellion of adolescence in which "a period of hardening of heart as wrong-doing became habitual," until "the word of God entered the experience . . . and began the process of return."[55] So, too, Chesterton's transformation began with a return to his childhood, for (as Kevin Morris says) Chesterton saw conversion "as the salvation of the boy Gilbert, as restoration to his infant state."[56] Chesterton himself referred to the metaphorical landscape of his first days—the little church of his baptism, the waterworks—as standing for "the acted allegory of human existence."[57] His adolescence—that transition from dunce to lunatic—found him in a "disturbed or even diseased state of brooding and idling" as his dabbling in the occult fed his "moral anarchy within."[58] Finally, Chesterton reached the age of adulthood, for the riddle of man is "hidden from boys and comes only to men in their maturity," taking on "more and more the nature of a religious enlightenment" preceding "the splendid attainment of second childhood."[59] We can see how Chesterton's creedal, biblical doctrines organized his autobiographical writings detailing his personal creation, fall, redemption, and new creation. We will see below how the scenario of Dorian Wimpole's change is similarly structured.

Considering Chesterton's wide reading of religious writers (and the fact that his own grandfather was a Wesleyan lay-preacher), it is not surprising to see him incorporating the confessional elements popularized in England by the Methodists. Alongside hymnody, the abundance of conversion literature is, according to Hindmarsh, "one of the greatest literary legacies of early

---

[55] Hindmarsh, "Early Methodist Conversion," 922-5.

[56] Kevin L. Morris, "Chesterton's Conversion: Hesitation and the Recovery of Infancy," *The Chesterton Review* 18, no. 3 (1992): 375-6.

[57] Chesterton, *Autobiography*, 38

[58] Ibid., 89, 96.

[59] Ibid., 234.

Methodism."[60] After all, this was the genre associated
with the time of such writers as the Clapham Sect evangelical Macaulay, whose *Essays* Chesterton devoured.[61]
No doubt the genre of conversion literature influenced
Chesterton himself. Dorian's narrative might differ from
popular evangelical testimony in its overtly fictional for-
mat, but the fact of its mirroring nature makes it a corollary to Chesterton's more standard works, such as *Autobiography* and *Orthodoxy.*

In order to more clearly understand the conversion of Dorian Wimpole in *The Flying Inn*, it is helpful to
examine its sixteenth chapter, "The Seven Moods of Dorian." The title of the chapter itself gives us a hint that
Dorian's conversion is referential, for the number seven
carries a biblical symbolism for completeness: consider,
for example, the seven sprinklings necessary to complete the Levitical blood sacrifice, or that Jesus made
seven "I am" declarations of His identity.[62] Even Dorian
gives a nod towards the title's biblical symbolism when
he refers to the blast of the Last (seventh) Trumpet her-
alding the resurrection of the dead and the return of
Christ.[63] Chesterton elsewhere indicated the number's
analogical meaning: the seven-day week as the structure of creation schematizes his early short story "A Picture of Tuesday" as well as *The Man Who Was Thursday*;
his poetry collection "The Queen of Seven Swords" typifies nations as the seven champions of Christendom.[64]
Chesterton's use of the word "moods" in the chapter title

---

[60] Hindmarsh, "Early Methodist Conversion," 910.

[61] Chesterton, *Autobiography*, 9.

[62] Leviticus 16:14, 19; John 6:35-15:1.

[63] See Chesterton, *The Flying Inn*, 596; cf. 1 Corinthians 15:52, Revelation 11:15.

[64] See "A Picture of Tuesday" in G. K. Chesterton,
*The Collected Works of G. K. Chesterton: Short Stories,
Fairy Tales, Mystery Stories, Illustrations*, ed. George J.
Marlin, Richard P. Rabatin, and John L. Swan, vol. 14
(San Francisco: Ignatius Press, 1993), 60-63; see also
G. K. Chesterton, *The Queen of Seven Swords* (London:
Sheed and Ward, 1926), 39-50.

is also suspicious, and we note its application in both *Autobiography* and *Orthodoxy* to connote stages of his own conversion.[65] Even though the phases of Chesterton's metamorphosis are not so obviously partitioned into Dorian's seven moods, the symbolism stimulates inquiry into a correlation between the experiences of character and creator.

The Moods

At his first appearance, Dorian is a milquetoast. He is a well-connected eccentric and "one of those who always tend to take their own fancies seriously."[66] His notoriety as "Poet of the Birds" was earned at the publication of his first book (an ingenious English interpretation of the birdsong of various species), but his creativity has dried up. An austere, academic bore with "too little of the juice of zest," he resembles in a way his cousin, Lord Ivywood, who "shared the mental weakness of most men who have fed on books"; that is, Dorian ignores the reality in favour of the representation.[67] His senses have been dulled. In promoting the worth of animals over humans, he has forgotten the taste of oysters. He has displaced Chesterton's "reality of being and its goodness" with a Manichean view of the oyster as an entity to be respected but not eaten.[68] Capitulating to the current trend as Chesterton was for a while "swept along with the prevalent philosophy of his day," Dorian has entered "the great Ivywood debate on vegetarianism," a religious philosophy of moral evolution also expressed in

---

[65] See, e.g., mood of brooding in Chesterton, *Autobiography*, 95-96; mood of reform in Chesterton, *Orthodoxy*, 310.

[66] Chesterton, *The Flying Inn*, 568.

[67] Ibid., 568, 543.

[68] See Christopher Derrick, "Chesterton and the Pursuit of Happiness," *The Chesterton Review* 6, no. 2 (1980): 232.

the progressive purification of teetotalism.[69] As Misysra says,

> It will always be asked by those who hate the very vision of Progress: "Where do I draw the line? May I eat oysters? May I eat eggs? May I drink milk?" You may. You may eat or drink anything essential to your stage of evolution, so long as you are evolving towards a clearer and cleaner ideal of bodily life.[70]

Vegetarianism thus represents wrong thinking and is the antithesis of Chesterton's theories on food and faith. Marshall McLuhan noted the "sacramental sense of the life of earth and sea and sky, of tillage and growth, and of *food and wine*, which informs his work" (italics mine).[71] The novel deals through fiction with a theme of evolutionary morality, this progressive cyclical nature of Misysra's philosophy previously discussed in *Orthodoxy*: "Certain of the idealistic vegetarians . . . say that the time has now come for eating no meat; by implication they assume that at one time it was right to eat meat, and they suggest . . . that some day it may be wrong to eat milk and eggs."[72] Vegetarianism is equated with religious heresy through Chesterton's fiction as well as his nonfiction.

As "a personality who could not be prevented from being anything he chose, from a revolutionist to a bore," Dorian chooses—at first—to be a bore.[73] He has, as Chesterton said elsewhere of the modern world in

---

[69] Chesterton, *Orthodoxy*, 262; Chesterton, *The Flying Inn*, 568.

[70] Chesterton, *The Flying Inn*, 532.

[71] H. Marshall McLuhan, "G. K. Chesterton: A Practical Mystic," in *G. K. Chesterton: A Half Century of Views*, ed. D. J. Conlon (Oxford: Oxford University Press, 1987), 1.

[72] Chesterton, *Orthodoxy*, 313.

[73] Chesterton, *The Flying Inn*, 568.

general, "a remarkable capacity for being content with half-truths that are rather hollow" and is in desperate need of transformation.[74] He sounds like the adolescent Chesterton himself in his lunacy (who possessed "a callousness, a carelessness, a curious combination of random and quite objectless energy with a readiness to accept conventions") just before he put his head "over the hedge of the elves" to take notice of the natural world, and to observe that rational facts of men are not as true as the imagination of fairyland.[75] But Dorian is not beyond hope. Although he is exhibiting *Orthodoxy's* "chief mark and element of insanity" that is a blind dependence upon reason, yet because he is a poet, like Chesterton, his shred of retained mysticism will allow him to face the coming twilight with "one foot in earth and the other in fairyland."[76]

Before the first mood comes upon Dorian, he is riding in his car through the woods on a moonstruck night, full of "a fury of omniscience" as he identifies with every squirrel and bird. Chesterton, too, maniacally plunging towards "spiritual suicide," suffered Dorian's God complex. In *Autobiography*, he explained: "It was as if I myself had projected the universe from within, with all its trees and stars; and that is so near the notion of being God that it is manifestly even nearer to going mad."[77] Dorian is shocked into stopping his chauffeur at the sight of Dalroy and Pump loading a donkey-cart with cask, cheese, and signboard.[78] With a "swelling omnipotence [that] went beyond the poetical," Wimpole demands justice for the animal, which he suspects is

---

[74] G. K. Chesterton, "On Change as Change," *G.K.'s Weekly* (November 7, 1935); reprint *The Chesterton Review* 19, no. 1 (February, 1993): 18.

[75] Chesterton, *Autobiography*, 61-62; Chesterton, *Orthodoxy*, 254.

[76] Chesterton, *Orthodoxy*, 230.

[77] Chesterton, *Autobiography*, 89, 95-96.

[78] Chesterton, *The Flying Inn*, 571.

also in danger of being ridden.[79] He accuses Dalroy of this equestrian intent.

>"No," answered the Captain inno-
>cently. "I never ride on a donkey. I'm
>afraid of it."
>   "Afraid of a donkey!" cried Wim-
>pole incredulously.
>   "Afraid of an historical compari-
>son," said Dalroy.[80]

Dorian, however, is not afraid for he, like Chesterton's maniac, is one of those "men who believe in them-selves," setting forth from the mad-house of sin on an intellectual journey.[81] For Chesterton, a maniac was one who neglected to begin inquiry with the fact of sin.[82] The synonymy between Dorian's incipient madness and the fact of his sin stands in contrast to the holy picture of Dalroy's donkey, reminding us of Chesterton's poem in which another donkey cried, "Fools! / For I also had my hour; / One far fierce hour and sweet: / There was a shout about my ears, / And palms before my feet."[83] The fictional Dorian meets this donkey as the real Ches-terton, too, met Christianity. Dorian's introduction on the forest drive provokes the first of his emotions, for he

---

[79] Ibid., 572.

[80] Ibid., 577.

[81] Chesterton, *Orthodoxy*, 216. For a treatment of Chesterton's themes of sanity and insanity in *The Ball and the Cross*, see Adam Schwartz, "G. K. C.'s Methodi-cal Madness: Sanity and Social Control in Chesterton," *Renascence: Essays on Values in Literature*, Fall 1996, vol. 49, no. 1, p. 23 (18) [database on-line] (Marquette University Press, 1996, accessed 28 August 2000); available from Infotrac.

[82] Chesterton, *Orthodoxy*, 217.

[83] "The Donkey" in G. K. Chesterton, *The Poems of G. K. Chesterton*, The Works of G. K. Chesterton (Hertfordshire: Wordsworth Poetry Library, 1995), 248.

is abandoned in the wood by his chauffeur and left in the sole company of the donkey.

"The **first mood** . . . was one of black and grinding hatred."[84] Dorian has been ignorant of the plight of his servant in the way the middle class of Chesterton's day "knew far too little of the working classes."[85] He has not noticed the common man's hunger because of the fullness of his own stomach; the recent banquet featured him as a speaker on "the tragedy of the oyster," a "forgotten creature" that some humanitarians shamefully considered as an exception in their otherwise vegetarian diets.[86] His stomach and his mind are full and preoccupied. He himself has forgotten a creature—the chauffeur, the commoner, "the creature whom man has always found it easier to forget, since the hour he forgot God in a garden."[87] Elsewhere, Chesterton mourned the plight of godless society wherein "every man has forgotten who he is. . . . We are all under the same mental calamity; we have all forgotten our names. We have all forgotten what we really are."[88] Chesterton's society of forgetfulness towards humankind is Dorian's state of mind, as well.

But Dorian is neither foolish nor evil, "only a man made sterile by living in a world of indirectness and insincerity" as Chesterton himself—in his "period of madness" and curiosity about the occult, before he had defined dogma—was intellectually right yet morally wrong.[89] Although the chauffeur has been a nonentity to Dorian, he now hates the man with a murderous hatred for abandoning him, and in his obsession Dorian kicks the stones and tears up the roadside bracken and beats upon the bark of the trees, for to him "the whole wood and the whole world had become a kind of omnipresent

---

[84] Chesterton, *The Flying Inn*, 594.

[85] Chesterton, *Autobiography*, 25.

[86] Chesterton, *The Flying Inn*, 570.

[87] Ibid., 579.

[88] Chesterton, *Orthodoxy*, 257.

[89] Chesterton, *The Flying Inn*, 594; Chesterton, *Autobiography*, 86.

and pantheistic chauffeur, and he hit at him everywhere."[90] This change in Dorian is a positive one, an
"upward stride in what he would have called the cosmic
scale. The next best thing to really loving a fellow-
creature is really hating him . . . . The desire to murder
him is at least an acknowledgement that he is alive."[91]
Dorian's phase sounds like Chesterton's own "mood of
unreality and sterile isolation" leading to his "moral anarchy within," during which time he progressed from a
dreamlike state of relative naivety to imagining the
worst of crimes.[92] The first stave, in which both Chesterton and Dorian gain awareness of their own limitation,
gives way to another mood.

"His rage also did him good merely as a relief;
and soon he passed into a **second** and more positive
mood of meditation."[93] Dorian discovers that he is rather fond of the donkey. This surprises him because, for
all he has been the champion of the forgotten creatures,
he has never before felt affection for them. His poems
about animals, though sincere, are cold and abstract.
Yet, now in the forest, he realizes that

> his love of creatures had been turned
> clean around and was working from the
> other end. The donkey was a companion,
> and not a monstrosity. It was dear be-
> cause it was near, not because it was dis-
> tant. The oyster had attracted him be-
> cause it was utterly unlike a man . . . .
> But in that maddening vigil among the
> mystic pines he found himself more and
> more drawn towards the donkey, because
> it was more like a man than anything else
> around him.[94]

---

[90] Chesterton, *The Flying Inn*, 595.
[91] Ibid.
[92] Chesterton, *Autobiography*, 95-96.
[93] Chesterton, *The Flying Inn*, 595.
[94] Ibid., 596. Note the correlation between Dorian's experience and the garden vigil of Gabriel Gale,

Chesterton, whose own "groping and guesswork philosophy" typified his real-life period of lunacy and isolation,
here formulated a fictional parallel between the donkey
and the spiritual side of Dorian Wimpole.[95] The donkey
bears the image of man as man bears God's image, and
as God in Christ bore man's image. This paradoxical
similarity/dissimilarity between the person and the animal hints at Chesterton's view of the incarnation, which
cherished the material world and found the highest value of a person or object in its own identity rather than in
an absorption of the individual into some greater unity.[96]

Dorian scratches the donkey's ears, quoting the
oft-spoken words of Jesus: "He that hath ears to hear,
let him hear"; this alerts Chesterton's readers to take
note of the underlying truth of the parable as it alerted
Jesus' listeners regarding the judgement to come upon
those who reject it.[97] If Dorian is referring to the Mark
7:16 passage, an interesting connection is made between *The Flying Inn*'s vegetarianism and the Pharisees'
promotion of certain formalities that neglected the
command of God while holding to the traditions of men,
for it is what is in the heart—not what goes in through
the mouth—that defiles.[98] In this way Chesterton draws
his readers' attention to the necessity of a heart conversion, to the relationship between ingesting foods in religious philosophy and the practice of true religion, to the
idea that not external practices but internal realities
save. Chesterton pits Ivywood's philosophy of food and
drink (legalism progressing to nihilism) against Dalroy's

---

which in its turn links Eden to Gethsemane, links sin's
enslavement to its horrible solution; see Chesterton, *The
Poet and the Lunatics*, 131.

[95] Chesterton, *Autobiography*, 105.

[96] See Coates, "Philosophy and Religious Background of *The Flying Inn*," 307.

[97] Chesterton, *The Flying Inn*, 596; cf., e.g., Mark
7:16 (KJV only), Mark 4:9, Matthew 13:43, 11:15.

[98] For further substantiation of the biblical principle, see also Peter's vision in Acts 10:9-15 and 1 Timo-
thy 4:3-5.

freedom to partake (grace resulting in Christian gratitude), for, as he wrote in *Orthodoxy*, "Christianity is the
only frame which has preserved the pleasure of Pagan-
ism."[99]

After his maniacal mood, like Chesterton Dorian
begins to meditate, resisting as Chesterton resisted the
"mental ruin . . . wrought by wild reason," to return
again as Chesterton returned to the "dangerous boyhood
of free thought" and the vigorous health of the free will
fostered by exercising the imagination.[100] Dorian con-
templates the beauty of nature, not in his former, inertly
intellectual sense but now glorying in the experiential
particular. He appreciates the donkey and the pine nee-
dles as Chesterton discovered the limitations that make
creation "something and not just anything."[101] Dorian
understands Chesterton's "root phrase for all Christian
theism," which is that God the Creator is separate from
His creation.[102] Through his new rapport with the donkey, Dorian identifies himself as part of the story and
not the Storyteller, as made and not Maker. The "Poet of
the Birds" has not listened to birdsong for a long while.
Donkeys were *meant* to pull carts, he now remembers;
oysters were *meant* to be eaten and not made into
something higher, for their worth is intrinsic. Dorian is
awakening from the Chestertonian slumber of adolescence to recapture the "implicit but unfolded" idea of
repentance and absolution.[103]

"The donkey had reconciled him to the landscape; and in his **third mood** he began to realize how
beautiful it was."[104] Dorian views nature in a new way,
feeling suddenly that it is not so inhuman or hostile as
first perceived:

---

[99] Chesterton, *Orthodoxy*, 350.
[100] Ibid., 240.
[101] Ibid.
[102] Ibid., 281.
[103] Chesterton, *Autobiography*, 57.
[104] Chesterton, *The Flying Inn*, 597.

Rather he felt that its beauty was at least half human; that the aureole of the sinking moon behind the woods was chiefly lovely because it was like the tender-coloured aureole of an early saint; and that the young trees were after all noble because they held up their heads like virgins. Cloudily there crowded into his mind ideas with which it was imperfectly familiar, especially an idea which he had heard called "The Image of God."[105]

In this stirring of sacramental awareness, Dorian sees his surroundings as "dignified and sanctified by their partial resemblance to something else . . . as if they were baby drawings; the wild, crude sketches of Nature in her first sketchbooks of stone."[106] Dorian's forest seems, as Syme's in *The Man Who Was Thursday*, to be "stooping and hiding a face"—the face of God.[107] Chesterton wrote into Dorian's story his own view of creation, in which (as Boyd put it) "apparently profane realities are really sacramental signs from God."[108]

In his reverie Dorian is reminded of "the little wood" of Eden, seeing himself as another Adam or what Chesterton described in *Orthodoxy* as "a statue of God walking about the garden."[109] Dorian spends pleasurable hours contemplating the creatures with "a new and realistic interest in them which he had not known before."[110] His sense of appreciation and curiosity reminds us of the point at which Chesterton, with "a mystical minimum of gratitude," clung "to the remains of religion by one thin thread of thanks."[111] But Dorian's aesthetic mood is disrupted by the appearance of a snake, which he chooses

---

[105] Ibid.
[106] Ibid.
[107] Chesterton, *The Man Who Was Thursday*, 150.
[108] Boyd, *The Legendary Chesterton*, 64.
[109] Chesterton, *Orthodoxy*, 298.
[110] Chesterton, *The Flying Inn*, 599, 598.
[111] Chesterton, *Autobiography*, 97.

to kill as the biblical Adam could have chosen to reject his Edenic serpent. The scene recalls another in which Chesterton (on his moorland walk with Father O'Connor) caught "a sudden glimpse of the pit that is at all our feet" when he came face-to-face with "those morbid but vivid problems of the soul."[112]

After the long night, sunrise "flung faintly across the broad foliage a wan and pearly light far more mysterious than the lost moonshine."[113] Although Dorian has written "a hundred times" about daybreak and read about it "a thousand," he is filled with wonder at his first sentient experience of dawn. Suppositional, scientific knowledge is not the same as the personal experience of daybreak in "the fullness of its shining fate" that allows him to see clearly the reality of the forest, the liveliness of the donkey, and the deadness of the viper.[114] Dorian sees the difference between life and death as Chesterton came to realize that "the Christian Church in its practical relation to my soul is a living teacher, not a dead one."[115] Something new has awakened in Dorian—an "affectual not merely intellectual response to God's offer of grace," as David Lyle Jeffrey explained conversion.[116] Dorian makes a choice beneath the trees, his daylight no longer the confusion of "shattered sunlight and shaken shadow" in Syme's "wood of witchery," but more like the "open space of sunlight . . . the final return of his own good senses."[117]

We see the same sensual imagery using light in Chesterton's poetry, in which the visual is a metaphor of the spiritual.[118] For example, as a "Babe Unborn," in

---

[112] Ibid., 319.

[113] Chesterton, *The Flying Inn*, 600.

[114] Ibid.

[115] Chesterton, *Orthodoxy*, 359.

[116] Jeffrey, *Dictionary of Biblical Tradition*, 160.

[117] Chesterton, *The Man Who Was Thursday*, 112, 114.

[118] See further Kevin L. Morris, "Chesterton Sees Red: The Metaphysics of a Colour," *The Chesterton Review* 21, no. 4 (1995): 505-17.

dark he lay dreaming of leaving "the empires of the night. I think that if they gave me leave / Within the world to stand, / I would be good through all the day / I spent in fairyland."[119] Again, in "Art Colours" he wrote, "On must we go: we search dead leaves, / We chase the sunset's saddest flames," in search of "God of the day-break."[120] As Chesterton claimed in *Autobiography* of his own experience, confession and forgiveness led to a "strange daylight . . . something more than the light of common day" in which he found that God "remade him into His own image" in "that dawn of his own begin-ning."[121] He had been "blundering about" since his birth, looking for a way of "loving the world without trusting it" when he experienced the relief of orthodoxy. [122] His Thomist elevation of the senses in the discovery of God criticized the Augustinian school for "treating the soul as the only necessary treasure, wrapped for a time in a negligible napkin." [123] As Dorian finds metaphysical meaning through his aesthetic contemplation in the woods, so Chesterton approached spiritual truth through the outer layers of a thing, through the senses working inwards to "reach what was in the inside from what was most conspicuous on the outside."[124]

"And then the **fourth mood** fell upon him like a bolt from the blue, and he strode across and took the donkey's bridle, as if to lead it along."[125] Dorian's return to good sense catapults him into action, into the quest of "the finding and fighting of positive evil," for "all the wild woodland looked jolly now the snake was killed."[126] He has "passed out of the mood of Maeterlinck into the mood of Whitman, and out of the mood of Whitman into

---

[119] "By the Babe Unborn" in Chesterton, *Poems*, 243.

[120] "Art Colours" in Chesterton, *Poems*, 282-3.

[121] Chesterton, *Autobiography*, 319.

[122] Chesterton, *Orthodoxy*, 282-3.

[123] Chesterton, *Saint Thomas Aquinas*, 37.

[124] Ibid., 121.

[125] Chesterton, *The Flying Inn*, 600.

[126] Ibid.

the mood of Stevenson" (that is, from listlessness through optimism to meaningful action, as Chesterton himself proceeded through "Leaves of Grass" into *Treasure Island*).[127] Dorian's change of heart propels him into activity: he leaves his erudite passivity for an experiential activism and "swashbuckling comedy"—the symbolic world of Chaucer and Cervantes in which even his travelling companion, the donkey, reminds him of Sancho Panza.[128]

Dorian's fourth mood reflects Chesterton's schema of adventure in the defense of liberty and human dignity through that paradoxical Christian belief system that "always forbade wars and always produced wars."[129] His real-life brooding gave way to action. He said in *Orthodoxy*, "The more I considered Christianity, the more I found that while it had established a rule and order, the chief aim of that order was to give room for good things to run wild."[130] In discussing the limits necessary to give maximum freedom, Chesterton considered the rejection of limitations by the anarchist who, thinking he is achieving liberty, is simply stepping outside of the protective definition of Christian civilization as described by its literature. Chesterton's own inward vivification resulted in action as he embraced the lively truths of Christianity, rejecting, for example, Impressionism and its philosophy of limitlessness in favour of biblically analogical fiction.[131] So, as Chesterton embraced liberty within the definition of creedal limitation,

---

[127] Ibid.; see also Chesterton, *Autobiography*, 97.

[128] Chesterton, *The Flying Inn*, 601.

[129] Chesterton, *Orthodoxy*, 291.

[130] Ibid., 300.

[131] See, e.g., Chesterton, *Autobiography*, 110. For the Christian influence of the "penny dreadfuls" Chesterton read, see further Chesterton, *Orthodoxy*, 288. For his own fictive expression (in a 1919 short story) of a change of heart, resulting in outward action, from defiance to the respectability of orthodoxy, see also G. K. Chesterton, "The Conversion of an Anarchist," *The Chesterton Review* 8, no. 1 (1982): 1-9.

Dorian enters into personal, adventurous freedom within the description of literary tradition.

"The **fifth** or unexpected **mood** . . . is called by the vulgar Astonishment."[132] A policeman and the journalist Hibbs, who are on assignment from Lord Ivywood to hunt down the renegade Dalroy and Pump, accost Dorian.[133] Hibbs is confused and hung over from a night of drunkenness that he is desperate to conceal, and with "strange, soft fear and cunning" he employs subjective relativism to defend his mistaken accusation of Dorian as the guilty fugitive.[134] Dorian is astonished over the allegation against him: "Well, of all the mad worlds! A pack of thieves steal my limousine, I save their damned donkey's life at the risk of my own—and *I'm* run in for stealing!"[135]

Dorian's astonishment (or "wonder," as *Oxford English Dictionary* proposes and that is in keeping with Chesterton's doctrine) is like Chesterton's amazement at the paradoxes of Christianity wherein "two opposite passions blaze beside each other," "love and wrath both burning."[136] Time and eternity, flesh and spirit, rationalism and mysticism find their connection in the justifying work of Christ. The agnostic rationalist, Dorian—who seems like Chesterton to be regaining the childish "elementary wonder" of fairyland over " 'a law' that he has never seen"—finds his ground of truth while he Is being accused of falsehood.[137] So the revelation that "Christianity was accused, at one and the same time, of being too optimistic about the universe and of being too pessimistic about the world" made Chesterton "suddenly stand still."[138] The inconsistency of the accusations levelled against Christianity by non-Christians puzzled Chesterton in the same way that the innocent Dorian is

---

[132] Chesterton, *The Flying Inn*, 601.
[133] Ibid., 601-2.
[134] Ibid., 604.
[135] Ibid., 602.
[136] Chesterton, *Orthodoxy*, 352, 296.
[137] Ibid., 256.
[138] Ibid., 278.

puzzled by Hibbs's vague accusations and changing truths. With a new optimistic realism, Chesterton asked: "What again could this astonishing thing be like which people were so anxious to contradict, that in doing so they did not mind contradicting themselves?"[139] Dorian makes a dash for freedom, is apprehended, and is locked in a temporary cell to experience his next mood much as Chesterton, with his own new "wild truth reeling but erect," entered a mood of determined reform.[140]

Under incarceration, Dorian experiences **mood six**, a clamorous and convincing complaining as he is taken for judgement before the magistrate (his aristocratic cousin Philip Ivywood) who "continued to look away as they entered, as if expecting, with Roman calm, the entrance of a recognized enemy."[141] The similarity to Pilate's judgement of the innocent Christ is heightened by the conditions of Dorian's accusers: the foolishness of Hibbs's lies, the inspector's blindness to Dorian's true identity, and Ivywood's "frigid forgiveness."[142] Dorian says, " 'I tell you frankly, Philip, if there really are, as you say, two men who are bent on smashing your schemes and making your life a hell—I am very happy to put my car at their disposal. And now, I'm off.' "[143] Forthwith he experiences the **seventh mood**—a celebratory feast of oysters—before he throws his lot in with the fugitives.

Dorian's trial before the authorities might mimic Chesterton's own pugnacious religious debate with atheist Blatchford, as both contests espouse Chesterton's doctrines "with adamantine gravity."[144] Recognizing Jesus Christ as the man of the "right shape"—the standard, the Truth against which all other truths must be measured—Chesterton held up his new thought (that is, orthodoxy) against the accusations of the agnostics and

---

[139] Ibid., 293.
[140] Ibid., 306.
[141] Chesterton, *The Flying Inn*, 606.
[142] Ibid., 607.
[143] Ibid.
[144] Chesterton, *Autobiography*, 173.

sceptics who presented him with all the contradic-tions.[145] As Dorian rejects vegetarianism, so Chesterton could no longer view Christianity as "a compromise" that "was merely sensible and stood in the middle." [146] Brought before his accusers, Chesterton, too, proclaimed himself innocent. Dorian's belief disallows him to stand in the middle of the road out of temperance, respect, or tolerance towards Ivywood's syncretism. In the same way, Chesterton's understanding of the paradoxical Christian truths so "central in orthodox theology" pro-pelled him, also, into the defense of his faith.[147] Chester-ton's condemnation of heretics sounds like Dorian's con-demnation of Hibbs and Ivywood as he proclaims his own allegiance to the fugitives, Dalroy and Pump. Ches-terton said that an atheist "cannot think atheism to be false and continue to be an atheist."[148] In the same way, Dorian's rejection of Ivywood's philosophy prohibits his continuing vegetarianism and condones his oyster sup-per in a Chestertonian celebration of "the glorious gift of the senses."[149] Dorian throws his caution to the wind and joins Dalroy, in the spirit of Chesterton's impulsive purchase of rail tickets to go "wherever the next train goes."[150] The reformation of Dorian is Chesterton's own "walking toward the New Jerusalem"; no longer does Dorian protect the prevalent, seductive philosophical vi-sion of Ivywood and Misysra, but he begins like Chester-ton to "change the world to suit the vision" as he joins the community of idealists, Dalroy and Pump, beneath the wooden sign of the Old Ship Inn.[151] The bore be-comes a revolutionary. As Chesterton reminded us, "For the orthodox there can always be a revolution; for a revolution is a restoration."[152]

---

[145] Chesterton, *Orthodoxy*, 294-5.
[146] Ibid., 296.
[147] Ibid.
[148] Ibid.
[149] Chesterton, *Autobiography*, 330-1.
[150] Ibid., 203.
[151] Chesterton, *Orthodoxy*, 310.
[152] Ibid., 315.

Conversion Accomplished

"The Seven Moods of Dorian" finds its denouement throughout the rest of the novel, which now foregrounds the symbolism of the cross. Dorian's conversion experience in the forest (when he comes "back to earth like a man fallen from the moon") is followed by his failure in the House of Commons (in a picture of "backsliding") and his final disgust with Lord Ivywood's solipsistic philosophy that would "deny that any limit is set upon living things."[153] Dorian then makes good on his threat of mood six to join Dalroy and Pump, completing their trinity in a portrait of Christian fellowship for, as Chesterton maintained, "Boys . . . wander in threes . . . the symbolic number for comradeship" because "to us Trinitarians . . . God Himself is a society."[154] With "something like a shout of laughter," Chesterton plunged into the next episode of his life that, like Dorian's, was one of "helping certain friends and reformers to fix the terrible truth called Responsibility, not on tramps or drunkards, but on the rulers of the State and the richest men in the Empire."[155] On their way to recapturing the country from the heretical invaders, the fictional rebels share a celestial experience in a huge tree "near to heaven" in which Dorian eats some of the "holy" cheese that itself has been on a "pilgrimage."[156] An illustration of the Kingdom of God, the branches of the tree in which Dorian finds

---

[153] Chesterton, *The Flying Inn*, 618, 615-24, 659.

[154] Chesterton, *Autobiography*, 63; Chesterton, *Orthodoxy*, 340. Note the contrast to the Miltonian antitrinity of Ivywood, Misysra, and Hibbs. The fellowship of Chesterton's Christian marriage also sustained his faith, and he described his wife, Frances, as the one "who brought the Cross to me." See Maisie Ward, *Gilbert Keith Chesterton* (London: Sheed and Ward, 1944), 76.

[155] Chesterton, *Autobiography*, 175.

[156] Chesterton, *The Flying Inn*, 671-2. His reference is to the inexhaustible milk of the legendary Dun cow.

rest spread out "to the four quarters of heaven" like "a bird brooding over its nest."[157]

Dorian is no longer coldly academic. In the "profound intellectual revolt of the poet against the politician," he sings a new and emotional song.[158] Dorian finds "his artist's love of beauty fulfilled as it never had been before," as Chesterton's own conversion incorporated a strong aesthetic element of imagination.[159] Dorian secures comfort in this tree at the sign of the inn as Chesterton (having searched "the land of void and vision") also found a temporary home in this world, the fallen Garden of Eden.[160] This picture in fiction of the branching tree "as a friend with arms open for the man"[161] sounds like Chesterton's depiction elsewhere of the posture of the crucified Saviour, with

> outstretched arms . . . truly opened wide, and opening most gloriously the gates of all the worlds; they were arms pointing to the east and to the west, to the ends of the earth and the very extremes of existence. They were truly spread out with a gesture of omnipotent generosity; the Creator himself offering Creation itself.[162]

The symbol of the cross becomes Dorian's fixed goal—that sign of the inn, which Captain Dalroy has "brandished in the air like a banner" against the corruption of "Babylon."[163] The signpost is metaphorical of the cross in its silhouette, its message of national religion,

[157] Ibid., 670-1; cf. Psalm 91:4, Matthew 13:31-33.

[158] Chesterton, *The Flying Inn*, 656.

[159] Ibid., 673-5; see also Leigh, "Psychology of Conversion."

[160] See Chesterton, *The Flying Inn*, 670-1; cf. Chesterton, *Orthodoxy*, 215, 359.

[161] Chesterton, *The Flying Inn*, 725.

[162] Chesterton, *Saint Thomas Aquinas*, 135.

[163] Chesterton, *The Flying Inn*, 475.

its composition of wood, and its function as a tree to be climbed and a weight to be borne.[164] Dorian follows the sign of the Old Ship Inn as it flies across the landscape calling the people to the exercise of their free will. He joins Dalroy's military "marching crowd" through the streets of London to retake Parliament and, "far off, at the head of the procession, he could see the sign with the ship and the cross going before them like an ensign."[165] As Chesterton once "saw suddenly the meaning of the shape of the cross," calling it "a blazon, a boast," so Dorian now recognizes his standard.[166] "The cross is the crux of the whole matter," Chesterton said.[167] The Old Ship Inn sign is the main image of Chesterton's novel as the cross is the symbol of Chesterton's own conversion:

> The Cross, though it has at its heart a collision and a contradiction, can extend its four arms for ever without altering its shape. Because it has a paradox in its centre it can grow without changing. . . . The Cross opens its arms to the four winds; it is a signpost for free travellers.[168]

Dorian has found his "second youth" as Chesterton gained his rejuvenating "second childhood" of spiritual birth.[169] The uprising of the commoners in *The Flying Inn* finally halts the evolution of England into an Islamic state; this plot action parallels Dorian's application of his

---

[164] Ibid., 689, 417-8, 694, 561, 696-8.

[165] Chesterton, *The Flying Inn*, 694.

[166] Chesterton, *Orthodoxy*, 359; Chesterton, *Autobiography*, 229.

[167] G. K. Chesterton, *The Everlasting Man* (San Francisco: Ignatius Press, 1993), 134.

[168] Chesterton, *Orthodoxy*, 231.

[169] Chesterton, *The Flying Inn*, 696; Chesterton, *Autobiography*, 234; see also Chesterton, *Orthodoxy*, 363.

own inward beliefs: "I will not be evolved. I will not be evolved into something that is not me," Dorian resolves.[170]

But Dorian has changed. His allegorical revivification—and Chesterton's own cycle of creation, the fall, redemption, and new creation—are complete. Dorian's first mood of emotional deadness followed by obsessive hatred for the chauffeur sounds like Chesterton's sense of unreality or isolation from the Creator and his teen-age diabolical "madness." The forest meditation of nature stimulated by the donkey reminds us of Chesterton's spiritual interest as he was drawn to metaphysical questions through his readings and acquaintances. The fictional man's recognition of beauty imitates Chesterton's own awakening aesthetic as he gratefully discovered the sacramental traces of God and His image in humankind. The optimistic sense of adventure Chesterton developed upon grasping Christianity parallels Dorian's taking to the road, and Dorian's astonishment over the subjective charges by Hibbs reflects the wonder Chesterton felt at Christianity's paradoxes. Dorian's complaints before the authorities can be likened to Chesterton's apologetic discourses. The seventh mood of celebrating with an oyster feast portrays Chesterton's jubilation over the freedom of grace received, the relief of orthodoxy, and the reclamation of his own joyous childhood. Dorian's former disinterest in the common man becomes an ardent communion as Chesterton, too, discovered Christian fellowship. Both stories are consistent with the biblical description of conversion: both characters have had a change of mind involving the intellect, emotion, and volition, and both have turned towards the central image of the cross resulting in a changed life.

Previously we defined conversion as a mysterious act initiated by the Creator whereby an individual turns from sin and towards God through faith in Jesus Christ. Dorian's conversion can be redefined as that mysterious act (initiated by his creator, Chesterton) whereby he

---

[170] Chesterton, *The Flying Inn*, 718.

turns from the madness of blindly following a foreign, syncretistic philosophy towards the commonsense freedom of western Christianity through faith in his redeemer, Captain Dalroy. "All Christianity concentrates on the man at the crossroads," Chesterton declared; "Will a man take this road or that?"[171] Dorian is the man at the crossroads looking for adventure in a land of authority for, as Chesterton said, "One can find no meanings in a jungle of scepticism; but the man will find more and more meanings who walks through a forest of doctrine and design."[172] Dorian's woodland journey is a fictional parallel to the spiritual quest of G. K. Chesterton; the character's rejection of the philosophy of vegetarianism is an allegory for Chesterton's rejection of contemporary false philosophies in favour of Christian orthodoxy personally appropriated.

Dorian Wimpole has had Gilbert Chesterton's change of heart.

---

[171] Chesterton, *Orthodoxy*, 341.
[172] Ibid., 362-3.

Sources

Alexander, T. Desmond. *From Paradise to the Promised Land: An Introduction to the Main Themes of the Pentateuch*. Grand Rapids: Baker Books, 1995.

Baxter, Richard. *The Autobiography of Richard Baxter*. New York, NY: E. P. Dutton, 1931.

Belloc, Hilaire. *On the Place of Gilbert Chesterton in English Letters*. New York: Sheed and Ward, 1940.

Boyd, Ian. "In Search of the Essential Chesterton." *Seven: An Anglo-American Review* 1 (1980): 28-45.

_____. "The Legendary Chesterton." In *G. K. Chesterton and C. S. Lewis: The Riddle of Joy*, ed. Michael H. Macdonald and Andrew A. Tadie, 53-68. Grand Rapids: William B. Eerdmans, 1989.

_____. *Novels of G. K. Chesterton: A Study in Art and Progaganda*. London: Paul Elek, 1975.

[Chesterton, Cecil]. *G. K. Chesterton: A Criticism*. American ed. New York: John Lane Company, 1909.

Chesterton, G. K. *The Collected Works of G. K. Chesterton: Autobiography*. Vol. 16, ed. David Dooley. San Francisco: Ignatius, 1988.

_____. *The Ball and the Cross*. Dover Publications: New York, 1995.

_____. *The Collected Works of G. K. Chesterton: The Return of Don Quixote, Tales of the Long Bow, The Man Who Knew Too Much*. Vol. 8, ed. George J. Marlin and Richard P. Rabatin. San Francisco: Ignatius Press, 1999.

_____. *The Collected Works of G. K. Chesterton: Short Stories, Fairy Tales, Mystery Stories, Illustrations*. Vol. 14, ed. George J. Marlin, Richard P. Rabatin, and John L. Swan. San Francisco: Ignatius Press, 1993.

_____. *Come To Think Of It.* Essay Index Reprint Series. Freeport, N. Y.: Books for Libraries Press, 1931.

_____. *The Complete Father Brown*. London: Penguin Books Limited, 1981.

_____. "The Conversion of an Anarchist." *The Chesterton Review* 8, no. 1 (1982): 1-9.

_____. *The Everlasting Man*. San Francisco: Ignatius Press, 1993.

_____. *The Flying Inn*. In *A G. K. Chesterton Omnibus*, 409-726. London: Metheun and Co., 1947.

_____. *The Man Who Was Thursday: A Nightmare*, ed. Stephen Medcalf. Oxford: Oxford University Press, 1996.

_____. *Manalive.* G. K. Chesterton Reprint Series. Beaconsfield: Darwen Finlayson, 1962.

_____. *The Napoleon of Notting Hill*. Ware, GB: Wordsworth Editions, 1996.

_____. "On Change as Change." *G.K.'s Weekly* (November 7, 1935); reprint *The Chesterton Review* 19, no. 1 (February, 1993): 17-19.

_____. *Orthodoxy*. In *The Collected Works of G. K. Chesterton*. Vol. 1, ed. David Dooley. San Francisco: Ignatius, 1986.

_____. *The Poems of G. K. Chesterton*. The Works of G. K. Chesterton. Hertfordshire: Wordsworth Poetry Library, 1995.

_____. *The Poet and the Lunatics: Episodes in the Life of Gabriel Gale*. London: Cassell and Company, 1929.

_____. *The Queen of Seven Swords*. London: Sheed and Ward, 1926.

_____. *Saint Thomas Aquinas: The Dumb Ox*. New York: Doubleday, 1956.

_____. *What's Wrong with the World*. London: Cassell and Company, 1912.

Clemens, Cyril. *Chesterton As Seen by His Contemporaries*. New York: Haskell House Publishers, 1969.

Coates, John. "Malaise at the Heart of *The Flying Inn*." *Seven: An Anglo-American Review* 8 (1987): 25-41.

_____. "The Philosophy and Religious Background of *The Flying Inn*." *The Chesterton Review* 12, no. 3 (1986): 303-28.

_____. "Symbol and Structure in *The Flying Inn*." *The Chesterton Review* 4, no. 2 (1978): 246-59.

Cock, Douglas. "A Protestant View of Chesterton." *The Chesterton Review* 17, no. 1 (1991): 25-31.

Crowther, Ian. *G. K. Chesterton*. Thinkers of our Time. London: The Claridge Press, 1991.

Dale, Alzina Stone. *The Outline of Sanity: A Biography of G. K. Chesterton*. Grand Rapids: William B. Eerdmans Publishing Company, 1982.

Derrick, Christopher. "Chesterton and the Pursuit of Happiness." *The Chesterton Review* 6, no. 2 (1980): 221-32.

Frye, Northrop. *The Great Code: The Bible and Literature*. San Diego: Harcourt Brace and Company, 1982.

Gusdorf, Georges. "Conditions and Limits of Autobiography." In *Autobiography: Essays Theoretical and Critical*, ed. James Olney, 28-48. Princeton: Princeton University Press, 1980.

Hindmarsh, D. Bruce. " 'My chains fell off, my heart was free': Early Methodist Conversion Narrative in New England." *Church History* 68, no. 4 (1999): 910-29.

Hollis, Christopher. *The Mind of Chesterton*. Coral Gables, FL: University of Miami Press, 1970.

Hunt, Peter R. "Dickens's Influence on Chesterton's Imaginative Writing." *Chesterton Review* 7, no. 1 (1981): 36-49.

Hunter, Lynette. *G. K. Chesterton: Explorations in Allegory*. New York: St. Martin's Press, 1979.

Jeffrey, David Lyle. *People of the Book: Christian Identity and Literary Culture*. Grand Rapids: Eerdmans, with The Institute for Advanced Christian Studies, 1996.

_____, ed. *A Dictionary of Biblical Tradition in English Literature*. Grand Rapids: Eerdmans, 1992.

Kenner, Hugh. *Paradox in Chesterton*. New York: Sheed and Ward, 1947.

Kerr, Hugh T., and John M. Mulder. *Famous Conversions*. Grand Rapids, MI: William B. Eerdmans Publishing Company, 1983.

Leigh, David. "The Psychology of Conversion in Chesterton's and Lewis's Autobiographies." In *G. K. Chesterton and C. S. Lewis: The Riddle of Joy*, ed. Michael H. Macdonald and Andrew A. Tadie, 290-304. Grand Rapids: Eerdmans Publishing Company, 1989.

Manganiello, Dominic. " 'Where in Hell Are We?': Chesterton on Dante." *The Chesterton Review* 20, no. 1 (1994): 65-81.

McLuhan, H. Marshall. "G. K. Chesterton: A Practical Mystic." In *G. K. Chesterton: A Half Century of Views*, ed. D. J. Conlon. Oxford: Oxford University Press, 1987.

_____. "Where Chesterton Comes In." In *G. K. Chesterton: A Half Century of Views*, ed. D. J. Conlon. Oxford: Oxford University Press, 1987.

Morris, Kevin L. "Chesterton Sees Red: The Metaphysics of a Colour." *The Chesterton Review* 21, no. 4 (1995): 505-17.

_____. "Chesterton's Conversion: Hesitation and the Recovery of Infancy." *The Chesterton Review* 18, no. 3 (1992): 371-83.

Pearce, Joseph. *Literary Converts: Spiritual Inspiration in an Age of Unbelief*. San Francisco: Ignatius, 2000.

Rambo, Lewis R. *Understanding Religious Conversion*. London: Yale University Press, 1993.

Sayers, Dorothy L. *The Mind of the Maker*. San Francisco: HarperCollins, 1968.

Schwartz, Adam. "G. K. C.'s Methodical Madness: Sanity and Social Control in Chesterton." *Renascence: Essays on Values in Literature*, Fall 1996, vol. 49, no. 1, p. 23 (18) [database on-line] (Marquette University Press, 1996, accessed 28 August 2000); available from Infotrac.

Tippett, Alan R. "Conversion as a Dynamic Process in Christian Mission." *Missiology* 2 (1977): 203-21.

Ward, Maisie. *Gilbert Keith Chesterton*. London: Sheed and Ward, 1944.

Witherup, Ronald D. *Conversion in the New Testament*. Collegeville, MN: The Liturgical Press, 1994.

EPILOGUE: A TRIBUTE

A Chestertonian Inversion of Mt 7:17

From Athena's olive triumph,
To the Trees of Tolkien's light,
From Matt's and Luke's lists of "begats"
To rooted branchings left and right,
The myths of Man are *arbor*-crowned
On Calvary's deathly height.
But in this, Deb Elkink's book,
Inverted, as in G. K.'s sight,
You will find, and I agree,
That *her* good fruit has borne a Tree.

Peter J. Floriani, Ph.D.
Computer Scientist and Author
www.debellisstellarum.com

www.ingramcontent.com/pod-product-compliance
Lightning Source LLC
LaVergne TN
LVHW041213080426
835508LV00011B/936